Myths & Hitches

4

MISCONCEPTIONS, FALLACIES & FALSE BELIEFS

about

Science & Philosophy
Art & Literature
Film & Music
Fantasy & Mythology

Don M. Ferry

DEDICATION

To my wife Olivia, our children Gia, Rica, Dondi, Bill and Manley, and all our grandchildren, and to those friends and associates who have supported us in this endeavor.

ACKNOWLEDGMENT

The author is highly indebted to his wife Olivia A. Ferry for editing portions of this work, and to his son Dondi A. Ferry for his contributions to the cover design of the book.

TABLE OF CONTENTS

3

PREFACE

This is the fourth volume in the series entitled *Myths & Hitches*, a comprehensive collection of misconceptions and fallacies culled from popular lore. Arrayed in its pages are more than 300 items of information in several genres, from *science and philosophy* to *art and literature*, and from *film and music* to *fantasy and mythology*. What they convey may seem ordinary, but only in the sense that most everything in this world is ordinary. In fact, they are a cut above common trivia, owing to a feature that makes them uniquely engaging: each is a pseudo-fact, a lie dressed up as a truth (or vice versa), a belief that's flawed to the gills. People love trivia because they entertain, and trivia debunked can do no less—like a pratfall, which signifies nothing except that it's amusing. A pratfall deflates the pompousness of human behavior, while a fallacy exposed deflates the pomposity of human knowledge.

Many profess to debunk for a higher purpose: to enhance education and promote general literacy by eliminating errors and fallacies from the vast reservoir of popular information. It's an ideal, of course, but in raising the bar, it turns what should be a fun-filled exercise into something truly demanding and, at times, hardly feasible. Very often, the lie to be excised may have already become entrenched as myth, a myth even more wholesome and beguiling than the truth. For instance, would Sherlock Holmes' image remain as the world's greatest detective of fiction if, to abide by the truth, we were to remove his cape and deerstalker cap and deny he ever said, "Elementary, my dear Watson"? Would we serve Charles Darwin's memory right by revealing, for the sake of truth, that he was not the first to theorize about evolution and did not coin the famous phrase "survival of the fittest"? Would history be any richer (at the expense of great literature) from the finding that Richard the Lion-Heart and Prince John never heard of a fellow named Robin Hood? And wouldn't Rome's rich tradition suffer even a notch were a truth advocate to knock down its celebrated sons Remus and Romulus from their perch as the legendary founders of that city?

We share in the ideal, too, but only where, by exposing the untruth, we are able to ferret out the corresponding truth. When we fail, as we often do, we can only take comfort in Von Goethe's words: "It is easier to perceive error than to find truth, for the former lies on the surface and is easily seen, while the latter lies in the depth, where few are willing to search for it." Sadly, even the few who do decide to search 'in the depth' find out soon enough that truth has many faces, that "what is true by lamplight is not always true by sunlight." For truth may vary as to place: the ancient Roman writer Suetonius often failed to agree with his Greek counterpart Plutarch on significant details, making the study of Greco-Roman history thoroughly confusing to one who is not a pupil of either. Truth may also vary as to time, a phenomenon that that archetype of reference books, the Encyclopedia Britannica, makes evident whenever it launches a new edition to update or revise an earlier one. In a sense, the 'untruths' presented in this book are just versions of the truth, which means that, unless we are sure of our grounds, we should not impose the ideal by banishing them from popular lore as falsehoods.

Still, while we aim primarily to entertain, we hope to leave the message that the inability or difficulty of finding the truth is no license to falsify it. Information, essential or not, deserves to be reported accurately or not at all, and the historian, journalist, screenwriter, artist and blogger who care enough for what they do must keep that trust. The way information is handled in a society impacts ultimately on that society's respect for truth as a value on which all other values must rest.

Don M. Ferry

N.B.: The above has been lifted essentially from the preface of a similarly themed book, *Untruths and Nothing But* (Infinity Publishing, 2009), by the author. The contents of that book have been greatly expanded, reorganized and carried over into this volume of *Myths & Hitches* as well as into three other volumes of the series (*Myths & Hitches 1, 2* and *3),* all available in eBook format. Please refer to the end of each volume for a detailed list of the topics covered. —DMF

Science & Philosophy

I

Those Who Cant, Preach

On Mathematicians and Philosophers

"A hallucination is a fact, not an error;
what is erroneous is a judgment based upon it."

•

Bertrand Russell

1. Gentleman of Leisure

Myth! **The Epicureans regard the utmost in pleasure and sensuality as the main pursuit of humanity.**

The Greek philosopher Epicurus (342-270 B.C.) held that pleasure constitutes the highest happiness, a philosophy that unwittingly produced the word 'hedonism' and is often mistaken for it. But, unlike a hedonist, what Epicurus had in mind was 'pleasure' other than the brass, materialistic and selfish kind, the kind that tends to be pursued immoderately and at all cost. Epicureanism as conceived by its founder called for peace of mind, freedom from pain through pursuit of cultural interests, development of inner serenity, and temperance in sensual pleasure. The happy feeling Epicurus sought was "not a transitory or momentary sensation, but something lasting and imperishable, attained chiefly by pure and noble thoughts." In all things he counseled moderation, since in the long run that afforded one greater delight than "the frenzies of bed and board."

It is a common misconception to think of the true epicurean as a hedonist, who professes to indulge in the excessive pursuit of sensual pleasure. Unfortunately, Epicurus' theory would become thoroughly corrupted and misinterpreted by students and practitioners alike so that it became hardly distinguishable from hedonism. For more than two hundred years after his death, Epicurus' pupils and disciples had staunchly defended his teachings against violent attacks by later philosophers. Eventually, however, the theory yielded to the various unsupported assertions that it was a mere excuse for the greatest debauchery and sensuality imaginable. From then on, says an author, "some men, who had devoted their lives to such vices (as hedonists), called themselves Epicureans." Even the great Roman writer, statesman and orator Cicero failed to grasp Epicurus' meaning and sided with those who held a mistaken notion. Largely through him, "epicure" came to denote, not a true follower of Epicurus, but one given over to sensual pleasures and extravagant living.

2. The Prize is Wrong

Myth! Albert Einstein and Bertrand Russell won the Nobel Prize for their breakthrough works in science.

Einstein won the Nobel Prize for physics in 1921, but it was not for the famous theory of relativity that he had published twice before, once in 1905 and again in 1916. What brought him the plum rather unexpectedly was his lesser-known work on the photoelectric effect of light. Apparently, the selection committee, which had wanted to honor Einstein for his body of work, could only focus on a single subject under the rules, and it felt that the theory of relativity was too controversial for consideration.

A couple of years later, in 1923, the Nobel people would fidget with the very same standards they had set for the nomination of Einstein. On this occasion, the coveted Prize went to US physicist Robert A. Millikan for his determination of the electrical charge on the electron, making him the most famous American scientist of his day. But according to Broad and Wade (*Betrayers of the Truth*, 1982), a careful study of Millikan's research revealed that he cheated on his way to the Prize. There were major gaps in the reporting of data, he fudged numbers and statistics, and he used only the best results from his experimentation.

Just as ironic if not more embarrassing is the fate that British philosopher-mathematician Lord Bertrand Russell suffered at the hands of the Nobel Prize committee in 1950. Russell had more than 40 books and as many popular essays in print at any time ranging over philosophy, mathematics, science, ethics, sociology, education, history, religion, politics and polemic. Each of these major expositions would have sufficed to have him nominated for the highest award, and his collective achievements in any of the historical, philosophical or socio-political fields could have easily bagged him the Prize. This is not to mention that the most prestigious of them all, the Nobel Peace Prize, was as ready for his plucking, considering that Russell was one of the world's greatest pacifists in his later years. Yet the Nobel Prize he did win in 1950 was not for any of these fields but for Literature, where he had not one single piece of writing at the time it was given. He would invade the literary world only two years later, at the age of 80, when, "mainly to amuse himself," he would write a bland, almost unreadable, collection of five weird short tales entitled "Satan in the Suburbs And Other Stories."

One could carp about the way Einstein and Russell were treated, but it would not be easy to suggest that, for this reason alone, they should have declined the honor of being called a Nobel Prize laureate, or simply a Nobelist. Three nominees in the past apparently mustered enough courage to refuse the award, but only one—Jean-Paul Sartre of France—actually did it (in 1964) without any compromises. Boris Pasternak of the Soviet Union would have wanted to accept in 1958, but was forced to decline by the Soviet Union, which considered the Nobel "a reactionary bourgeois award." In the 1918 case involving Eric Axel Karlfeldt of Sweden, the Nobel Prize committee decided to renew the offer after his death in 1931, and this time his estate accepted.

3. In One or the Other, Mobs Rule!

Myth! Anarchy is a system that promotes the breakdown of law and order and the eventual demise of government.

The ordinary man on the street will tell you that anarchy is a term he is not comfortable with. He will say anarchy bats for the complete absence of government, or for that matter of any method by which the state tries to control society, and putting such a philosophy into action creates chaos, lawlessness, disorder, rioting and social breakdown. He would rather live in a democracy under a government of his own peers, as this is the only system that guarantees an orderly and peaceful environment.

As a practical matter, anarchy and democracy are the antithesis of each other. As political theories, they still are, but their positions are reversed. What our practical democrat doesn't realize is that democracy is in fact the least peaceful of all political ideals because it presupposes an environment of conflicting interests. On the other hand, entirely in contrast to its popular meaning, anarchism is probably the most idealistic and peaceful of political systems. That system sees free individuals coexisting in peace within a framework of voluntary associations. Government or regulation is eschewed, as it will only stifle the desire of individuals to reconcile their interests and resolve their differences at their own initiative.

Quite obviously, the anarchist's view and that of the democrat proceed from different assumptions. The first believes authority is the source of the evil, and that man, being rational, cooperative, and basically good when given the choice to act freely, will coexist in complete social harmony. On the other hand, the democrat thinks of anarchy not in terms of the evils of authority but of the chaos that may result if man is left to his own doing, considering that man by himself will breed violence, greed and deception.

Anarchism is sometimes identified with Marxism or Leninism, which shouldn't be. Anarchism in fact rejects the Marxist-Leninist theory of the dictatorship of the proletariat, in the same manner that it rejects any theory involving control of one class or individual by another. As a theory, it does not advocate revolution or even unrest.

4. The Tao of Mao

Myth! Lao-tzu wrote the Tao-te-Ching.

Out of China's mystical past emerges the towering figure of Lao-tzu, which tradition regards as the first philosopher of the Taoist school and the author of the Tao-te Ching. The latter, probably the most famous book of ancient China, is not just a great philosophical treatise but also one of the most sacred scriptures of Taoism, with Lao-tzu himself as its principal saint and divinity. The man cuts a mysterious figure with no definite or reliable links to any historical source. His life story is a patchwork of fables and legends, the most popular, like his meeting with Confucius and his voyage to the west, where he disappeared, being also the most suspect.

Many scholars feel there is no need to establish the historical authenticity of Lao-tzu because he may not be the real author of the Tao-te-Ching. If at all, he may have been one of several contributors to the book, which appears to consist of materials from different periods. Although the Tao-te-Ching dates from about 300 BC, some of its sayings can be dated to the time of

Confucius, while others are much later. It is due to these discrepancies that experts have assigned the authorship to several individuals.

Lao-tzu, in fact, may not even be a proper name but a generic term for a certain type of sage. Nonetheless, the figure is one of the most generally respected in all of Chinese philosophy and literature. Says a writer: "To the Confucianists he was a venerated philosopher; to the people, he was a saint or a god; and to the Taoists he was an emanation of the Tao and one of the greatest divinities."

5. Confucian Confusion

Myth! **Confucius founded one of China's greatest philosophical systems.**

The man who is generally considered China's greatest teacher was born in 551 BC in Shantung province and lived until 479 BC. The distinctively Oriental name evokes a figure standing in the mist like a demigod, whose teachings introduce us to a philosophical system that lays the foundation of a great eastern religion. But in fact Confucius is nothing of the sort. "Confucius" is a Western misnomer, a rather careless Latinization of the simple honorific K'ung Tzu, which translates as Master K'ung. According to Carl Crow, Portuguese Jesuit scholars made a mistake when, around the fifteenth century, they tried to approximate the sound of K'ung Tzu with the letters of the Latin alphabet. The original Master K'ung referred to a "sincere, lovable entirely human scholar and gentleman who lived a blameless life, suffered more disillusionment and disappointments than usually fall to the lot of men, and died feeling that his life had been a failure." Unfortunately, the corrupted name Confucius became "a bloodless deification, an intellectual Frankenstein monster created by readers who had lost track of the man."

While it is not right to credit Confucius with the founding of a religion or philosophical system, what he did was nevertheless commendable. He posited principles of right conduct in society, emphasizing the family as the basic social unit to implement such conduct. The fifth-century teacher is considered the father of

13

etiquette. And, of course, the legendary author of hundreds of epigrams, mostly ribald, each carefully couched in broken English and introduced by the line, "Confucius says."

6. An Ass of a Dog

Myth! The principles called "Buridan's ass," "Ockham's razor" and "Gresham's Law" were named, respectively, for the persons that devised them.

Two celebrated but controversial theorems are oddly named Buridan's Ass and Ockham's Razor. Behind the phrases are the Frenchman Jean Buridan and the Englishman William of Ockham, both scholastic philosophers and logicians of the fourteenth century.

Jean Buridan (1300-1358) asserted that man desires that which appears to be for the greater good, but because of free will, he will delay his decision until he can look into his motives. The dilemma, a variant of the theory of determinism, is illustrated by the allegory of "Buridan's ass," which states: "If a hungry ass were placed exactly between two haystacks in every respect equal, it would starve to death, because there would be no motive why it should go to one rather than to the other." As it happens, the theory is not really Buridan's but a statement originating with Aristotle's *De caelo* ("On the Heavens"). Buridan's view merely commented on Aristotle's position, which used as its example a dog sitting before two equal amounts of food. For local color, Buridan's free-minded and imaginative interpreters opted for an ass and bales of hay, and "Buridan's ass" has since become a synonym for a man of indecision.

William of Ockham (1285?-1349?), leader of the school of nominalism, was the teacher of Buridan who constantly debated with him. "Ockham's razor," the principle honoring his name, is sometimes called the Law of Economy, which states that "entities are not to be multiplied unnecessarily." This means, in lay terms, that anything needing an explanation should be discussed using the simplest elements and the fewest assumptions. Despite the tag, "Ockham's razor" does not appear anywhere in the philosopher's works, indicating that Ockham had no hand in its formulation.

14

There were, in fact, earlier proponents, including one of Ockham's contemporaries, the French Dominican theologian and philosopher Durand de Saint-Pourcain. The principle is a generalization that took on various forms both before and after Ockham's time, depending on the discipline to which it was applied. Nicole d'Oresme reasserted it in science, Pierre de Maupertuis and Galileo in astronomy, Ernst Mach in physics, and C. Lloyd Morgan in psychology. Ockham mentioned the principle so frequently and employed it so sharply that it was eventually named for him.

Sir Thomas Gresham (1519?-79) was not a philosopher, but like Buridan and Ockham, he lends his name to a celebrated principle that is not exactly his. To support a plea for the restoration of the currency of England, Gresham, then founder of the Royal Exchange, explained to Queen Elizabeth I that "bad money drives out good." His financial expertise notwithstanding, Gresham made no further development or theoretical exploration of this thesis. It soon became obvious that his statement was a mere reiteration of a principle of economics already known to merchants, financiers, and political leaders well before the sixteenth century. Some believe Copernicus, the Polish astronomer behind the heliocentric theory, originated the notion, although it is also possible he only adopted it. The idea remained generic for at least 300 years after Gresham's death, and only in the latter part of the nineteenth century did it become known as Gresham's Law.

7. Philosophical Distemper

Myth! Diogenes "lived in a tub like a dog," but still held his own in debates with fellow philosophers like Zeno.

"Cynic" is a word that comes from the Greek adjective "dog-like." It appears Diogenes was called a cynic, and imparted that name to his philosophical sect, because he lived like a dog. According to *The American Heritage Dictionary of the English Language* (Third Edition, 1996), this Greek oddball proclaimed his presence with such actions as "barking in public, urinating on the leg of a table, and masturbating on the street." He is said to have lived most of his adult life in a barrel that served as a tub, though some suspect this last antic "probably started as a simile or a metaphor and then became corrupted and was soon reported as fact by the free-wheeling historians of the times." That the man was a cynic (or, as we understand the word today, a faultfinder or disbeliever) is beyond dispute, but it is highly questionable that anyone could have led an actively cynical life in such cramped quarters. It was Seneca, Diogenes' biographer, who started the whole idea when he wrote about Diogenes' disreputable personal habits, noting that "a man so crabbed ought to have lived in a tub like a dog." Since then, the expression has been carried over the centuries as fact, citing Seneca as authority.

False stories may have also been used to sensationalize Diogenes' celebrated penchant for finding flaws in others in his pursuit of virtue. For instance, contrary to many biographical accounts, he could not have confronted Zeno of Elea at a public lecture to refute the latter's paradox of motion because they were not even contemporaries (this Zeno is different from Zeno of Citium, who was reportedly so despondent about his physical well-being that he strangled himself to death). That Diogenes spent weeks walking the streets with a lantern in daylight searching for an honest man was no doubt also a simile or metaphor in the beginning but ended up as an integral part of the man's legend.

8. Praise Allah and Pass the Ammo

Myth! Islam preaches violence against non-believers and promotes *jihad* against its enemies.

The stock criticism against Islam is that it is a violent and persecutory religion, one that propagates itself through holy war, or *jihad.* The Arabic concept of *jihad,* which by tradition imposes a duty on Moslems to crush non-believers who do not wish to be converted, has assumed larger importance in modern times because of social strife in the Middle East during the last two decades.

It is probably unfair that Islam should be branded for this perceived militancy while other religions are not. As social historians have noted, the early aggressions committed in the name of Islam were mainly due to the Arab character, which was "earth-

16

bound to the Bedouin law of violence and revenge." Islam itself preached tolerance and moderation, with Mohammed leading the way by saying: "Let there be no violence in religion...Give a respite to the disbelievers. Deal thou gently with them for a while." Indeed, *jihad* was not any more violent than the Crusades or the campaign of proselytizing by the Church during the Age of Discovery. In the long run, it was even less severe because, unlike Christianization, it usually did not entail colonization. Keenly aware that Mohammed never intended to wage holy war against non-Arabs of other faiths, the practitioners of *jihad* directed it mostly against Arab unbelievers who did not peaceably submit

The modern interpretation of *jihad* has to do less with conducting an actual war than with making war with one's inner self. The word more correctly means to struggle or to make an effort in behalf of oneself. The external kind of *jihad* has rarely been invoked since the earliest days of the faith because of the many conditions for waging it. Any Moslem holy war today would be sanctioned only as a defensive measure in order to preserve the faith. *Jihad* should not be confused with the acts of militant fundamentalists like the Shiites, who are a small minority compared to the orthodox Sunni Moslems representing the conservative, static establishment of Islam.

9. Jerry Pandering

Myth! Jeremy Bentham coined the phrase "the greatest good for the greatest number."

Bentham was thought to have originated the principle of "the greatest good for the greatest number," which underlies the theory of Utilitarianism. In his *An Introduction to the Principles of Morals and Legislation* (1789), Bentham used the phrase, saying the idea should be the object of all legislation.

Actually, Bentham's book merely gave new application to an old and tired concept. The ingredients of Utilitarianism are found in the history of thought long before Bentham, its origins dating back to the hedonistic theory of the ancients. Frances Hutcheson, a British 'moral sense' theorist, was among the first in the late 17th century to avail of the phrase "the greatest happiness for the greatest numbers" to define his moral philosophy. Bentham himself confessed that Joseph Priestly was the one who had given him the words, and the principle they describe was actually taken from the 18th-century writings of Priestly and various other thinkers such as Claude-Adrien Helvétius, Cesare Beccaria and David Hume.

10. Evolutionary Road

Myth! Charles Darwin amassed empirical evidence over a 14-year period to prove what he called "evolution," the process by which a higher form develops from a lower one.

In the popular mind, evolution is the process by which a higher or more complex form of life develops from a lower or simpler one. Charles Darwin is widely believed to have originated the theory and established it empirically in his books on the matter.

All is not as simple as that, however. First, while it is generally assumed that the 'higher' forms have evolved from 'lower' ones, Darwin thought no such thing. What he said is that evolution occurs through "natural selection," which "includes no necessary and universal law of advancement or development—it only takes advantage of such variations as arise and are beneficial to each creature under its complex relations of life." Critics point out that, if only for this reason, it is inaccurate to call his book 'Origin of Species'. Its real and fully descriptive title is The *Origin of Species by Means of Natural Selection, or the Preservation of Favoured Races in the Struggle for Life.*

Second, Darwin's pioneer work, which he completed in 1871, was formulated without any physical evidence and was built mainly on supposition and speculation. According to Alex Paterson ("A Critique of Darwin's Theory of Evolution," 2008, at *www.vision.net.au/*), "close examination of a whole raft of scientific data reveals the <u>absence</u> of virtually any empirical scientific evidence in support of the theory, either regarding the alleged spontaneous generation of life in first place, let alone the evolution of life forms from one species into another." Philip Johnson, in *Darwin on Trial* (cited by Paterson), concludes: "The philosophically important part of the Darwinian theory—its

18

mechanism for creating complex things that did not exist before—is therefore not really empirical science at all, but rather a deduction from naturalistic philosophy. In brief, what makes me a 'critic of (Darwinian) evolution' is that I distinguish between naturalistic philosophy and empirical science, and oppose the former when it comes cloaked in the authority of the latter."

Third, Darwin may have spent as many as 14 long years conceiving his theory of evolution and trying to amass evidence for it. But, in what historians say is a classic case of simultaneous research leading to a common conclusion, Alfred Russel Wallace formulated the same theory independently of Darwin within a period of only three days. Wallace was living in the Malay Archipelago when he wrote his paper entitled "On the Tendency of Varieties to Depart Indefinitely from the Original Type" and sent Darwin a copy in February 1858. Later in the same year, the two agreed to present a paper jointly to the Linnaean Society, and both were credited as joint originators of the theory. The only difference of note was the fact that Darwin was much more empirical than Wallace's. Nevertheless, as a writer notes, "the unfortunate thing is that history has given all five stars to Darwin and the scraps to Wallace."

Fourth, contrary to what most people think, Darwin did not coin the word "evolution," and no one really knows who did. The word could have been as old as the concept, which started in antiquity. And the one who popularized it was neither Darwin nor A. Russel Wallace but the English sociologist Herbert Spenser.

Finally, Darwinians may not easily accept the fact that during their hero's own time, evolution was not a new idea to science. The early Greeks, notably the philosophers Anaximander and Empedocles, had already entertained a theory of mutation through adaptation, before 18th century thinkers—from Newton to Carolus Linnaeus—took up the idea of an evolutionary process in the animal world. In the 1600s, Leibniz and de Maillet both hinted that the 'great chain of being' had been forged by mutating links. Even Darwin's own grandfather, the great naturalist Erasmus Darwin, had an inkling some fifteen years before he was born, and the idea became mod in scientific circles in the mid-19th century. Darwin himself, in the third edition of his *The Origin of Species by Natural Selection*, nominates Aristotle as the father of the theory.

11. Our Cousin Hairy

Myth! Charles Darwin was the first to suggest the phrase 'survival of the fittest'.

We have all heard of "the missing link" but are not quite sure what to make of it. The name suggests a being, half-human and half-primate, that stands between man and the apes in the evolutionary chain and has remained elusive or undiscovered—like Yeti and Bigfoot, perhaps.

Rejecting the suggestion, scientists say this is not even good science fiction. Man's evolution was an enormously long and complicated chain in which no one "link" could possibly vary so much from any other that it would stand out. The concept that man descended from and was a later development of apes was invented by Darwin's detractors and assigned to him to make him look foolish. It is completely at odds with what Darwin postulated, which is that man and ape evolved from a common ancestor several million years ago. In his own words, "man is the co-descendant with other mammals of a common progenitor." There is only the slightest hint in Darwin's works of a "missing link" between man and ape, and that is when he describes (in his *Descent of Man*) their common progenitor as "a hairy quadruped, furnished with a tail and pointed ears."

The phrase "survival of the fittest" is similarly associated with Darwin, although he had nothing much to do with it. Herbert Spencer, founder of evolutionary philosophy and himself a Darwinian, used it in his book, Principles *of Biology* (1864), to encapsulate Darwin's theory of natural selection as it applies to social development. Darwin's reaction to this restatement of his theory was obviously favorable, for he wrote in *The Origin of Species,* "The expression often used by Mr. Herbert Spencer of the Survival of the Fittest is more accurate, and is sometimes equally convenient." But he would also say there were others who had suggested the phrase earlier, the two most prominent being William C. Wells in 1813 and Patrick Mathew in 1831.

James Trefil (*Sharks Have No Bones*, 1993) notes that Spencer's application of "survival of the fittest" in a social context is quite different from Darwin's own understanding of the phrase.

Darwin "used the term 'fit' to describe individuals who are successful in producing offspring in the next generation, nothing more." On the other hand, the connotation given it by Spencer and other proponents of Social Darwinism is that of "best," which has a moral overtone. Thus, "(t)he rich, according to Spencer, got where they are because they are fit while the poor are where they are because they were not fit."

12. Darrow on the Defensive

Myth! After obtaining his law degree from Dartmouth, Clarence Darrow undertook many unpopular causes without pay, winning most of them using his unexcelled power of argument and oratory.

The famous criminal lawyer Clarence Darrow has been described as a social philosopher, agnostic and free spirit "who chose to become involved, who cared and who gave of himself." Most people believe he was a defender of unpopular causes and persons, and that his defense of John T. Scopes, undertaken without pay, was wholly in character.

The more accurate view of Darrow shows a half-baked lawyer (he was a law school dropout) who was cynical, atheistic, opportunistic and generally unfriendly. The Scopes defense was the only case he undertook for free, and he accepted it because he smelled a publicity breakthrough for himself. Besides, he wanted to embarrass William Jennings Bryan, who excelled him in oratory.

Darrow was reputedly fond of courtroom gimmicks, but the anecdote about his using his cigars to disrupt his opposition's summing up is too contrived to be true. It is said that Darrow would insert a wire in the cigar, allowing the ash to grow longer and longer, and the suspense would distract the jury from the other lawyer's word.

The film *Inherit the Wind* (1960) did much to immortalize the clash in the Scopes trial, but it would not have taken much of a Darrow to defeat Bryan. Although the statesman-politician of 'Cross of Gold' fame was a great orator, he was also an ignorant fundamentalist in his waning years. It was once reported that, as

21

US secretary of state, Bryan invited the Swiss navy to the opening of the Panama Canal, unaware that Switzerland, a land-locked country, did not support a navy.

---

13. Pin Dancing

Myth! St. Thomas Aquinas started a famous debate among medieval scholars when he posed the question, "How many angels can dance on the head of a pin?"

Other than the fact that its original wording was, "How many angels can dance on the point of a needle?," there is no fallacy involved in the question, as this is basically a metaphysical issue that may have been argued in the past as part of a theological exercise. However, there are conflicting reports on who first thought it up and whether it was indeed debated by medieval scholars.

Many assume St. Thomas Aquinas was the origin since only he had the profound intelligence and authority to delve into the problem without making it look like an utter waste of time. Indeed, in his *Summa Theologica*, he paid considerable attention to the nature of angels and how they relate to space and other elements of the physical world. For instance, Aquinas argued whether an angel moving from A to B passes through the points in between, and whether one could distinguish "morning" and "evening" knowledge in angels. Finally, he inquired whether several angels could be in the same place at once, and this was the closest he got to the dilemma of angels dancing on a pinhead.

Actually, most if not all of the top theologian of the Middle Ages supported Aquinas' view that angels are 100 percent pure spirits, having no matter or mass and taking up no space. Naturally, when the question cropped up in post medieval times, Aquinas was cited as the philosopher who asked the question and, by way of answering it himself, also said, "Infinitely many." According to the Internet, most who write about angels "assume that this question was one of the many mind-game riddles of subtle logic by which medieval churchmen quibbled over angels' finer points."

However, modern-day philosopher Mortimer Adler, head of the

Institute of Philosophical Research, takes exception, insisting that neither Aquinas nor any of his contemporaries asked the question. In his book *The Angels and Us*, he says this was a cliché cooked up by early modern types to ridicule and satirize the intense speculations about angels during the Middle Ages. Others claim it was a latter-day fabrication to discredit scholastic philosophy at a time when it still played a significant role in university education. Adler is apparently correct, as there is historical evidence to prove that the real debate on the question began only in the 17th century, waged by philosophers, writers and playwrights that included Richard Baxter, Joseph Addison, Ralph Cudworth and Isaac D'Israeli. James Franklin mentions a seventeenth century reference in William Chillingworth's *Religion of Protestants*, where he accuses unnamed scholastics of debating "Whether a Million of Angels may not fit upon a needles point?" H. S. Lang, author of *Aristotle's Physics and its Medieval Varieties* (1992), says: "The question of how many angels can dance on the point of a needle, or the head of a pin, is often attributed to 'late medieval writers' ... In point of fact, the question has never been found in this form". In the twentieth century, the issue has been kept alive mainly by such luminaries as mystery novelist Dorothy Sayers, who has argued that the answer "usually adjudged correct" to what is "simply a debating exercise" was that "angels are pure intelligences, not material, but limited, so that they have location in space, but not extension."

---

14. Counter Reformation

Myth! The Arabs invented Arabic numerals for their own use but introduced them to Europe in the ninth century.

They are known almost everywhere as Arabic numerals, but the Arabs did not invent them. They were so-called only because the Arabs were the ones who brokered their introduction into Europe.

Arabic numerals were in use in India since the third century BC. They were brought to a higher level of sophistication during the Gupta Dynasty (AD 320-550), when two innovations became part of the system. First was the idea and symbol of zero, and

23

second was the decimal method by which the positional value of the numbers increases tenfold to the left and decreases correspondingly to the right.

The early Muslims, who had a genius for borrowing ideas and developing and refining them, were especially fascinated with Hindu mathematics. In the 8th century Baghdad caliphs started bringing Hindu works to their capital, so that by the following century, some had spread and were in common use in Arabic and Persian regions. The technology transfer was noted by Baghdad scholar Mohammed ibn-Musa al-Khowarizmi, whose famous treatise *Al-jebr wa'I-muqabalah* gives us the word "algebra," and three centuries later, his piece on it was translated into Latin as *De Numero Indorum (On the Numbers of the Hindus)*. This introduced algebra into the capitals of Europe and served as the principal mathematics textbook there until the 16th century. It is said al-Khowarizmi's book "gave so full an account of the Hindu numerals that he probably is responsible for the widespread but false impression that our system of numeration is Arabic in origin." In fairness to this sage, however, he never made any claim that he invented the system.

Although already popular in Europe by the 12th century, Arabic numerals did not generally supersede Roman numerals until the 16th century. Why this was so is not easily explained, considering that the Hindu system is obviously far superior to the Roman when dealing in large numbers in an efficient way. The latter, as most everyone agrees, is cumbersome, being expressed either with full words or alphabetical letters. Though they used fewer symbols and were just as accurate, they were not suitable to rapid written calculations and the needs of advancing science. Even harder to understand is the fact that Arabic numerals, with their proven advantages and all, have never been used by the Arabs, who continue to maintain a language that has its own symbols for numbers.

15. Anonymous / Eponymous

Myth! Pythagoras, Euclid and Plato devised the famous geometrical conventions named after them.

24

Everyone who has had their fill of high school geometry must have heard of the theorem that the square of the hypotenuse of a right angle equals the sum of the squares of its two sides. They were probably told it was the Greek mathematician Pythagoras (ca. 540 BC) who devised it, hence the name 'Pythagorean Theorem'.

Some say Pythagoras only initiated the idea and others developed it later, but even that may not be accurate. There is evidence to suggest that the Pythagorean model goes back to the Babylonians of Hammurabi's time, over 1000 years earlier. It appears Pythagoras was given credit only because the first recorded proofs of the theorem came from the Pythagorean School consisting of the many students, associates and followers that succeeded their teacher in his beliefs and preaching. What is called the Pythagorean Theorem should probably have been called the Pythagorean Proof, as it is just one of the many validations of $a2 + b2 = c2$ (where c is the hypotenuse) that have appeared throughout continents, cultures and centuries. It is reckoned that more proofs of the theorem, each with a singularity of its own, have probably been offered than any other, with the book *The Pythagorean Proposition* containing 370 alone! Euclid had his own proof, and so had US president James Garfield who, when he was still a major general, published a novel algebraic approach based on the area of a trapezoid.

Like Pythagoras, Euclid boasts a name that is almost synonymous with his science. In fact, he is often recognized as the Father of Geometry, mainly for putting together a book titled *Elements*, which contains a host of geometric principles that were worked out of a set of axioms. It turns out, however, that there is hardly any result in Euclid's collection that he formulated himself or was not produced by earlier mathematicians. His accomplishment, according to Wikipedia, was merely "to present (these results) in a single, logically coherent framework, making it easy to use and easy to reference." Worse, there is some doubt that Euclid himself wrote the *Elements*, as there is no mention of him in the earliest surviving copies. Those copies say they are "from the edition of Theon" or the "lectures of Theon", while the primary text kept in the Vatican Library mentions no author at all. The ancient philosopher Proclus had mentioned Euclid briefly in a pseudo-history he wrote nearly 800 years after the fact, thereby establishing himself as the only source for the claim that Euclid authored the *Elements*.

On Platonic solids, the verdict of mathematicians and historians alike is that, contrary to what the term suggests, Plato had nothing to do with their discovery or creation. These geometric figures date back to antiquity, when ornamented models can be seen among the carved stone balls created by the Scottish people in the late Neolithic age at least 1000 years before Plato. The ancient Greeks immediately took an active interest in the shapes after they were discovered, some say by Pythagoras, others by Theaetetus, a contemporary of Plato. Later, Plato featured them prominently in his philosophy, thus their name. In the dialogue *Timaeus* c.360 B.C. Plato associated each of the four classical elements (earth, air, water, and fire) with one of the regular solids. Earth was associated with the cube, air with the octahedron, water with the icosahedron, and fire with the tetrahedron.

II

Protean Man

On Benjamin Franklin

"An investment in knowledge pays the best interest."

•

Benjamin Franklin

1. Shocking Results

Myth! Franklin initiated the experiment that successfully extracted electricity from a cloud.

Ben Franklin was ahead of the competition when he proposed that lightning was electricity in an anonymous 1748 publication. He followed this up three years later by publishing instructions on how the theory might be proved.

Most history texts relate that Ben proceeded with the experiment in 1752, thus setting a scientific milestone that changed the world forever. But by heaping all the praise on Ben, these same texts tend to exclude the work of a Frenchman named Thomas-Francois Dalibard, who only a month before did a similar experiment and came up with the same spectacular results. Dalibard actually beat Franklin to the punch in their simultaneous quest for proof that electricity is present in the air.

According to their biographies, the two scientists first met in 1776 during one of Franklin's visits to France, and immediately became friends because of their common interest. Dalibard translated the American's proposal into French, and in May of 1752 the work became the Frenchman's frame of reference for performing an experiment using a 40-foot-tall metal rod at Marly-la-Ville. Attaching wine bottles to ground the pole, he successfully extracted electricity from a low cloud. It is said that, unaware of Dalibard's work, Franklin achieved the same result from his famous kite experiment, although, luckily for him, his findings were made public earlier than Dalibard's. Luckily for Franklin too, both history and science have been slow to concede that, while it was undoubtedly his theory, he wasn't the first to prove it.

2. Experiment Perilous

Myth! Franklin's 1752 experiment involved flying a kite in a thunderstorm.

What's worse than everyone saying that Ben wasn't the first to prove his theory is some saying he didn't prove it at all—at least not in the way the experiment was described in later accounts.

Tradition more than history tells us that one day in June of 1752, Ben Franklin was in Philadelphia, hoping to use the steeple on top of Christ Church as the lightning rod in his experiment to extract electricity from storm clouds. When the steeple couldn't be completed in time, he decided that a kite flown close to the clouds should do just as well. Ben attached a metal key to the kite to serve as the leader, then tied the kite string to an insulating silk ribbon for the knuckles of his hand.

Tom Tucker (*Bolt of Fate: Benjamin Franklin and his Electric Kite Hoax*, Parsecs, 2003) insists this kite incident never happened, and that Franklin perpetrated the hoax to earn a false honor for himself. The arguments in support of his thesis boil down to the following:

(1) Franklin was known to mix facts with fiction in his literary works, particularly those appearing in the *Pennsylvania Gazette* and *Poor Richard's Almanac*. If his "pseudo predictions and plagiarized proverbs" show Franklin was capable of hoaxing in the realm of popular culture, then he must also be so capable in the realm of science and natural philosophy.

(2) The only mention in writing **Franklin** made of the kite experiment was in a *single* statement published in *1788*. Everything that is known about what happened is provided by Joseph Priestley's somewhat detailed description in his 1767 *History and Present State of Electricity*. However, Priestley's account, besides being hearsay, does not specify the date of occurrence and was published fifteen years after the supposed fact.

(3) Franklin claimed his 21-year-old son William, misrepresented in popular lore as a boy, was a witness—in fact, the only witness— to the event. But there is no extant testimony regarding the incident from William as much as there is no documentary evidence—only tradition—to show that William was a son of Ben (presumably illegitimate) and that there was a strong father-son relationship to justify his presence in a risky venture.

(4) The kite experiment was actually impossible to do as described. Even if it were possible, it was a very dangerous experiment, one that would most likely have seriously injured Ben. Similar efforts by later scientists have been uneven and some have resulted in major injuries and, in one case, death.

Franklin's defenders argue back—rather weakly, it seems—that he would not have risked his scientific reputation, which he had carefully built in America and abroad, by inventing the incident. Ben "appreciated the penalty that the gentlemanly establishment of natural philosophy would have meted out had the fraud been exposed—banishment from the realm he had just entered on good terms." Moreover, Ben may not have performed the experiment in exactly the way it is often described; that is to say, he didn't conduct his test during the worst part of the storm; the kite drew an electrical charge from the air but was not struck by lightning as is generally thought; and he stopped at the first sign of the key receiving the charge. A good number of investigators successfully repeated Franklin's experiment in the decades ahead with all kinds of kites, proving that obtaining atmospheric electricity in this way even on a cloudless day is a feat easily accomplished.

3. Saturday Night Fervor

Myth! Franklin founded the Saturday Evening Post.

There's no doubt that The Saturday Evening Post was someone's popular legacy to the 20th century. Until its demise in 1969, the magazine had carried a reminder in its masthead that former postmaster Benjamin Franklin took out the very first issue one day in 1728.

The phrase most intimately connected with The Saturday Evening Post—"Founded A.D. 1728 by Benjamin Franklin"—is completely untrue, meaning that the venerable postmaster never made it as the Post's master. The Post was founded on August 4, 1821, when Charles Alexander and Samuel Atkinson, printers, took over the print shop that began to publish the magazine. Cyrus H. K. Curtis bought the Post in 1897, with its masthead confirming that it had been founded "A.D. 1821." Later, on the cover of the January 29, 1898, issue, printed while the magazine was under the guidance of its first editor, William George Tordan, the phrase "Founded A.D. 1728" appeared, superseding the previous one. Then, in September of 1899, when George Horace Lorimer was starting his long editorial career with the Post, the cover carried the complete phrase "Founded A.D. 1728 by Benjamin Franklin" for the first time.

The story that Ben 'founded' the magazine, or any other magazine from which the Post could have descended, is nothing short of pure imagination. True, in 1729 (not 1728), Franklin, who was then in his early twenties, bought a faltering newspaper, the Pennsylvania Gazette, and, with his characteristic genius, turned it into a flourishing success. The Gazette closed in 1815, twenty-five years after Franklin's own death in 1790, and the Post was established by a different group six years later. The only relationship between the Gazette and the Post is that "both publications were printed in the same shop at different times."

The Franklin connection was apparently invented as a way of drumming up business in the midst of the yellow-press news wars at the turn of the century. The idea was to trade in on Franklin's printing experience, which started at age 13 with his apprenticeship to his brother James, a printer, who in 1721 published a newspaper called the New England Courant. Franklin left Boston, settled in Philadelphia, Pennsylvania, in 1723, where he worked as a printer, and in 1729 bought the Pennsylvania Gazette.

As one critic noted, it is ironic that a magazine so sternly dedicated for so many years to the old-fashioned American virtues should lend itself to deceit. Especially abused were the early covers, like the one for March 7, 1903, on which the artists J.J. Gould and Guernsey Moore painted Franklin as a young man at his printing press, with the caption "Franklin's First Number." Contrary to popular belief, however, the Post did eventually acknowledge the non-existence of its Franklin link, although only implicitly. Starting with the issue of April 18, 1942, and until the magazine's cessation in 1969, the phrase "Founded A.D. 1728 by Benjamin Franklin" was completely eliminated. Franklin continued to have his image featured on the cover once each year, as was the policy, but for the other months, according to Time Magazine, "(t)he cover was redesigned to eliminate all memories of the past but Norman Rockwell."

It is equally ironic that the appropriately named Post should honor Franklin as a pioneering publisher when it could have honored him instead as a pioneering postmaster general. And doubly ironic is that the Pony Express, which blazed a trail of 157 relay stations through five states in 1860, continues to be recognized as the first US postal service to use mounted riders and relay stations. Thanks to Franklin, his post office used the same system in 1775 and was actually the very first to do so.

4. Who was Minding the Stove?

Myth! **Franklin invented the circulating stove that continues to be marketed today with his name on it.**

Ben is often credited with an invention that continues to be marketed as the Franklin stove alongside its modern counterpart, the fireplace. In truth, the circulating stove had been in use more than 70 years prior to Franklin's experimentation with the product. What Franklin did was to improve on the contraption well enough to give it his name.

In his original 1742 design Franklin made two changes. First, he recast the stove using more advanced metallurgy. Earlier the stove was made of bricks, plaster and stone, and later of an inferior type of cast iron, which cracked when fired. This caused smoke to pass through the crevices in the materials and into the room. Second, Franklin dragged the device out of its nook and into a freestanding position in the center of the room. It was claimed that, with these improvements, the product started giving off twice the amount of heat as would a normal wall-bound fireplace for a third of the wood consumed.

But not really. Scientists say Franklin misunderstood the laws of heat convection when he designed the stove to vent smoke from the bottom instead of the top. Where the intention was to make the product more heat-efficient, Ben's concept actually left no way to draw in fresh combustion air, and the whole thing became hardly operable. Thus, in the thirty years since the stove was invented, twenty years of that in marketing, Ben's brother, Peter, succeeded in selling only two to the public.

But the invention remained unpatented, and eventually a man named David Rittenhouse took an interest in modifying Ben's design by devising what is now considered its most vital feature. He added an L-shaped pipe to the back of the stove, which directed the smoke up and out of a chimney—the stovepipe, as we have come to know it—at the same time allowing air in from the bottom of the stove to create airflow through the fire. By 1790 Rittenhouse's version was selling successfully and was widely used, and with further improvements from various manufacturers over the years, it continues to be a fixture in American homes more than two centuries later. Historians say the Franklin stove should have been called the 'Rittenhouse stove', as Ben's original invention was practically worthless.

5. Don't Grind the darn Thing, Bury it!

Myth! **Franklin coined the phrase "an axe to grind."**

The expression "an axe to grind" is defined in usage dictionaries as "an ulterior or selfish motive; a favorite topic for promotion; a private end to serve." In modern times, it has acquired an additional meaning, namely, "a reason for feeling hostile against somebody."

The phrase as originally conceived is commonly attributed to Benjamin Franklin, who is said to have based his coinage on a story called 'The Whistle', which he sent to a friend in 1779. A similar anecdote appeared in Franklin's autobiography, written between 1771 and his death in 1790 and first published in 1791. However, while both stories involve a child, an axe and a grindstone, neither mentions the phrase *an axe to grind*.

The story that is now often told is titled "Too Much for Your Whistle" and has Young Ben as the child protagonist. In it, a man appears to praise Ben's father's grindstone and asks Ben to demonstrate how it works. As Franklin complies, the stranger places his own axe upon the grindstone, this time praising the boy for his skill and vigor. When the axe has been sharpened, the stranger just laughs and without a word of thanks walks away. The lesson of the story is believed to have given rise in popular usage to the expression "an axe to grind."

But critics say that, while Franklin may have originated the story, it was the humorist Charles Miner who, after Franklin's death, coined the phrase. Miner's text entitled *Who'll turn Grindstones?* explicitly mentions "an axe to grind," but is similar enough to Franklin's earlier stories to suggest that Franklin was the real inventor of the phrase. Its first publication, an anonymous

33

piece in a Pennsylvania newspaper in 1810 or 1811, is listed as having been reprinted from the Luzerne Federalist, of which Miner was co-founder. The story was published again in 1812 with a slightly different text, but this time bearing Charles Miner's name. The story was reprinted later in a collection, *Essays from the Desk of Poor Robert the Scribe*, which is confused by many with Poor Richard's Almanac and associated for that reason with Franklin. Whether or not Miner plagiarized his story from Franklin, there seems to be no doubt he was the first to put the phrase into print.

6. Spare the Rod and Spoil the Works

Myth! Franklin invented the type of lightning rod that is currently in favored use worldwide.

As early as 1750, or two years before his purported kite experiment, Franklin began to conceive of the lightning rod as a means of protecting people, buildings, and other structures from lightning. There are, of course, speculations that lightning conductors were used in Nevyansk Tower in Russia, believed to have been built sometime between 1725 and 1732 and proving that Russian craftsmen created the first lightning rod some 25 years before Franklin did. But nothing is known about the architect or origin of the building and not even the time of construction is clear.

Franklin began to advocate lightning rods with sharp points over the objections of his English adversaries, spearheaded by Benjamin Wilson, an electrician, who favored blunt-tipped lightning rods. The latter reasoned that sharp ones attracted lightning and increased the risk of strikes, whereas blunt rods were less likely to be hit. Citing experiments and actual incidents in support of this observation, the English were able to convince King George III to have his palace equipped with a blunt lightning rod. When it came time to adopt the device for the colonies' buildings, the decision assumed a political nature and Franklin's version prevailed.

In modern times, field evidence and the laws of physics have shown that a blunt rod with a hemispherical end is more effective than a sharp lightning rod because it is able to maintain a stronger electric field. This was proved as late as 2000 in an experiment conducted by the Langmuir Laboratory for Atmospheric Research, New Mexico Institute of Mining and Technology, in Socorro, New Mexico. As a result, US standards have been changed to express a preference for blunt rods, which are now installed the majority of the time on new systems in the United States.

7. Proverbial Weatherman

Myth! **Franklin composed the proverb, "A penny saved is a penny earned," to proclaim his thriftiness as a virtue.**

This man of protean dimensions exhibited his knack for predicting the weather while reciting proverbs in that wonderful miscellany called *Poor Richard's Almanack*. Many of the sayings that ran in the collection from 1733 to 1757 still appear in modern books of quotations under Franklin's name, on the premise that he made them up or at least adapted them from longer works by others.

Franklin himself conceded, though sometimes only impliedly, that a few of the gems drew on sources not his own, such as the adage, "An ounce of prevention is worth a pound of cure," which he called "an old saying" or "an English proverb." Ditto for "There are no gains without pains" and "A word to the wise is enough." Actually, while Franklin's reputation was there to assure that most of the sayings were original, they amounted to no more than 5 percent of the 1,044 proverbial texts appearing in his almanacs.

Ralph Keyes recounts how a University of Maryland Ph.D. candidate by the name of Robert Newcomb spent years delving into the history of Franklin's sayings, only to discover the sad fact that most of Poor Richard's wisdom was borrowed from already existing collections. In some cases Franklin improved on the original, but on the whole, he simply published other men's work with little or no revision. He was especially partial to George Herbert's work, of which he adopted nearly four-dozen lines virtually unchanged, and to those of James Howell and Thomas Fuller. By the time Newcomb completed his research, he had located three quarters of Franklin's sayings in these previously published compilations.

Of the many proverbs Ben popularized, "A penny saved is a penny earned" would be the most in keeping with the man's character—that is, if it's true, as most modern Americans believe, that Franklin was a very thrifty person, a penny-pincher even, during his lifetime. But if there is one fact emerging from his various histories and biographies, it is that Franklin was just the opposite. He was known for his profligacy while living abroad as a US diplomat, admitting in 1782 that frugality was "a virtue I could never acquire myself." The false belief may have stemmed from the equally wrong notion that the adage was a Franklin original and therefore heartfelt. Actually, Ben merely improvised on G. Herbert's "A penny spar'd is twice got" (1640) and T. Fuller Worthies' "A penny sav'd, is a penny got" (1661).

8. The Long Hot Summer

Myth! Franklin invented Daylight Saving Time.

Once, to amuse his friends, Franklin penned a discourse on the thrift of natural versus artificial lighting, including some proposed funny regulations that Paris might adopt to help. In it, he parodied himself, his love of thrift, his scientific papers and his passion for playing chess until the wee hours of the morning, then sleeping until midday. He suggested whimsically that Parisians economize on candles by rising earlier to use morning sunlight, and proposed taxing shutters, rationing candles, and waking the public by ringing church bells and firing cannons at sunrise.

Unbelievably or not, popular readings and school texts have used the foregoing, entitled "An Economical Project," as their basis for concluding that Franklin was the first to conceive of daylight saving time (DST). Few realize that Ben, who wrote the essay during his sojourn as an American delegate to France in 1784, intended it to be a spoof to while away the time he was spending languishing at his post because of gout and other ailments. His friends, among others, were taken in initially by the proposal but later realized Ben was only musing and wasn't serious about carrying it through.

Some insist that, nevertheless, Franklin's playful piece should be credited with providing the spark that ignited the theory of DST. Others say there are no points of similarity between Ben's 'project' and DST to warrant such claim. Ben's strategy was to adjust working and sleeping habits; DST's is to advance clocks in order to extend the day and shorten the night. Also, while Ben's objective was to save on lighting facilities such as candles, DST's purpose is to lengthen the time for economic activity and, consequently, increase power usage. As a final note, it has been observed that Europe in the 18th century, with its rail and communication yet to be modernized, wouldn't have been ready for DST. As it did not keep accurate schedules, the convention would not easily have fit in that setting.

Critics hammer in the point by arguing that if Ben's idea was so stimulating, it would not have taken another 100 years for DST to take hold. Instead, it died a quick death, and DST itself would only be taken seriously beginning in 1895, when George Vernon Hudson, a New Zealand entomologist/astronomer, aware of the value of after-hours daylight, proposed a two-hour daylight-saving shift in a paper presented to the Wellington Philosophical Society. Ten years later, a prominent English builder and outdoorsman, William Willett, independently conceived of DST during a pre-breakfast ride, when he observed with dismay how many Londoners slept through a large part of a summer day. His proposal, which was published in 1907 under the title, "Waste of Daylight," is sometimes regarded as the first formalization of the DST concept. Actually, it was the second, having been presented a good many years after Hudson, once a Londoner himself, made his breakthrough in another part of the world.

9. Trotting out the Turkey

Myth! Franklin fought publicly to have the bald eagle replaced with the turkey as America's national symbol.

"Turkey" is US slang for failure. The word is usually applied to a play or a movie that has flopped, although its coverage is broad enough to include almost any person or event that has failed. The turkey's association with a very negative concept apparently stems from that animal's known tendency to act stupidly even in simple situations. Some say it's really because the ungainly bird cannot fly, but it's not exactly true that the turkey is an earthbound fowl. Although domestication through selective breeding has deprived the common variety of the power of flight, those untouched in the wilds remain excellent flyers.

Most people find it amusing, if not ironic, that Franklin would find favor with a bird so disreputable as the turkey—and promote it vigorously as his country's icon! A year and a half after Congress adopted the Great Seal on June 20, 1782—with the bald eagle as its centerpiece—Franklin wrote a letter from France to his daughter Mrs. Sarah Bache in Philadelphia and shared some thoughts with her about this new symbol of America. In his letter, Franklin cast doubt on the propriety of using the Bald Eagle as "the Representative of our Country" considering that "(h)e is a Bird of bad moral Character. He does not get his Living honestly...like those among Men who live by Sharping & Robbing he is generally poor and often very lousy. Besides he is a rank Coward." In the same breath, he praised the turkey as an alternative, saying, "(T)he Turkey is in Comparison a much more respectable Bird, and withal a true original Native of America . . . He is besides, though a little vain & silly, a Bird of Courage..."

Contrary to popular belief, Ben did not express these personal musings elsewhere, and they formed part of the lore only after they were revealed by his daughter. Moreover, many historians suggest Ben said all these with tongue in cheek, "for on previous occasions, he had published opinions favoring other unlikely symbols." Thus, in a 1775 letter printed in a magazine, he made a good case for the Rattlesnake as an appropriate representation of "the temper and conduct of America." Not any less whimsical was the "official preference" he expressed in 1776 when he was on the committee that Congress appointed to design the Great Seal, which eschewed an animal emblem in favor of an action scene with Moses and the Pharaoh.

Other historians surmise that Ben's unsolicited praise for the turkey and his dismissal of the bald eagle was just a reaction to the hasty manner in which the latter was officially adopted. Contrary to the suggestion that there was "great debate amongst the Founding Fathers" on the choice of the national bird, Congress approved Charles Thomson's eagle design from among those presented by the preliminary committees on the same day he submitted it—June 20, 1782.

In fairness to those who value the gobbler as more than just thanksgiving fare, the word 'turkey' does not always connote bungling. In the game of bowling, a winning streak of three consecutive strikes is called a turkey. In some metaphors, the term also carries a positive connotation, e.g., to "talk turkey" is to talk plainly or seriously, and "that's cold turkey" means the true details, the straight truth.

10. Alarming Trend

Myth! **Franklin founded the first volunteer fire department and the first fire insurance company.**

The proverb, "Three removes is as bad as a fire," is a rare Franklin original, and in the modern sense means that moving residences more than twice is like losing one's house to a fire. It shows Ben's continuing concern with fire and a reputation for thinking of various ways to protect against the hazard.

Thus, according to the *Scripophily.com* website, "His invention of an iron furnace stove allowed people to warm their homes less dangerously and with less wood...Interestingly enough, Franklin also established the first fire company and the first fire insurance company in order to help people live more safely." The part concerning the stove may have some truth in it, but everything else is wrong. Contrary to the claim, the Philadelphia's Union Fire Company that Ben founded in 1736 wasn't the first of its kind. While it was the first volunteer fire department in the City of Brotherly Love, Boston and other cities had put up their own earlier. In 1659, almost a half century before Franklin was born, Peter Stuyvesant started what may well be the first organized effort at fire fighting by distributing 250 buckets, plus ladders and hooks, in New Amsterdam, and appointing a 'brentmaster' or fire chief to lead it.

Ben is oftentimes given the credit for designing the first fireman's coat, notwithstanding that early Philadelphia firemen had no uniform and wore whatever was handy. The first fire departments that employed *uniformed* firemen on a full-time salaried basis did not appear on the US scene until 1850.

In 1752, Franklin and some friends founded The Philadelphia Contributionship for the Insurance of Houses from Loss by Fire, purportedly the oldest fire insurance company in America. Actually, it was the second oldest, the earliest being the Friendly Society of Mutual Insuring of Homes against Fire, a mutual company founded by Charleston residents in 1735. But because it lasted only until 1741, when a major fire put it out of business, Ben's company 11 years later had the appearance of being the first. The first successful joint-stock company, as opposed to a mutual, was the Insurance Company of North America, which began business in Philadelphia in 1792 to sell marine, fire, and life insurance.

---

11. Richard on Richard

Myth! Franklin composed a proverb based on the fate of Richard III.

The Franklin proverb partly reads: "For the want of a horse the rider was lost; for the want of a rider the battle was lost; for the want of a battle the kingdom was lost." It makes no specific reference to Richard III, however, nor to any historical event involving this last Yorkist king. Only Shakespeare made some allusion in his play *Richard III* when he quoted Richard as saying, "A horse! A horse! My kingdom for a horse!"

In the preface of *Poor Richard's Almanack* for 1758, Richard Saunders, Ben's alter ego, tells of a man known as Father Abraham who says, "And again, he Richard adviseth to circumspection and care, even in the smallest matters, because sometimes a little neglect may breed great mischief, adding, for want of a nail, the shoe was lost; for want of a shoe the horse was lost; and for want of a horse the rider was lost, being overtaken and slain by the enemy, all for want of care about a horseshoe nail."

It is not probable that Franklin had any particular true incident in mind when he wrote the above, or even that he drew upon his imagination for an illustration of his precept. This is because Franklin appropriated the proverb in its entirety from George

Herbert's collection. Herbert was the Bartlett of Franklin's day, and the one from whom Franklin sourced many of his Poor Richard sayings. As Herbert put it in his *Jacula Prudentum*, "For want of a nail, the shoe is lost; for want of a shoe, the horse is lost; for want of a horse, the rider is lost."

III

Their Electric Moments

On Inventors, Scientists and Entrepreneurs

"I have not failed.
I've just found 10,000 ways that won't work."

•

Thomas Edison

1. The Light that Failed

Myth! Edison invented the electric light bulb.

Many, including Thomas Edison himself, regard the electric light bulb as his greatest invention. Edison is so closely identified with his 'masterpiece' that one can almost see the face of this homegrown genius imprinted on a burning filament.

But never mind what Edison believed. While he admittedly did a lot for the electric light, he did not invent it. In fact, he was sued for making the claim—and lost. It was Sir Humphrey Davy who first came up with the device in 1802, when he passed electricity through a platinum wire. Unfortunately, the filaments burned out too soon, forcing the Englishman to abandon his discovery. Others, mostly Europeans, continued the task, so that by the 1860s short-lived light bulbs with filaments were strong enough for some application. Although incandescent light had yet to be perfected, by the 1870s arc lighting (light that is created when a spark "arcs" across two highly charged electric rods) was already in use in lighthouses and in the street lamps of some major cities. The only problem was that they used too much energy and generated too much light to be practical in homes.

Enter the late Edison. Beginning work in 1877, Edison made thousands of attempts towards producing a long-lasting filament. Finally, in 1879, after placing a carbonized cotton thread in a bulb from which the air had been pumped out, he succeeded. But he was a year too late. A fellow inventor by the name of Joseph Swan, who had made independent and similar progress in incandescent lighting, was able to patent his work in 1878. Although Swan won the patent infringement action he filed against Edison, the two rivals decided on a settlement by joining forces in the Edison and Swan United Electric Company. Edison later bought out Swan's interest in the venture, and on his own established the first large-scale commercial lighting system.

We are told that Edison made his critical breakthrough on October 21, 1879, known for many years as 'Electric Light Day'. Supposedly on this occasion, he kept a light bulb lit for a minimum 40 hours. This is totally untrue. According to lab notes, another full year went by before the inventor could produce a 40-hour bulb. A reporter who needed copy for the Christmas season faked the whole story about the October 21 event in a December 1879 issue of his paper.

Edison, like Swan, merely improved on what others had achieved earlier. However, it is only fair that he alone gets the credit for the development of public lighting, for establishing an electrical distribution system that could be operated economically, and for promoting the general use of electricity.

| 2. Current Events |

Myth! Edison developed and promoted the use of alternating current in American homes.

Thomas Edison remains foremost in the minds of most Americans as the man responsible for the type of electric current that powers their homes.

In fact, what Edison championed was the use of direct current, in the process fighting off competition from alternating current at every turn. The latter ultimately prevailed, thanks to the superb efforts of another pioneer, George Westinghouse. Alternating current (AC) is generally the one proposed for modern power systems, from houses to factories, because, unlike direct current, it can be easily converted to higher or lower voltages.

Edison initially succeeded in getting the whole of America to accept direct current as the standard. To do it, he had to discredit alternating current in a most underhanded way—by promoting Westinghouse's version as the more efficient current for the electric chair! When the state of New York abandoned the gallows for the chair as the favored mode of execution in 1890, Edison connived with officials to have a Westinghouse AC generator installed at the prison to effect the killing. The first ever execution by electricity was deliberately botched to make a martyr of the victim, William Kemmler, and Edison the winner of the 'War of the Currents'. By 1882 Edison Electric Light Company's Pearl Street Station was up and running in New York City. This early electrical system, running on direct current, would serve as a model for the rest of the country. Fortunately for everyone, Edison's power grid did not last. In the end, AC proved to be more useful for industrial purposes than DC and eventually became the national standard.

Contrary to the movie myth, throwing the switch of the electric chair to start an execution has no effect whatsoever on the main power system of the prison. The flickering and dimming of the lights on death row when an electrocution is in process is shown on the screen purely for effect. According to an observer, "(t)he chair works by creating a massive short circuit so it is utterly impossible to have the thing linked up to the regular supply without blowing everything in the place. It runs off its own generator."

3. The Don of Movie Making

Myth! **Edison invented the movies.**

Edison usually gets the credit for inventing motion pictures. The greatest single proof of his accomplishment was the kinetoscope process, which debuted in the late 1800s.

This happens to be one more wobbly trophy for the Wizard of Menlo Park. The first motion picture films were taken with a camera patented in Britain by French-born Louis Aimé Augustin Le Prince in 1888. Edison's invention was admittedly more sophisticated, but it did not appear until 1891. Unfortunately, Le Prince disappeared with his invention after boarding a train at Dijon bound for Paris.

Assuming Le Prince's contribution does not qualify for lack of substantiation, it still cannot be said that Edison's kinetoscope process is the original. The Englishman William George Horner in 1833 invented the zoetrope, or 'wheel of life', a rotating slotted cylinder that made pictures appear to move when the device was turned. In 1879, a San Francisco photographer, Eadweard Muybridge, patented 'a method and apparatus for photographing objects in motion'. His purpose was to corroborate the claim of California governor Leland Stanford that a running horse lifts all four of its feet off the ground simultaneously. Then in 1882, a Frenchman, Etienne Jules Marey, devised a photographic 'gun' to record the flights of birds.

It is not widely known that Edison's personal attempts at inventing motion pictures were never successful. His failures in 1887 prompted him to direct his assistant William Kennedy Laurie Dickson to develop a device "which should do for the eye what the phonograph does for the ear." Two years later Dickson came up with the first model of the kinetoscope, with its accompanying camera, the kinetograph. "In other words," one writer notes, "Edison may have instigated the first commercially developed movie process, but he did not invent it." It was Dickson who completed the kinetoscope almost single-handed at Edison's laboratories in West Orange, New Jersey.

Even the Vitascope was not an Edison invention, as is generally believed. It was designed by Jenkins and Armat and given to Edison under an exploitation contract. This machine is often honored for having screened a film for the first time before a paying audience on 23 April 1896. That event, however, was actually preceded a year earlier, on 20 May 1895, when a cruder type called the Eidoloscope, designed by one Eugene Lauste, screened a film before paying customers.

4. Merchant of Phonography

Myth! Edison invented the phonograph as a device for playing music.

Some biographers claim Edison originally intended his phonograph to bring music to the masses. This is evident, they say, from the fact that soon after constructing the device, he had it play the simple tune "Mary had a little lamb." Others insist Edison could not have had this purpose in mind because he was somewhat deaf and did not care particularly for music. Besides, he did not play music on the contraption, as is popularly believed, but only shouted into it the words 'Mary had a little lamb' to test the sound.

In 1878, Edison confided in the North American Review that the principal use of the phonograph was for "letter writing and all kinds of dictation without the aid of a stenographer." He had been convinced apparently that his original plan to use the invention as a telephone-answering device was premature. The telephone was proving to be an economical and convenient tool for the average

American family, and Edison saw no need to enhance its application.

Edison limited his early marketing efforts to the phonograph's business and office prospects as a dictating machine. To help launch this purpose, he recorded various voices, one of them purportedly that of Abraham Lincoln. As expected, no copy of the President's historic pressing has ever been found; the inventor's first successful sound-recording device came out only in 1877, or twelve years after Lincoln's death. However, Edison succeeded in getting the voice imprints of a few luminaries of the era, among them Robert Browning, P. T. Barnum, William Gladstone and Alfred, Lord Tennyson.

Music was tentatively played into the machine when Johannes Brahms did a Hungarian rhapsody for the representatives Edison sent abroad armed with phonographs and cylinders. But the first real breakthrough for the phonograph as a music-recording device would occur only a decade later. A Polish pianist and child prodigy, twelve-year-old Josef Hofmann, made the first classical recording at Edison's New Jersey laboratory in 1888. That same year the German pianist and conductor Hans von Bülow invited Edison to the Metropolitan Opera House in New York City, where the two collaborated on reproducing symphonic music for the first time.

5. The Man who Wasn't There

Myth! Edison was a scientific genius, if an absent-minded one.

Edison is popularly regarded as a rags-to-riches genius with a generous share of the eccentricities associated with inventors. "In Thomas Edison's case," says a writer, "the confusion has been over not the invention but the inventor himself." Myths flourish about his personal life, like growing up poor and doing badly in school. According to a story that imitates the opening scene of Walt Disney's *The Absent-Minded Professor*, Edison became so engrossed with his experiments that he forgot his own wedding day. Another story recounts how a train conductor, annoyed by Edison's dangerous experiments, struck him on the ear and made him deaf. These events and circumstances have been proven spurious, but not some of the idiosyncrasies. The inventor did believe in office anarchy, telling a recruit in his laboratory who asked about the rules, "Hell! There ain't no rules around here! We are tryin' to accomplish somep'n."

People think Edison was a genius, something that not even his super-sized ego would admit. He was an industrious innovator without much technical qualification but with a lot of marketing savvy. Two of his famous quotations were designed to give most of the credit for his accomplishments to toiling, not brilliance. The first: "Genius is one percent inspiration and ninety-nine percent perspiration." The second: "There is no substitute for hard work."

6. Global Movement

Myth! After recanting at his trial for heresy, Galileo muttered, "And yet it moves."

Legend has it that at his trial before the Inquisition in 1633, the Italian mathematician, physicist and philosopher Galileo Galilei muttered the phrase, *Eppur si muove*, after being forced to recant his belief that the Earth moves around the Sun. The English equivalent, "And yet it moves," is often used in modern speech to indicate that, although someone who is in a knowledgeable position may discount or deny something publicly, that does not stop it from being true.

At the time of Galileo's alleged trial, it was the dominant view among theologians, philosophers and scientists that the Earth is the stationary center of the universe "as ordained by God." For his contrariness, Galileo's adversaries brought him before the Inquisition on a charge of heresy, a capital offense, but Galileo is said to have recanted to save his skin and was only put under house arrest until his death nine years later.

According to some historians, Galileo never spent so much as a day in prison, not because he recanted but because there was no real trial or Inquisition to pressure him into making a recantation. Galileo was merely asked to explain his science before some royalty and elders at a forum where he stated that "if the Pope insists that he (Galileo) must not affirm what he happens to know, he would obey to avoid a scandal among the faithful." These same historians cast doubt on the belief that the hearing was an attack on heliocentrism, considering that Galileo was not the founder of the theory but only supported it by observations made using a telescope. Moreover, heliocentrism dates back to Aristarchus of Samos in the 3rd century BC, and was already a developed mathematical model in Nicolas Copernicus' time in the 16th century. The theologian Thomas Schirrmacher notes that Galileo and the Copernican system were actually well regarded by church officials—until this luminary fell victim to "his own arrogance, the envy of his colleagues, and the politics of Pope Urban VIII."

There is no contemporary evidence that Galileo muttered the expression, *Eppur si muove*, at the time of the supposed trial, and although the earliest biography of the scientist, written by his disciple Vincenzio Viviani, depicts Galileo as having sincerely recanted, it does not mention the phrase. Logic dictates that had he been in an Inquisition and his grumbling heard and recorded, any recantation would have been nullified then and there and he would have been sentenced to death. Researchers have traced the beginnings of the legend to a tale recounted by an Italian living in London in 1757, or 124 years after the supposed incident, and published in *Querelles Littéraires* (1761). In 1911, the famous line was found on a Spanish painting owned by a Belgian family and dated 1643 or 1645. Though falsely depicting Galileo in a dungeon, the art piece strongly suggests that the legend had already been circulating for over a century before *Querelles Littéraires* was published and may even have been current during the physicist's lifetime.

7. Three from Galileo's Proofs

Myth! Galileo invented the telescope and conducted experiments at famous Pisa landmarks leading to the discovery of the laws of the pendulum and of falling bodies.

In one of the several pseudo-historical bits about Galileo, the twenty-year-old fledgeling scientist was mooning about in the cathedral of Pisa when he noticed a lamp swinging freely from a

49

long chain overhead, making an arc to the left and then another to the right. Curious to find out how long it took the lamp to swing back and forth, he felt his pulse to time the swings and concluded that the period of each swing was exactly the same. It is said that from this observation the law of the pendulum, which would eventually be used to regulate clocks, was born.

It is true Galileo avidly studied the motion of a pendulum and realized that its swing is constant regardless of amplitude (at least to small angle approximations). But he did not come by the theory as a result of observing a swinging lamp in the cathedral of Pisa or anywhere else. Britannica, which reported the false story, apparently did not check the previous works of biographers and historians, which had already exposed it as myth. William Shea, a leading authority on Galileo, says there is no evidence outside Vincenzio Viviani that Galileo knew how to count a pendulum's pulse. Viviani was the Italian scientist's first biographer who idealistically misrepresented Galileo's early interests and became the Britannica's unwitting source.

Viviani was again the advocate of a second myth as prominent as the first, tending to give the impression that Galileo was an experimentalist more than a mathematician. This time Galileo is reported as employing the scientific method to prove that objects of different weights fall at the same velocity, contrary to Aristotle's thesis that the heavier the object, the faster it will fall. Proceeding to demonstrate the uniformity of acceleration, the Italian dropped a cannon ball and a wooden ball simultaneously from his native city's most famous landmark, the Leaning Tower of Pisa. The entire faculty of the university who were assembled there walked away convinced not only of the new principle but also of Galileo's scientific prowess.

And the Britannica once more took up the story, not realizing that neither Galileo himself nor any of his contemporaries had mentioned it specifically. Years before the Encyclopedia's entry, Lane Cooper, in his book *Aristotle, Galileo and the Leaning Tower of Pisa* (1935, Cornell University Press) had expressed doubt that the episode, assuming it happened, involved Galileo. Joe Milana of the University of Maryland's Department of Physics voiced the same sentiment, saying: "While some of his earlier predecessors actually performed this experiment, Galileo did not." Milana went on to note that, "when Galileo was an old man, one of his students did perform the demonstration to an audience of

Aristotelian scholars and found in fact a slight difference in the time the two balls struck the ground." This difference was totally consistent with Galileo's own finding that viscosity (wind friction) affects the speed of falling bodies. But to the Aristotelian scholars, who were completely ignorant of the scientific method, it was proof that their old master Aristotle had been correct after all!

William Shea, for one, concludes that, except for his incursions into astronomy, Galileo's approach was fundamentally mathematical, as he was, in fact, a professor of mathematics and did not depend on "detailed observation of natural phenomena." Yet in a third myth, the famous Pisan is presented as having invented the telescope by the use of advanced laboratory skills. Actually, Galileo had nothing to do with the instrument except to announce its existence, improve on the original, and use it intensively for his astronomical experiments. The real inventor, at first thought to be the Dutch optician Hans Lippershey, was Lippershey's apprentice who, in 1608, "while playing games, suddenly found that he could make far-away things look nearer by combining certain lenses. He reported this to his master, who enclosed the lenses at the two ends of a tube and created the first telescope." But having heard of the Lippershey breakthrough despite efforts by the Dutch government to keep the invention a secret for military reasons, Galileo set out to duplicate the device and did so within one year. His version was treble the power of Lippershey's model and enabled him to conduct experiments that eventually led to his famous astronomical discoveries.

8. Henry and Lizzie: A Love Story

Myth! **The philanthropist Henry Ford, who originated the moving assembly line in automotive manufacturing, returned much of his wealth to his workers and the public.**

Ford, an icon of the American capitalist system, is admired for several things. He passed on his profits to the buyers of his products through lower prices and to his workers by doubling their wages to $5 a day in 1914. He upheld the old rural values of honesty, thrift, and hard work, and was an avowed pacifist who sponsored a peace ship to Europe in 1915 to talk world leaders into ending the war. He left behind Greenfield Village in Dearborn, Michigan, so future generations of children could see how people lived in pre-industrial America.

But many who look at the underside of the icon are disappointed to see a different man. Professing to scorn history, Ford was actually ignorant about it. He was a rabid anti-Semite, using the Dearborn Independent weekly newspaper, which he acquired in 1918, to publicize his hate. The tycoon exploited his workers and pioneered in the art of union busting. The extra pay to his workers was Ford's way of justifying the dehumanizing drudgery of the assembly line (Ford workers were "forbidden to sit, whistle, sing, lean against the machinery, smoke or talk while working"), and of preventing them from joining a union.

Ford recaptured the wages he paid—and more—from the prices of cars the workers bought themselves, and he made millions in profits during both world wars. His vaunted philanthropy was worth no more than the $40 million or so he distributed between 1908 and 1947, a measly amount relative to the wealth he accumulated. Contrary to the image it projected, the Ford Foundation he and his son Edsel established in 1936 was not a recipient of much Ford wealth during his lifetime.

Ford's moving assembly line, which enabled the efficient mass production of his automobiles, wasn't really original. People think so only because he installed one of the earliest types. The very first one can be traced to Eli Whitney (1765-1825), who applied the technique to the manufacture of small arms for the US government. Even Frederick W. Taylor was ahead of Ford when he described the idea in a book he wrote in 1911. In the automotive industry, the originator was Ransom E. Olds, who, with his innovation, boosted production of the Reo and Oldsmobile brands from 425 cars in 1901 to over 2,500 the next year. What Ford did was improve on Old's system of wooden platforms on casters passing between lines of workers who added parts until the car was completed. Ford introduced the conveyor belt, which moved both the cars and needed parts along the production line, cutting Ford's production time for the Model T from a day to about two hours.

Within the Ford Company itself, no single individual conceived the idea of a conveyor belt. According to Ford biographer Robert Lacey, the invention was the joint effort of several of Ford's top engineers who were being pressured by the need to increase the output of Model T units immediately. Sales had gone from eighteen thousand cars in 1909-10 to thirty-five thousand in 1910-11 to seventy-eight thousand in 1911-12. People had begun buying the car in such great numbers that Ford could not meet the demand.

Historians believe that if Ford is to be honored, it should not be for any manufacturing breakthrough. Rather, it should be for his ability to recognize the necessity for something new and his willingness to try it.

9. Oil Alone

Myth! **John D. Rockefeller conceived the future monopoly called the Standard Oil Company.**

John D. Rockefeller has always been regarded as the founder of the Standard Oil Company, the fountainhead of many of the major oil companies now operating in the United States and around the world. But a closer scrutiny of this once great monopoly reveals that he was not the one who first thought of it.

When asked once about the origins of the company, John D. said, "I wish I'd had the brains to think of it. It was Henry M. Flagler." Flagler's long partnership with Rockefeller began in 1865 when Rockefeller rented desk space in his office to the young commission merchant who had just arrived in Cleveland. Flagler put in a modest amount—about $50,000—into the firm, but it was not his money that was so important as his abilities. At a time when demand for oil was low, Flagler suggested expanding the business through the formation of a joint stock corporation in 1870. As secretary and treasurer, Flagler handled the organization of the new firm with precision, and was also instrumental in developing a working relationship between the fledgling trust and the railroads.

Flagler in his later years would become known as the 'Father of Florida', for his role in building the Florida East Coast Railroad in the 1890s from Daytona to Miami and for converting large areas of swampland along the way into fabulous resorts. He extended the tracks more than 100 miles over a loose string of islands to Key

West, and another line into central Florida that opened the state's richest agricultural region.

10. Down-to-Earth Principle

Myth! Newton discovered gravity from seeing an apple fall from a tree.

Sir Isaac Newton was taking tea under some apple trees in the family gardens at Woolsthorpe one summer afternoon in 1665. Suddenly, an apple fell from an overhanging branch and hit him on the head. Eureka! Thus was the principle of gravity born (or, more precisely, discovered).

One could believe that a falling apple inspired the formulation of perhaps the greatest law of physics if the scientist himself had admitted it. This was precisely what Newton did, according to some historians, except that no confirmation can be found in any of the great man's writings. It is alleged that the apple fell on the ground (not on his head, as some would have it) in the light of the crescent moon, setting Newton to wondering if the same force affected both the apple and the moon. A report states that in 1936, a publisher brought out the memoirs of one of Newton's closest friends, W. Stukely, and on page 19 was revealed 'the old apple anecdote'. Much earlier than this, a Newton biographer, Sir David Brewster, had perpetuated the story as originated by Voltaire (*Eléments de la Philosophie de Newton*, 1738). "One day," writes Voltaire, "in the year 1666, Newton, then retired to the country (at Woolsthorpe, visiting his mother), seeing some fruit fall from a tree, as I was told by his niece, Mme. Conduit, fell into profound meditation upon the cause which draws all bodies in a line which, if prolonged, would pass very nearly through the center of the earth."

Casting a pall on all these postulations, *The People's Almanac #2* states that "important early biographies of Newton by Pemberton, Whiston, and Colin Maclaurin include no mention of the incident at all." Others that do are based solely on hearsay. For one, the aforementioned Stukely, a physician, cleric and prominent antiquarian, vaguely reminisced on a meeting in which Newton had mentioned about the apple, but never claimed to have

54

witnessed the incident firsthand. For another, Voltaire relied completely on the gossip provided by Mme. Conduit, who in some accounts is identified as Catherine Barton, Newton's niece and housekeeper during his affluent days. A source reveals that, although Voltaire may have been a rabid advocate of Newton, they never actually met. The Frenchman himself was one of the first to confess that people tended to attribute to Newton things that he never did. About a century later, the great German astronomer Karl Fredrich Gauss would resort to the same hearsay tactics to finish off the apple theory. Doubting that any part of the story is true, he called it silly and alleged it was only invented by Newton to put down a 'stupid, officious' inquirer.

While this has nothing to do with the apple, it may be worth noting that in a report personally written by Newton as its president, the Royal Society announced in 1712 that he had invented calculus and that Gottfried Wilhelm Leibniz' own claim was a plagiarism. It is now well established that both, acting independently, are the inventors.

11. Looking Over one's Shoulder

Myth! Newton quipped, "If I have seen a little farther than others, it is because I have stood on the shoulders of giants."

Sir Isaac Newton, whose fine intellect led him on to some of the greatest scientific discoveries ever made, had his share of false credits too. One of these had to do not with a bum achievement but with a bad quote. In order to show the scientist and much-published author as modest and unassuming as Galileo before him and Einstein after him, historians and biographers have dreamed up one of his more famous aphorisms, "If I have seen a little farther than others, it is because I have stood on the shoulders of giants."

Newton is said to have made the remark on February 15, 1676, in a letter to his rival Robert Hooke. It was supposedly to call attention to the latter's slight build and severe stoop, as the scientist's way of spiting Hooke for being highly critical of his ideas. Newton enjoyed his reputation as author of the quote for nearly three centuries until sociologist Robert Merton wrote an entire book debunking it. According to Merton, the saying about dwarves seeing farther from the shoulders of giants had been around in some form or other for centuries before Newton used it. John of Salisbury wrote in his *Metalogicon* that the metaphor was first heard in the twelfth century (ca. 1126) from Bernard of Chartres. Robert Burton repeated the phrase in his 1624 *Anatomy of Melancholy*, citing his contemporary, Didacus Stella, who in turn pointed to Luke as his source (in 1891, John Bartlett misattributed Burton's version of the saying to the Roman poet Lucan, an error that persisted through Bartlett's 1980 edition fifteen years after Merton's book was published). Only a couple of decades before Newton's letter, George Herbert in his *Jacula Prudentum* (1651) had given his own spin on the saying, and in the 19th century, Samuel Taylor Coleridge in *The Friend* (1828) wrote, "The dwarf sees farther than the giant, when he has the giant's shoulders to mount on." Friedrich Nietzsche would later controvert Coleridge, arguing that the dwarf (the academic scholar) brings even the most sublime heights down to his level of understanding. Or alternatively, as in *Thus Spoke Zarathustra* (1882), one climbs to great heights with a dwarf on his shoulders to show him his greatest thoughts.

Variations on the theme appeared frequently thereafter in a wide range of genres and cultures. The portrayal of dwarfs on shoulders was common in medieval religious art, including some stained-glass windows of the cathedral at Chartres. In Asia among Malays and Filipinos, the dwarf is a lowly fly that, when standing on the head of a water buffalo, presents a prouder and more masterful figure than its host. In modern times, a bestselling book by British scientist Stephen Hawking is called "On the Shoulders of Giants," while his country's two-pound coin bears the inscription "Standing on the shoulders of giants" on its edge. Google Scholar, a search site for scholarly literature, has adopted "Stand on the shoulders of giants" as its motto. The last three instances of the aphorism have Newton to thank for, whether or not he originated it.

Merton has a good word for Newton, though. In Merton's words, the saying "became Newton's own, not because he deliberately made it so but because admirers of Newton made it so."

12. Rub-a-dub-dub

Myth! Archimedes discovered the principle of buoyancy while soaking in a bathtub.

The tale is told that King Hiero II gave some gold to a smith to be made into a votive crown. Seeing the finished crown, the king suspected that the gold had been adulterated with an inferior metal, and so asked Archimedes to test it. The Greek mathematician and scientist, deciding he would ponder over the problem while relaxing in his bath, got into a tub that was filled to the brim. Upon noticing that some of the water ran over, he reportedly exclaimed, "Eureka!" He had realized that his body, while immersed in the water, lost weight equal to the weight of the amount of water that it displaced. Applying this finding to Hiero's problem, he concluded that since gold is heavier than silver, a floating vessel holding a pure-gold crown would displace more water than one holding a crown made of mixed metals. Thus did Archimedes find that the crown was deficient in gold and that the smith had tricked the king.

Archimedes' discovery is a science factoid, but modern historians believe the story woven around it is a fabrication. The principal author, a biographer named Vitruvius, is one of the many Greek pseudo-historians who in their days popularized their works by blurring the line between reality and myth.

13. Pressure in the Right Places

Myth! Charles Atlas founded his success in the bodybuilding business on a system called dynamic tension.

Charles Atlas (1894-1972), whose real name was Angelo Siciliano, started out as a husky boy in his native Sicily, then became anemic, weak and underweight after settling in Brooklyn at age 11. Sick of being made fun of, he resolved to build himself up through dynamic tension, a system he himself had developed. He acquired a powerful physique and soon won the title of 'The World's Most Perfectly Developed Man'. Opening his own gym where he offered his system in person or by mail order, an imaginative advertising campaign by his marketing assistant, Charles Roman, and the novelty of his system combined to make the business a success. He drew tens of thousands of responses yearly from individuals interested to attain the Atlas physique as a way of escaping from a life of weakness and inferiority.

The centerpiece of Roman's ad was a comic strip in which Atlas is a 97-pound weakling who gets sand kicked into his face by a muscled beach bum before his miracle transformation. The cartoon treatment was apparently necessary because the incident never happened and Atlas did not weigh 97 lbs. when he made his crucial decision to undergo physical development. He was, in fact, skinnier, a puny 80 pounds, raising his base weight to 97 lbs. only to make his claimed rate of improvement more credible. Whatever it took Atlas to put on a new appearance, most physical culturists believe he could not have done it except by a balanced regimen that included diet, weights and exercise, and only a little of his patented dynamic tension.

14. Mr. Smithson Goes to Washington

Myth! The Smithsonian Institute is a museum and learning institution established in Washington, DC, under John Smithson's last will and testament.

It's the Smithsonian Institution in accordance with the terms of its creation—until someone slips and calls it the Smithsonian Institute. The error arises likely because the Institution, which was founded in 1846, has under its aegis the Smithsonian Tropical Research Institute. A British chemist and mineralogist bequeathed the greater part of his estate amounting to £100,000 "to the United States of America, to found at Washington, under the name to [of] the Smithsonian Institution, an establishment for the increase and diffusion of knowledge among men." When the gift was made, it was not clear that the federal government could legally accept it, and eight years of wrangling, mostly between the forces of John Quincy Adams, who was in favor, and John C. Calhoun, who was against, ensued before Congress gave its final approval.

Another misconception about the Smithsonian is that it is a

museum. Its more famous features include an array of museums, such as the National Air and Space Museum, the National Museum of American Art, and the National Museum of History and Technology. But these are entities existing independently under the Institution and none of them is identifiable with the Institution itself. For the same reason, it is erroneous to call the Smithsonian an establishment of learning, as writers often do, although it has under its administration the aforementioned Smithsonian Tropical Research Institute as well as the Science Information Exchange and the Radiation Biology Laboratory. It also frequently sponsors scientific research and exploration and publishes books and periodicals. Rather than being a corporation, as this is normally understood, the Institution is an incorporated board consisting of the US vice president, the chief justice, three senators, three representatives, and six non-officials as regents.

The Smithsonian is not named for someone called Smithsonian, or Smith, or for that matter anyone originally named Smithson. Our philanthropist was a self-made Englishman born in France in 1765 and christened James Lewis Macie. His father, Hugh Smithson, was a wealthy Briton who legally changed his name to Hugh Percy and later became the 1st duke of Northumberland. Being an illegitimate child, Macie was able to assume his paternal name only when he was in college. Two oddities about the bequest stand out: first, the US was only an alternate to Smithson's primary beneficiary, a nephew who died heirless; and second, Smithson never saw Washington or any part of America, and apparently did not correspond with anyone there until he died in 1829 at age 64, seventeen years before the Institution was founded.

IV

Nature Studies

On Nature and its Laws

"All truths are easy to understand once they are discovered;
the point is to discover them."

•

Galileo Galilei

1. Ole Blue Cheese

Myth! "Blue moon" is a metaphor and has nothing to do with a real moon.

In the Rodgers and Hart song "Blue Moon," the word "blue" conveys mood. The title itself is a metaphor that describes the unhappiness of lonely people who endure life "without a love of (their) own."

Obviously, not mood but color underlies the literal connotation of "blue moon." Reference is to an optical illusion that occurs when large quantities of sulfuric dust or fine debris from a volcanic eruption or forest fire travel high enough into the atmosphere to filter the moon's reflected light. The moon looks bluish from an angle through the chemical mist, but it never really assumes a bluish hue. The earliest known "blue moon" came out in 1883, its face hazed in volcanic dust spewed thirty miles into the air by a volcanic eruption on the island of Krakatoa near Java. The latest appeared on September 26, 1950, when a forest fire in northern British Columbia sent up enough sulfur to make the moon look blue to people from Great Britain.

An older explanation for the origin of "blue moon" has to do with the time of the moon's appearance. Back in the early sixteenth century, jocular writers claimed that the moon was made of blue cheese. Actually, they were not alluding to the color of the moon but to its similarity to stale cheese. When full and just rising, the moon resembles newly pressed "green" cheese both in color and shape. However, it rarely appears in this manner on unusually clear nights. Rather, with the entire surface remaining visible despite just a thin edge being illuminated, it looks like cheese that has become blue with mold.

A more recent connotation of "blue moon" is the lunar condition that occurs when two full moons appear in the same month. Since the full moon is seen once every 29.53 days, it is possible to have a "moonless" month, which under the present calendar can only be a February. To compensate for the loss of a full moon in February, another month, usually January or March, may have two full moons, one at the beginning and the other at the end of the lunar cycle. A "blue moon" of this type occurred in 1885, 1915, 1934 and 1961, although what happened in 1866—two "blue moons" in the same year—was even more spectacular. That year February had no full moon but the preceding January and the following March had two full moons each. According to astronomers, this remarkable sequence happens only "once in a blue moon"—that is to say, not for another 2,500,000 years.

2. The Moon has Two Faces

Myth! **Fifty percent of the moon is perpetually dark.**

There is no "dark side of the moon," the popular expression notwithstanding. True, a good part of the moon is never visible from the earth, but that doesn't mean it's an area perpetually devoid of light. The sun shines on it, in fact on the entire moon, at some particular conjunction of the three bodies during the lunar day (or earth month). It's just that we can't see when it's high noon on the backside.

Experts believe that in the distant past, the moon was much closer to the earth than it is now and rotated much faster, so that the entire lunar surface could be seen from earth at various times. But action from the earth's gravity caused the side of the moon closest to us to bulge outward, just as the moon's gravity causes our oceans to bulge and create tides. Eventually, this continual deformation of the lunar crust as it rotated relative to the earth slowed the moon down so that the same side always faced toward the earth.

The perception is nonetheless wrong that exactly half of the moon's surface is hidden from human view. Although a stabilized position of gravitational forces has been achieved between the earth and the moon, the velocity of the moon's orbit is not uniform. This eccentricity results in the phenomenon known as 'libration', which enables us to see more than half of the moon's surface in its orbit. In all, about 59 percent of the moon's surface is visible at some point, while only 41 percent is actually never seen from earth.

Incidentally, the word 'quarter' as used to describe the moon's phases refers to time—one-fourth of a lunar month—and not to the shape of the visible moon. Quite often calendars, newspapers, authors, and artists offer sketches of these phases showing each quarter incorrectly as one-fourth of a full moon. A correct moon diagram would show, from left to right, a black circle (new); a circle half-black on the left (first quarter); a white circle (full); and a circle half-black on the right (last quarter).

3. Look, Sky Walkers!

Myth! **The constellation Twins is in the sign Gemini.**

The zodiac is an astronomical belt in which the sun, the moon and the major planets, as viewed from the earth, apparently move. It is divided into parts called the signs of the zodiac, each sign occupying 1/12, or 30 degrees, of the great circle. We see from the horoscope that a sign has the same name as that of the constellation located within its boundaries.

Many people still believe that the signs are in exact correspondence with the 12 constellations bearing the same names—for example, the lion sign with the constellation Leo and the crab with Cancer. This is no longer true. Each constellation is now in the sign that has the name next following its own. Thus, the constellation Leo has moved to the sign Virgo, Cancer to Leo, and Gemini to Cancer. Formerly, the constellations had fixed boundaries, and each was related to a specific time period during the year when the sun was supposed to pass through it. However, these star formations are actually irregular in size and shape, and the sun regularly passes through one—Ophiuchus—that is not considered a member of the zodiac. Consequently, the constellations have effectively shifted eastward over the last 2,000 years, a phenomenon called the 'precession of the equinoxes'. There has been no effect on the horoscope, however, and the dates continue to be used for astrological purposes despite the mismatch between sign and constellation.

The ancient Greeks called the belt *zodiakos kyrklos*, 'circle of animals', or *ta zodia*, the little animals'. Why they did this after naming only seven of the signs after animals is not clear. Four humans—the Gemini twins, Virgo and Aquarius—represent three other signs. Of the remaining two, one is Sagittarius the centaur, which is half-human and half animal, and the other is Libra the scale, an inanimate object. In short, the zodiac consists of seven and a half animals, four and a half humans, and one object. Quite possibly, the ancients saw the matter as scientists would, that is to say, they considered all the signs of the zodiac, including Libra, which was originally called 'the Claws' and attached to Scorpio, as belonging to the broad category of animals that includes humans.

4. 24 Carrot Sticks and a One Pound Cake

Myth! Wet sand is heavier than dry sand, a pound of feathers weighs the same as a pound of gold, and 'carat' is another way of spelling 'karat'.

Wet sand is heavier than dry sand. One pound of feathers equals one pound of gold. A carat is a karat. Each sounds like a truism, a statement you would bet your bottom dollar on as though you heard it from Einstein.

Bead of water or bead of sand? Your science teacher may tell you that sand to which an amount of moisture is added becomes heavier than when it was dry. But it's not always so. In certain cases, the wet sand will actually weigh less than an equal measure of dry sand. This is because of a reaction called bulking. The film of water that forms around the individual grains prevents them from flowing together, and this gives rise to an increase in volume out of all proportion to the amount of water added. Thus, a cubic foot of average wet river sand will weigh from twelve to fifteen pounds less than a cubic foot of the same sand in a dry condition. Of course, bulking depends on the quality of the sand. As a rule, fine sand bulks more than coarse sand does. But more important is the percentage of water added. Sand bulks noticeably from a dry condition to about five per cent of moisture. The US Bureau of Public Roads has noted that if sand is thoroughly saturated so that all the voids are filled with water, it will approximate its original weight measure for measure. A cubic foot of sand can tolerate a moisture content of about fourteen per cent without gaining weight. At this point it is said to be inundated and weighs about the same as an equal measure of dry sand. Beyond it, the wet sand becomes heavier than dry sand measure for measure as more and more water is added.

Bed of feathers or bed of gold? Feathers weigh less than gold volume for volume. Regardless of volume, however, a pound of feathers should weigh the same as a pound of gold. This is where Tricky Dickey gets tripped up. A pound of feathers actually weighs more than a pound of gold, using the different systems for measuring the weight of these objects. The avoirdupois pound contains sixteen 437.5-grain ounces, or 7,000 grains, while the troy weight pound contains only twelve 480-grain ounces, or 5,760 grains. Feathers and most other large and coarse commodities, including people, are measured by avoirdupois weight. Gold and other precious metals and stones are measured by troy weight. The difference between the two measures is an impressive four ounces.

Pile of bricks or pile of stones? Finally, many assume that the words 'carat' and 'karat' are simply different spellings of the same word. The fact is they have different meanings, although both are measures of valuable commodities. A carat is a unit of weight used for measuring precious stones and gems. The international standard, or metric, carat is 0.2 grams, which means that a twelve-carat diamond weighs 2.4 grams. Karat, on the other hand, refers to the purity of gold regardless of weight. Pure gold is assigned twenty-four parts, or karats, and anything less than pure gold is measured as a proportion of these twenty-four parts. For example, eighteen-karat gold contains eighteen parts gold and six parts alloy. Gold in an object that is only half-pure is 12 karat strong.

5. To the Ends of the Earth

Myth! The compass always points to the north.

The compass always points to the north, which is the North Pole. We don't need anyone to tell us that there's absolutely no chance, any time and anywhere, of the needle doing a sudden 180-degree turn and pointing south.

It is not the case, of course, that when the compass points north, it is pointing to the North Pole that we see on the globe. The geographic North and South Pole, where the earth's axis of rotation ends on both sides, should not be confused with their magnetic counterparts. The magnetic north pole is the northern pole of the earth's geomagnetic axis where the magnetic lines of force converge at the earth's surface. The magnetic north pole (near latitude 760 N, longitude 1010 W) is far from the North Pole (at 900 N latitude) by several degrees. The former lies near Bathurst Island in Canada, about 1600 kilometers (or 1000 miles) from the latter. The magnetic south pole is near the Adélie Coast of Antarctica, about 2600 kilometers (or 1600 miles) from the South Pole.

The compass does not point to the North Pole, and surprisingly, it does not always point to the magnetic north pole either. This is because the magnetic lines of force that encompass the earth and converge at the magnetic north are not straight, like the artificial meridians on a globe; anomalies produced by compression from solar wind and from the geographic and geologic features of a particular location cause them to meander. A compass needle simply aligns itself with these lines of force wherever they are located, even though some of these lines may not be pointed towards the magnetic north pole at the place where the compass is being used. If one were to follow the needle all the way to the north, his path would be a somewhat irregular course that would, true enough, end at the magnetic pole. That pole is where all lines of force, including the one being followed, come together after their more or less wandering journey.

It sounds improbable, but people may one day find the compass needle pointing south where it should be north, and vice-versa. This is because Earth's magnetic north pole and magnetic south pole occasionally trade places, as they have nine times over the last 4 million years. The changes occur at random intervals and could happen at any time. The phenomenon is not so easy to understand. The poles act on some of Earth's components in exactly the same way they do on compass needles. Minerals in molten rocks, in particular, can become magnetized when they cool, and as they harden, they will align themselves toward the magnetic north pole in the Northern Hemisphere and with the magnetic south pole in the Southern Hemisphere. By studying the magnetic fields in ancient volcanic rock formations, such as basalt, in the north, scientists have learned that at certain times in history, all the basalt of a particular age had been magnetized to the south. Since the rocks hadn't moved from the moment they were formed, the only explanation for the southward orientation is that Earth's magnetic poles must have reversed, causing the minerals to lean in the exact opposite direction. The theory is that its molten metal core generates Earth's magnetic field, and internal changes in the movements of this core cause the sudden shift.

6. Round as an Egg

Myth! **The earth is round and revolves on its axis while it orbits a stationary sun.**

Common sense tells us there is no way to survive a cosmic fluke, such as the earth getting squashed into an ovoid, or the sun suddenly moving in orbit. People will indeed continue to speculate until they realize that both are not "ifs" but facts. That is to say, the earth is an ovoid flattened at the poles and the sun moves in an orbit.

When the Vanguard satellite launched in March 1958, it went into orbit to discover, along with many other truths, that the Earth is not really round. Astronomer John O'Keefe saw from Vanguard's orbit that the Earth is slightly pear-shaped with a bulge in the southern hemisphere—though not to the extent Columbus imagined. The polar diameter of the earth is about twenty-six miles less than its equatorial diameter. As a result, the equator is about thirteen miles farther from the center of the earth than are the North and South Poles. Otherwise stated, the earth is an oblate spheroid, which means it is slightly flattened at the poles and bulges at the equator. This fact was predicted in 1687 by Sir Isaac Newton, based on the effects of centrifugal forces resulting from the rotation of the earth. While this difference may seem significant, it really has little practical consequence, since this flattening, as reported by astronauts from space, is not even visible. Incidentally, the sun isn't round either. Like the earth, its shape is a sphere flattened on top and bottom.

Clarence Darrow argued that the Biblical story of Joshua commanding the sun to stop couldn't be true, but it's his refutation that's fallacious. For one, the sun revolves around the galaxy one complete orbit every 255 million years, and also moves on its axis like Earth in the same direction but at an uneven rate. For another, the sun could stop in its orbit without endangering the earth, which would continue to revolve on its axis and around the sun. Incidentally, it is not just the sun and the planets that move but the entire galaxy, which hurls outward as part of the expansion of the universe.

---

7. How Levelly the Sea

Myth! Water seeks its own level, and sea level, where air meets sea, is the same all over the globe.

The idea that sea level is the same everywhere is utterly wrong. Sea level is in a constant state of change, as evidenced by the action of the tides, which may vary from one to two feet to as much as fifty feet. Aside from tides, sea level is also affected by less regular and predictable factors, such as atmospheric pressure, wind and waves, long-term climatic changes, coastline configurations, gravitational pull of mountains, and currents. Other variations are not easy to understand, e.g., why the sea level of the Pacific is about two feet higher than at the same latitude in the Atlantic, and why the level of the oceans in the Northern Hemisphere drops about eight inches in the spring without rising anywhere else. Sea level, which has risen and fallen several hundred feet through geological history, is rising this century at the rate of .05 inches per year, probably due to the melting of polar ice. Sea level is not a precise term, and when one speaks of it, the reference is to a theoretical figure, a mean sea level obtained from the average sea level measurements at various locations over a certain period.

Low tide in one place may be compensated by high tide in another only in a comparatively small part of the ocean. But if the two places under comparison are oceans apart, it is no longer that simple. As one writer observes, "the sea doesn't just slosh back and forth between the two sides of the ocean like water in a barrel that's being rocked back and forth." Tides are the regular rise and fall of coastal water levels, caused mainly by the attraction of the moon. But centrifugal force also has something to do with it. What happens is that the oceans on the side of Earth facing the moon are "pulled" toward the moon, causing a bulge or high tide. At the same time, the oceans on the opposite side of the Earth—facing away from the moon—also bulge in the exact opposite direction, the result of centrifugal force. These two bulges produce high tides on opposite sides of the Earth, and their action of drawing away water from the areas halfway between them produce the compensating low tides at the other quadrants. These bulges and depressions literally travel around the world as the moon orbits the Earth in the same direction the latter is spinning.

8. The Long and Short of 24 Hours

Myth! A day is always twenty-four hours long.

It is ironic that our age-old convention for measuring time, the calendar, can't always be relied upon for precision. A year is a fraction more than 52 weeks and February occasionally has 29 days. Fortunately, we still see days of exactly 24 hours arriving like clockwork.

Until the 18th century an hour was usually taken as the 12th part of the period between sunrise and sunset or between sunset and sunrise. Its length varied with the seasons. Modern clocks now measure the hour with electronic accuracy, marking it every 60 minutes or 3,600 seconds. Each second is the time it takes an electron to spin on its own axis inside an atom of cesium. However, this is calendar time, which is different from time as it exists in nature. The latter, called solar (or astronomical) time, is measured by the movement of the earth relative to the sun. A solar day is represented by one revolution of the earth upon its axis; it varies in length because of the variation in speed of each revolution, and is usually a few seconds more than 24 hours. A solar year, on the other hand, is the total time it takes for the earth to make one complete orbit around the sun. As this is approximately 5 hours, 48 minutes, and 45.5 seconds more than 365 calendar days, the excess time is lumped together every four calendar years to make up February 29 of a leap year.

Thus, when we say that the days are longer in summer than in winter, our basis is solar and not calendar time. Under the calendar, a summer day still consists of 24 hours even though daylight may last longer than usual. In the solar year, however, the summer and winter solstices determine the longest and shortest days. These are the times of the year when the sun reaches its farthest or nearest point in its swing northward or southward from the Equator.

Incidentally, one of the most universally held misconceptions about summer is that its relative warmth, particularly in the Northern Hemisphere, is caused by the closeness of the sun to the earth during that period. Actually, the planet's distance from the sun (which is determined by the shape of its orbit around the sun) has little to do with the temperature difference between summer and winter. January 3 is a rather chilly day, yet the earth's elliptic orbit makes it closest to the sun on that day, when it is 91,410,000 miles away. On July 4, one of the warmest days of the year, the earth is at its greatest distance from the sun—94,519,000 miles. What accounts for the longer hours of sunshine and more direct rays of sunlight in summer compared to winter is the tilting of the earth's axis of rotation of about 23° from the plane of its orbit while it moves around the sun. The more nearly perpendicular rays of light this tilting elicits provide more energy in given areas (with less of that energy being reflected back into space by atmospheric gases and particles) and generally produce warmer weather. As the earth moves in its annual orbit the Northern Hemisphere is tilted toward the sun during the summer half of the year and away from it during the winter half. Thus, for example, although about 7 percent more heat is received when the earth is closer to the sun in late December than early January, the effects of tilting are so much greater that distance becomes almost negligible as a factor.

9. Somewhere under the Rainbow

Myth! **Most rainbows end in large bodies of water.**

Some people finally realize there's no pot of gold at the end of the rainbow. But ever wondering where the colors come from, they simply shift to the belief that rainbows spring out of the sea.

The possibility of seeing the end of a rainbow is totally nil, of course, for the reason that there isn't one. Theoretically, the light continues to bend into a complete circle—a circle that cannot be seen totally because it is cut off by the horizon. Elusive, therefore, is not the word for that legendary pot of gold at the end of the rainbow; quite simply, it is non-existent, just like its fabled location.

The US Weather Bureau assures us that rainbows due to showers of rain are never seen as complete circles by observers at ordinary elevations. The phenomenon may be seen in full sometimes, but only from points well up in the air, as from a balloon, an airplane or a mountaintop. Aviators may see it at a considerable altitude when the sun is near the horizon. Circular rainbows that are seen occasionally at ordinary elevations are not produced by rain but by mist or spray. Peculiarly colored circles that sometimes appear around the sun and the moon are not true rainbows.

Incidentally, the common notion that a rainbow is bowed because the earth or the sun is round is not true. The shape of the bow is not due to the spherical form of any planetary body, but to the refraction and reflection of light by the individual raindrops.

10. The Straight Story

Myth! The shortest distance between two points is a straight line.

An arc or a crooked line, when straightened out, becomes longer and will extend beyond the two points it connects. This demonstrates an indisputable truth in Euclidean geometry, i.e., the shortest distance between two non-contiguous points is a straight line.

Proving that indisputable does not necessarily mean absolute, there are non-Euclidean situations in which the principle is compromised. For instance, on curved surfaces such as the earth, the shortest distance between any two locations is the great circle that passes through those locations, and not the straight line drawn between them on a flat map. Those familiar with terrestrial navigation know that a straight line is not the shortest distance between, say, New York and Tokyo. Rather, the shortest is the so-called great circle route, which is the arc on the surface of the globe that stretches between these two cities. The northern great circle route that passes over Alaska is the one used by airlines and ships on long-distance trips between the US and Japan. When shown on a map, the line looks like an arc because a map is a flat representation of a round world. However, viewed directly from

71

overhead, it will be straight enough, though not straight in geometric terms. A truly straight line between New York and Tokyo would go right through the earth and under the ocean, "as if carved out by an unimaginably powerful laser beam."

The ground distance between two points on level land is a straight line, and it is always shorter than the ground distance between the same points on hilly land. Therefore, it would take more posts to fence on hilly land than on level land. Wrong! The shortest distance between two posts placed on hilly land is measured not by their distance on the ground but by their horizontal distance. This is the same as the horizontal distance between the two posts placed on level ground. The curvature of the land will not affect the number of posts provided they are placed parallel to one another and the same horizontal distance apart. It would, of course, be different if the posts were placed perpendicular to the ground and apart from each other based on ground distance. Note, too, that wire strung across a hill fence does not follow horizontal distance but the actual curvature of the ground.

A more mundane explanation goes like this: "When rolling or mountainous land is surveyed for division purposes it is treated as a plane surface and the surveys are made exactly as if the hills or mountains did not exist. Although there are more actual square rods of surface area in a section of hilly or mountainous land than there are in a section of level land, both contain the same acreage from the standpoint of the surveyor." Therefore, a fence will be of the same length regardless of hills and valleys.

11. Snap Judgment

Myth! The sound of finger snapping is produced by the friction between the thumb and the middle finger.

Using the hands is probably the most straightforward means of non-verbal human communication. It's quick, quiet, graphic and easily apprehensible. Take finger snapping, for example. It's common especially among the musically inclined, since it's a natural way of attaining rhythm or synchronization. Many people assume that friction between the thumb and the middle finger causes the familiar snap they hear. In reality, the sound is not produced by any action between the middle finger and the thumb, but by the middle finger striking the palm near the base of the thumb. The almost silent snap against the thumb merely provides enough speed or momentum to the finger so that its impact with the hand creates what may well be 'the sound of one hand clapping'.

A few other fallacies about hand movements may be worth mentioning. Historical research shows, for instance, that laying one hand on the other in prayer is not religious or Biblical in origin. And it was not part of Christian tradition before the 9th century. Until that time, in both Hebrew and Christian worship, the most common posture of prayer had consisted of arms and hands spread toward heaven. Painters and sculptors commit an anachronism when they paint praying hands in scenes that date to Biblical times. The gesture signifies subjugation or submission, and is traceable to when prisoners offered their hands for shackling and soldiers as a sign of surrender. The Christian Church later appropriated it on the justification that it originally represented a church's pointed steeple.

Pontius Pilate was the first character known to perform hand washing as a way of disclaiming responsibility for an act about to happen. In his case, it was for the murder of Jesus Christ. Pilate's ablution offers the suggestion that the gesture was typically Roman. But in fact, washing of the hands by a priest was part of an ancient Jewish ritual preceding a sacrifice, to demonstrate his lack of responsibility for the bloodletting to follow. The practice is alluded to in *Psalms* 26:6 and 73:13 of the Old Testament.

People instinctively place their hand on their mouth in an apparent attempt to stifle a yawn. At times it is just a sign of politeness and at other times a desire not to spread germs. But in most cases, there is a 'supernatural' significance. According to 'Sperenza' Wilde in her book *Superstitions of Ireland*, it used to be the habit of common folk to make the sign of the cross before the mouth when yawning. This was to prevent the devil from rushing into the body and taking up residence there. For babies who yawned and didn't know any better, their mothers would make the sign of the cross before their open mouths. Eventually, the gesture devolved into a simpler method, that of covering the mouth.

73

Finally, the handshake as a form of greeting is apparently a fairly recent Western invention. There is a finding that the gesture is unknown to modern-day primitive tribes, disproving the theory that it is a natural way of expressing civility, friendship, or affection. Sociologists believe the practice of nose rubbing, which is still prevalent among the Eskimos and the Polynesians, has had an older history and a wider following.

12. Hair to Dye for

Myth! The color of one's hair depends on the kind of hair pigment that produces it.

The ordinary layman might see six basic hair pigments in the human body: black, brown, yellow, tawny, buff and red. He might then think that each pigment acting independently of the others produces the specific hair color corresponding to it. Perhaps a pigment might combine with one or more of the others to account for some variation in the same hair color.

This is simply not the case. Scientifically speaking, there are not six pigments but only one, which is called melanin. Melanin is extractable and is oftentimes the basis of artificial dye, but acting naturally it produces all the colors of human hair, including blond, red and brunette. As each gray hair is pushed out of the skin follicle, certain amounts of melanin granules, depending on the individual, are attached to the hairs, giving each person their particular hair color. The particular color that results is determined by the size of the melanin-producing cells, the number of melanin granules coming from each cell, and the manner of formation of those granules. For instance, very small ellipsoidal or spherical granules of melanin are randomly distributed within the dried cortical cells, imparting buff, brown, or black colors. Both the size of the cells and the number of granules decrease over time, and eventually, when the granules are no longer available, as in old age, the hair resumes its original, uncolored, grayish-white appearance.

13. Horrorscope Signs

Myth! **Fear or terror can turn hair white overnight but cannot make it stand on end.**

We have all heard of hair turning white overnight from fear, shock or other traumatic experience. In 1976 'Ripley's Believe it or Not' carried an item about Annie Oakley, the famed sharpshooter, who saw her hair turn snow-white a few hours after being involved in a railroad accident near Wheeling, West Virginia. Time reported that on March 2, 1942, a certain C. Yates McDaniel suffered a similar change in hair color after witnessing the collapse of Singapore at close hand. In the same issue, the news magazine noted that Ernie Pyle's head became visibly white on May 31, 1943, during the African campaign. Earlier celebrated cases include those of Marie Antoinette, St. Thomas More, and Henry of Navarre.

Scientists dismiss these incidents as more hysterical than historical, asserting that, *firstly*, there is no way hair can be truly white unless it's a wig or is dyed. That is to say, when hair does any color turning, it becomes gray, not white. Or more precisely, it reverts to gray, as this is its original color.

Secondly, the natural process of hair coloration takes as much time as normal hair growth, proving that there is no such thing as hair turning gray overnight. Whatever its present color, hair on the head is dead tissue and no longer susceptible to any chemical reaction underneath the scalp. Only a new growth of hair totally lacking in the pigment called melanin can be gray, and by definition, this appears only gradually. Finally, no bodily fluids are capable of bleaching melanin, and even if there were, no mechanism exists by which these can get from the hair follicle into the hair shaft to bleach the previously formed melanin.

There are only three possible explanations for hair turning gray: (a) the hair has been bleached or dyed overnight; (b) there is a sudden loss or removal of artificial hair color; and (c) the individual suffers rapid and selective loss of normal colored hair, revealing gray hair underneath. This last condition usually occurs when trauma triggers an autoimmune disorder called *alopecia areata*. For still undetermined reasons, *alopecia* seems to affect mostly pigmented hairs, leaving white ones untouched. While the

75

impression is that of an overnight graying, it is really over a longer period.

The claim that fear or terror can make hair stand on end may be stretching the hair metaphor even more, but in the general case it is true. Early medical reports of executions mention the hair of criminals standing on end when they are being prepared for the electric chair. The reason apparently is that hair muscle stiffens when stimulated at the roots by nerve fibers acting simultaneously in response to stimulus. For hair on the head, the kind of fright necessary to act as stimulus must be severe, but for body hair, even moderate or casual fear can cause the erection of the papillae, the tiny nipple-like projection at the hair root. This gives the appearance or feel of the hair standing on end, and explains the crawling sensation one feels on the arms and back of the neck during a fright session.

14. Father Of The Pride

Myth! If the lion is the king of beasts, the tiger is the prince.

Although the lion is commonly called 'the king of beasts', it is not the largest of the great cats but only the second largest after the tiger. Male lions are typically eight to ten feet long (including the tail), about three feet high at the shoulder, and four to five hundred pounds in weight. Their striped cousins can exceed that by a foot in length, several inches in height, and a hundred pounds in weight. Guinness says that individually speaking, the real king of beasts is the Siberian tiger, an endangered species, which can grow up to 12 feet long and 3 ½ feet tall and weigh between 400 to 650 pounds. The lion has a thicker body fur than the tiger, but it is principally the mane that makes the former look bigger than it really is.

Samuel Johnson's paean to the lion as "the fiercest and most magnanimous of the four footed beasts" is probably better addressed to the lioness. This quiet and humble creature (compared to her mate, that is) actually does 90 percent of the hunting, while the male, afraid to risk his life or simply preferring to rest, reluctantly does the other 10. In addition to her killing job, the lioness performs a dominant administrative role and provides much of the pride's leadership.

And yet, maybe because of his sexual prowess, the male is allowed to grab the biggest share of the kill, leaving only a small portion to the lioness and her cubs. In contrast, male tigers share generously with others in their territories, and more often than not will allow the females and cubs to feed first. Female tigers share even more than the males, being much more tolerant in this respect with individuals of the same sex.

Disney's *The Lion King* gives a hint of what's liable to happen when the king of beasts gets caught in a stampede. Both the lion and the lioness are poor runners, unlike certain other members of the cat family, such as the leopard and the cheetah. As to who would win a land race between the lion and the tiger, the answer is fairly obvious. Though both felines are not known runners, the tiger is quicker and more lithe and should beat the lion over any given distance. Lions can reach speeds of 80 km/h, but only for short bursts, which is why they prefer to stalk to get near their prey before starting their attack.

A land race between the lion and the tiger would be purely hypothetical, of course, since a lot of geography separates the natural habitats of the two. Lions are found in western India and Africa, while tigers exist only in the Soviet Far East, Korea, Southeast China, and Northeast India. Tigers once did range over most of Europe, Africa and Asia hundreds of years ago, but they are now extinct in these areas.

There are other reasons the two felids are hardly compatible with each other. For the lion, the popular phrase 'king of the jungle' is a misnomer because the creature belongs to the open country; on the other hand, the tiger prefers denser vegetation, for which its camouflage is ideally suited and where a single predator is not at a disadvantage compared to a pride. Moreover, the lion thrives in organized social groups that roam far and wide, whereas the tiger is fiercely individualistic and territorial. Male tigers are usually intolerant of other males within their respective areas, and because of their aggressive nature, territorial disputes can be violent and may end in the death of a participant.

However, it is entirely possible for the two cats to meet even if only casually. Both can be found in India, the lion in the west and the tiger in the northeast. There have been recorded instances of the lion walking great distances in search of food, affording an opportunity for a chance encounter with the tiger. But even if they meet, and one is male and the other female, nothing is liable to happen, as they will likely just ignore each other. Nevertheless—and this should come as a surprise to many people—the animals can breed together in captivity, producing tigons (from a male tiger and a female lion) and ligers (from a male lion and a female tiger). The liger is more common than the tigon because the mating process is easier.

Despite incidents of attacks on humans, lions have enjoyed a positive depiction as strong and noble in various cultures, particularly in Asia. The name Singapore, for instance, is the Anglicized form of the original Sanskrit-derived Malay word *Singapura*, meaning 'Lion City'. The derivation is based on Malay mythology, describing how the founder-prince of Singapore (then called Temasek) renamed the island after sighting a maned red and black beast when he first set ashore on the island, believing it to be a lion and a good omen. The lion is a principal feature of the Singapore national coat of arms and is also the nickname of the national football team. This is rather odd, inasmuch as lions have never been known to live anywhere near Singapore and historians believe the beast seen by Sang Nila Utama was likely a tiger. The latter has been sighted as late as the 20th century in the city-state's environs and is in fact the national animal of neighboring Malaysia, where it abounds.

15. The Sssssound of Music

Myth! The snake charmer uses music to control the cobra's movements.

Word mavens say the popular saying, "Music soothes the savage beast," should read, "Music soothes the savage *breast*." Be it beast or breast, however, it's apparently not the mellifluous sound of music that does the soothing. Snakes, particularly cobras, can't hear the sound of the flute enough to respond to it. This is not because they lack ears. A zoologist reports: "Snakes don't have normal ears like those of other creatures, but they have ears nevertheless. Resting beneath the surface of the face, covered by skin and muscle, is a thin bone plate called the quadrate bone.

While once part of the skull, it is now detached and is held in place by ligaments to act as a pressure plate for sound. On the inside surface of the quadrate bone is an attachment called the columnella; this conducts vibrations to the expanded inner ear, which lies in the oval window of the cochlea." However, snakes are generally not sensitive to vibrations either, whether from the ground or through the air. In particular, vibrations from a flute are well beyond the snake's sensing range, which is in the low frequency band between 100 and 700 hertz.

Fortunately for the charmer, the snake can detect the tapping of his foot and perceive the movement of his arms and the side-to-side motion of the flute. The creature sways in rhythm, seemingly mesmerized, but experts say it is actually engaged in some form of shadow boxing. With the motion, the snake is able to remain erect while it tries to estimate the distance between the charmer and itself and establish an opportunity to strike.

The snake charmer is quite aware that, his skills notwithstanding, his art is not 100 per cent safe. Thus, he resorts to certain forms of insurance, like having the snake's mouth sewn shut or the fangs removed. He knows cobras are night hunters and cannot see well enough in daylight to strike accurately; still, he subtly remains outside the striking distance of the snake as it is coiled up in the basket. Finally, the cautious charmer avoids using the aggressive king cobra, which is quick to lash out at almost anything. The Asiatic cobra is preferable because it is quieter and less likely to lunge at a large target, especially one too large for it to eat.

Another of the myths that surround the cobra is that, like other snakes, it has the power to hypnotize animals and even people. The snake does not really hypnotize; its glassy eyes just seem to stare while it sways from side to side, a physical necessity to keep the upper part of its body off the ground. When it stops swaying, it is forced to slide back to the ground. The victim–a small bird or rodent–may become curious or even freeze with fear, and appear to be 'charmed' by the snake.

In *The Jungle Book*, Rudyard Kipling tells the story of Rikki-Tikki-Tavi, an Indian mongoose that becomes a household pet. Among Rikki's more memorable adventures is his fight with two cobras, Nag and Nagina, which he eventually kills. In telling the tale, Kipling was drawing on a popular belief that the mongoose and the cobra are sworn enemies and that in any fight the mongoose always wins.

But the truth is somewhat different. Mongooses will kill and then eat almost anything—small rodents, birds, shellfish, eggs, fruit—but snakes are not a major part of their diet. Indeed, one Indian species of mongoose eats almost nothing but crabs, while an African species feasts on crocodile eggs. So reluctant is the mongoose to engage the cobra in battle that snake charmers sometimes stage fights between the two just to see what happens. In reality, if the quick-footed mongoose does not break the cobra's back with its sharp teeth, it is swiftly killed by the venomous bite of the snake. The mongoose is even less lucky with other snakes, such as the pit viper, which almost always wins in a West Indian staged fight. That the mongoose is immune to snake bite is pure hokum.

16. Suicide Kings

Myth! Man and the lemming are the only animals capable of mass suicide.

The Masada and the Guiana incidents are grim reminders that man, despite strong cautionary instincts and highly developed social traits, is capable of mass suicide given the right circumstances. Documentaries reveal that the lemming is the only other animal that has a penchant for group self-destruction when motivated.

Not much can be said about these small, thickset rodents from the Arctic regions except that they tend to move en masse, but are so prolific that when they do, it takes some time before any part of the path they are treading becomes visible again. Fiction writers and documentary filmmakers would embellish the picture by showing the hordes ending their journey by callously hurling themselves over the cliffs and into the sea to drown. Theirs is an offer of proof that what we are seeing is an example of mass suicide in the natural world, and the actors are possibly the only animals of the lower variety that have an instinct for self-destruction.

However, scientists say only one species of lemmings does

this, and the purpose is not ritualistic suicide but mass migration. The animals run, climb and swim in a supreme effort to get somewhere; many die along the way, but never for a suicidal cause. Lemming expert Arne Semb-Johansson of Oslo University infers that given their large numbers, many lemmings are bound to overshoot the land and somersault down into the killing waters. But their plunge is not intentional, only unfortunate. The idea, in fact, is survival; overpopulation depletes their food supply and they must move to newer grounds in search of sustenance. Their numbers mushroom to upward of 100 million, as was the case in Hardanger, Norway, in 1975. The journeys last for many weeks until, their numbers having been sufficiently depleted, the urge to migrate ends and the colony takes up residence at their last location.

According to a 1983 investigation by Canadian Broadcasting Corporation producer Brian Vallee, the 1958 Walt Disney documentary *White Wilderness,* showing a pack of lemmings marching to the sea and ultimate destruction, was a sheer fabrication. The lemmings were first brought to Alberta, a landlocked province that isn't their natural habitat, where Disney folks put them on a giant turntable piled with snow to film the migration segment. "Then, Vallee reports, they recaptured the lemmings and took them to a cliff over a river. 'When the well-adjusted lemmings wouldn't jump…the Disney people gave Nature a hand [and tossed them off]'" (*Uncle John's Fifth Bathroom Reader,* 1992).

17. When Giants Swam the Seas

Myth! The dinosaur is the biggest animal to ever inhabit the earth.

The initial impression was that dinosaurs were the largest animals that ever lived, until this was totally dimmed by the image of a blue whale roiling the ocean in the animation film *Pinocchio* (1940). In the early 1900s, a blue whale that was found near Antarctica was 38 meters (124 feet) long and weighed about 170 tons, or "as much as 2,300 people." According to a science writer,

81

"a fully grown blue whale is so large that an elephant could walk into its opened jaw and a basketball could pass through its largest arteries." In comparison, the largest known dinosaur was the Diplodocus, which was only 28 meters (91 ft.) long and a little more than 30 tons heavy. The vaunted Brontosaurus was 20 meters (65 ft.) long, while the most famous dinosaur, the Tyrannosaurus, was a mere forty feet in length. Much larger, but not large enough, is the vegetarian Sauropod named Brachiosaurus, which weighed fifty tons.

The data clock moved back to where it started when it was reported that in the 1990s, Utah's state paleontologist, David Gillette, had been painstakingly excavating a 43-meter-long (141.08 ft.) sauropod. The tentative name given to this potential creature was Seismosaurus, "because it must have created a minor earthquake with every step." Some of its brethren, notes Gillette, "may have been even longer." In fact, huge bone fragments discovered in the past several years have led paleontologists to speculate about the possibility of other colossi variously dubbed Supersaurus and Ultrasaurus. Members of the Sauropod group, any one of which could have surpassed the dimensions of the largest blue whale, have been likened to suspension bridges, with their legs acting as pylons to carry their great weight and the backbone the roadway between them. Gillette surmises, however, that because of their long necks, which extended up to 11 meters, blood would reach their uplifted heads only if they had as many as eight hearts, spaced out in the chest and along the neck, though that would multiply the risks of heart disease and stroke. Fossil hunter Jack Horner notes also that the greater they needed sustenance to support their size, the more vulnerable they would have been to extinction.

Be this as it may, the notion that the largest animal ever is the blue whale and not the dinosaur seems to have turned full circle with the finding that David Gillete calculated wrong. When he first described the Seismosaurus in 1991, he gave it a maximum 54 m (177.05 ft) length, making it the longest known dinosaur (excluding those known from especially poor remains, such as *Amphicoelias*). But recently, it was shown that the giant tail vertebrae were actually placed further forward on the tail than Gillete originally estimated. The study shows that the complete *Diplodocus* skeleton at the Carnegie Museum of Natural History in Pittsburgh, Pennsylvania, on which the dimensions of

Seismosaurus were based, had a 13th tail vertebra from another dinosaur, throwing the purported size of *Seismosaurus* off by up to 30%.

18. In the Company of Man

Myth! The dinosaur was a contemporary of man.

Any comic strip aficionado knows what a dinosaur is. It's the pet animal in Alley *Oop, Fred Flintstone* and *B.C.*

But comic strips are only meant to pander to one's fantasy and should not be blamed entirely for popularizing a scientific lie. The bigger culprits are the movies because they give the lie a veneer of reality with absolutely no feeling of remorse. Once Ray Harryhausen's step-animated dinosaurs appear on screen with the fur-bikinied Raquel Welch in *One Million Years B.C.* (1966), everything we know of man's prehistory goes down the drain. For dinosaurs died out 61 million years before the earliest man, meaning to say that, contrary to the impression created by this Hollywood film, cavemen or any other form of humans never lived while dinosaurs existed. The misconception may have been due to the fact that, as recent fossil discoveries show, man once coexisted with now extinct wildlife brutes, some of which were once thought to be prehistoric, e.g., the mammoth, the mastodon and the giant sloth.

With this false impression come others that are just as absurd. One is that the dinosaurs were short-lived creatures that could not successfully adapt to their environment. Another is that they finally became extinct with the onset of the Ice Age. In fact, dinosaurs antedated the Ice Age by millions of years. They were a very successful life form on earth, having existed for over one hundred fifty million years, during which time they constantly changed, progressed, and evolved. In comparison, humans even in their most primitive forms have existed for only about fifty thousand years. During their reign, these unusually large reptiles lived on every continent except Antarctica, dominating all other life forms, including mammals. They probably disappeared only after the earth's climate drastically and suddenly changed, or when a huge asteroid that hit the earth wiped them out.

19. Bye bye Birdie

Myth! The swan sings just before it dies.

The swan is known for its long, curving neck, accounting for "swan's neck" as a word of admiration or ridicule for that part of a woman's body. Similar metaphorical phrases do honor to this bird's dive and the way it sings at the moment of death.

The belief that swans sing at their death may be traced through much of the literature of Europe, including that of England, where we find the birds doing their thing in Chaucer, Shakespeare, Byron, and many other works. The English poet Samuel Taylor Coleridge wrote, "Swans sing before they die; 'twere no bad thing / Did certain persons die before they sing." Another layer is added to the myth with the claim that the first time the swan sounds off is also the last. The song, says the Britannica, "is sung only once by a swan in its lifetime, as it is dying." The early Greeks fostered the idea that a swan, unable all its life to sing like other birds, would burst forth into glorious song when it felt the approach of death. Says a commentator: "According to Plato, Socrates explained the song as one of gladness because the swan, sacred to Apollo, was shortly to be able to join the god it served. As Apollo was the god of poetry and song, it was also the belief that the souls of a poet passed after death into the body of a swan." From this we owe the allusion to the farewell or final appearance, action, or work of any poet, writer, or orator as his 'swan song', supposedly the culmination of all his artistry, his finest work.

We hate to disappoint, but modern authorities say it is quite rare for a wounded or dying swan to sing, and even more improbable for its sound to be mistaken for anything musical. A swan utters a variety of sounds from the windpipe; even the mute swan (*Cygnus olor*), the least vocal species, often hisses, makes soft snoring sounds, or grunts sharply. After repulsing an enemy, swans, in particular the trumpeter swan (*Cygnus buccinator*), utter a note of triumph, as geese do. There is also a so-called whistling swan (*Cygnus musicus*), but like the rest, it cannot be claimed to sing.

The other thing swans are wrongly admired for is their dive. Called the swan dive, this is performed by humans with the legs straight together, the back arched, and the arms stretched out from the sides. Swans, however, do not really dive. While no other waterfowl moves as fast on the water or in the air, swans merely dabble in shallows for aquatic plants. Sometimes they do a fancy act that looks like a swan dive, performed with head tilted back and arms held like the wings of a swallow until near the water. However, this is really a swallow dive and deserves to be only called such.

20. Whither the Winter Weather?

Myth! Groundhogs can predict the onset of spring 75 to 90 per cent of the time.

The fact that badgers were originally used for the purpose should alert us to what many weather commentators have been saying, namely, that the vaunted ability of groundhogs to predict the onset of early spring is, well, ground hogwash. But the love of (and curiosity for) Old World traditions among Americans, or at least among the thousands who observe Groundhog Day in many towns in the US and Canada, continue to nourish their belief in the special talent of Punxsutawney Phil and other animals of his genre.

One of the planting superstitions in sixteenth-century Europe was that, if badgers saw their shadows when they emerged from hibernation, they would be frightened and return to their den—a sure signal that spring would be delayed by another six weeks so that farmers should postpone planting for that period of time. When German settlers in the late 19th century began to transplant the idea to Pennsylvania, there were no badgers, and the groundhog, being the closest animal in appearance in the area, was substituted. Thenceforth, Groundhog Day has been almost invariably observed in most of North America on February 2, which happens to be about the time groundhogs emerge from their burrows after winter in the vicinity of Punxsutawney, Pennsylvania. Groundhogs, of course, begin to stir in the spring at different dates depending on their geographic latitude and the local climate. But the largest audience for Groundhog Day as one of the US' most popular rites of spring is attracted to Punxsutawney primarily because of the antics of its resident groundhog called

Punxsutawney Phil. This popularity has been further improved by the Hollywood treatment given to Phil as a subject of interest in the 1993 movie production *Groundhog Day* starring comic actor Bill Murray.

Actually, weather has nothing to do with the groundhog (or badger) emerging from its burrow after months of hibernation. According to one observer, Punxsutawney Phil "does not really come out on February 2 in order to check the weather as folklore would have us believe. Hunger and an interest in acquiring a mate are what really make the groundhog come out of his burrow. If neither desire is sufficiently strong, the animal will stay in its burrow for more sleep."

Groundhog Day proponents fix the rate of success of the groundhog as a weather animal at 75% to 90% of the time, while official studies put it at a much lower 37% to 39%. Actual records indicate that the groundhog scores a mere 28 percent of the time. But analysts say the exercise is close to meaningless because of the difficulty of projecting these statistics forward. For one, Phil's behavior in the positive cases may only be suggesting a 'spell of spring weather in winter' and not an early spring. As TV meteorologist Mike Randall put it, "there are *always* six more weeks of winter after Groundhog Day, and the concept of early spring in the astronomical sense simply does not exist." For another, since it is likely for Phil to see his shadow on a spring-like day when the sun is out, it is as likely for him to reenter his burrow and announce more days of winter. At other times the shadow may be there but Phil fails to see it, or he sees it but does not go back into his burrow. Or Phil may refuse altogether to come out of his burrow, as has happened on a number of occasions to the disappointment of his admirers. All these indicate that Phil's success rate, whether high or low, makes no real sense as it is based on accidental (and coincidental) acts and establishes no pattern that the superstition can be anchored on.

21. Up and down the Poles

Myth! Superman flies up and away to the North Pole faster than the speed of sound.

We never hear of Superman flying *down* to the North Pole to seek temporary refuge in his Fortress of Solitude. This is because, for some reason, people think north is up and south down, and, consequently, the North Pole is the uppermost part of the globe as the South Pole is the lowermost. The reason may well be that printed maps have long been oriented in this manner—with the north at the top and the east on the right—since it was first laid out by the ancient Greeks, of whom the earliest known was Eratosthenes ca. 200 BC. Ptolemy in the second century AD produced the *Geographia*, a collection of principles still followed in modern cartography, in which he showed an atlas of the known world based on the experiences of the Roman legions as they spread the Roman Empire. But Ptolemy's choice of north as up for his maps was purely arbitrary; the world being a sphere, he could have chosen any other direction and still be right. Historian Daniel Boorstin can only offer one explanation: "Perhaps this was because the better-known places in his world were in the northern hemisphere, and on a flat map these were most convenient for study if they were in the upper right-hand corner."

Superman's legend does claim he is faster than a speeding bullet, and since most bullets are faster than the speed of sound, this may tell us that the Man of Steel is faster than the speed of sound *all the time*. Actually, the most we can deduce from the boast is that our superhero is faster than the slowest speeding bullet, which is almost certainly not the supersonic kind. It may even be assumed that Superman can go well above the *minimum* speed of sound, but this is no assurance that he can exceed its *maximum*. It is a misconception to think that the velocity of sound is an absolute constant like the speed of light and has the same rate of speed under any condition. Sonic speed depends on the medium through which sound travels and, as a result, has widely varying rates. Density and temperature are important factors, so that the speed rate, say, at sea level and at higher temperatures, would significantly differ from that of sound as it traverses the Fortress of Solitude.

The trickier question, of course, is how long Superman can keep himself up in the air while flying directly to the North Pole. Physicists who have examined the superhuman phenomenon agree that the Kryptonian can fly only because the gravity of his home planet, to which he has remained adapted, is about fifteen times stronger than earth's. Nevertheless, at some point during a flying episode, earth's gravity, however puny compared to Krypton's, must pull him down. It has long been established that a bullet discharged from a horizontal gun, no matter its speed, begins to fall as soon as it leaves the muzzle. In a normal case, where there is no force interfering with the earth's pull, the bullet will reach the ground just as quickly as if it were dropped from the hand at the same height. This may not be so in Krypton, but Superman flying level from the spire of the Metropolis building would almost surely become grounded as fast as if he were Clark Kent doing a free fall from the same height. If there is some physical force or energy stronger than air lift or speed thrust that allows him to fully resist earth's gravity, and to turn it off when he wants to alight, we are still waiting for DC Comics or any related literature to reveal it.

22. Horns Aplenty

Myth! There is no animal in real life that has one true horn like the unicorn.
\

Even in the realm of fantasy, the unicorn is considered rare. The single horn located on this animal's forehead has magical qualities, and is the reason for its mythification.

However, the unicorn may not be as uniquely horned as we think it is. In real life, the African rhino has one horn, as opposed to its Asian counterpart, which has two. The rhino's, of course, is positioned on the upper surface of the animal's snout, unlike the unicorn's horn, which is centered on its forehead. Also, while we assume that the unicorn's is a bony structure, that of the rhino is not a true animal horn but simply matted hair hardened by secretions of keratin.

In any case, while both the rhino and the unicorn are singular animals, it is not entirely correct to think of the unicorn as just an odd-looking horse. Like most other mythological beasts, it is actually a composite of several animals. It has the head (red) and body (white) of a horse, the legs of an antelope, the tail of a lion, and the beard of a goat (until modern innovations, fanciful unicorns looked more like goats than horses). The fifth part of the

88

combination is the rhino's horn, which is the most conspicuous. Evidence shows unicorns were first drawn in Europe from the verbal descriptions of the African animal.

Both the horns of the unicorn and the African rhino are said to have magical properties, the first for nullifying the effects of poison and the second for curing certain diseases. Myths concerning the rhino's horn are largely responsible for its now being an endangered species. The persistent belief that this horn even contains an aphrodisiac has resulted in extensive killings of the animal and in poachers posing an immediate threat to the survival of the species. Illegal activities have not been prevented by warnings that there is no evidence to support any of the miracle stories concerning the powers of the rhino's horns.

---

23. They Live?

Myth! The hair and nails on the human body are capable of growing after death.

This is a fallacy caused by an illusion. As the human body shrinks soon after death, the most obvious parts that shrivel during its mummification are the skin and the tips of the fingers and toes. In the process, the hair and nail covering of the affected tissues appear to have grown longer. The dubious claim that the dead body of Elizabeth Siddal grew luxuriant red hair after death has become legend only because of the eminence of her husband Dante Gabriel Rossetti. The poet purportedly obtained permission to have his wife's grave in Highgate Cemetery opened to retrieve the only perfect copy of his best poems. "In the light," so the story goes, "he noticed that his wife's golden hair had continued to grow after death, filling the coffin, and the scene so unnerved him that despite the fact that he wrote about it in his sonnet 'Life in Love', he left instructions in his will that he be cremated and not buried beside Elizabeth."

The rest of the body may be alive, but the visible nail and hair are dead tissue. What grow during one's lifetime are those parts of the nail and hair under the skin. This is obviously the answer to the riddle: What growing tissue can be cut off without causing damage or pain?

Art & Literature

I

The Folly In Leonardo's Folio

On Leonardo da Vinci

"Art is never finished, only abandoned."

•

Leonardo da Vinci

1. The Smile becomes Her

Myth! Mona Lisa's smile was posed.

According to art historian Giorgio Vasari, who wrote in 1550, Leonardo's model for the *Mona Lisa* could not bring herself to smile as the painter wanted. It was agreed to put her in the right mood by hiring musicians and jesters to perform while she was being painted. Aided by Leonardo's coaxing and happy banter, the technique succeeded in eliciting the beautiful expression that graces the now celebrated painting.

A spiced-up version of the story claims the smile had something to do with the only romance in Leonardo's life. It is said that Leonardo as a young man fell in love with the real Mona Lisa and made her his mistress. At the time he was starting on her portrait, she was in the throes of an unhappy marriage and was so distressed that she couldn't smile. During the project, however, their illicit romance blossomed and she repaid Leonardo's affection with her famous expression. Of course, this version ignores the fact that Leonardo was gay, and the only relationship he could have had with Mona Lisa, assuming she was a woman, was of the platonic kind.

Both tales are considered myth mainly because of the finding that Renaissance artists did not paint directly from live subjects. They first made a sketch, or cartoon, from which they developed the paintings later in their studios. It is believed Leonardo made his master sketch of the *Mona Lisa* in Florence before taking it to Milan c. 1504, and then transferred it to a panel in preparation for the painting. The costume, the veil, and the background landscape were later added to complete the picture. There may have been a 'sitter' for the initial sketch, but she obviously didn't stay too long; Leonardo spent a leisurely seven years or more developing the *Mona Lisa*, something he could or would not have done had he been largely dependent on a live model.

Leonardo's sketch, which has not been lost, is noteworthy for showing an unsmiling Mona Lisa, a further indication that the nuanced expression was painted only later. The smile may not have been entirely a product of Leonardo's imagination, but copied from other sources. Experts point out that this kind of furtive smile on paintings was not uncommon during Leonardo's time, and was nothing unusual even for his lesser contemporaries. Quite likely, it was from the master Andrea del Verocchio, to whom Leonardo and many of his colleagues were apprenticed in the early days, that the technique was learned. At the least, it has been established that Leonardo did not originate Mona Lisa's 'sitting' posture but lifted it from other images of the seated Madonna, which were widely adopted at the time.

That Mona Lisa's smile was not posed is strongly disputed by others. An Internet source notes that the subtle formation of Mona Lisa's lips could not have been created by any other human being, even by a great artist. This is made obvious by the strange and powerful fascination the smile has had on the artist and on all who have looked at it for the last four hundred years. From the date she 'flashed' it, the captivating smile reappears in all of Leonardo's pictures and in those of his pupils. As the *Mona Lisa* is a portrait, "we cannot assume that he added on his own account such an expressive feature to her face—a feature that she herself did not possess. The conclusion seems hardly to be avoided that he found this smile in his model and fell so strongly under its spell that from then on he bestowed it on the free creations of his phantasy."

2. This Lady was no Dame

Myth! Leonardo gave the *Mona Lisa* its name.

The *Mona Lisa* is popularly called just that—the *Mona Lisa*—in the belief that this was the nickname of the lady who sat for it. In professional circles, it oftentimes carries the descriptive title 'Portrait of Lisa Gherardini, Wife of Francesco del Giocondo'.

However, neither title seems to have been used at the beginning of Leonardo's project. We are told the picture was commissioned as the *Madonna Lisa*, after the full first name of Mona Lisa. Later, on whose initiative we are not certain, it became the matronly *La Gioconda*, or *La Joconda,* which was first mentioned in 1525 in a heritage list of the painter Salai, Leonardo's student and heir. The name Mona Lisa probably didn't catch on until the finishing stages or after the painting had already left Leonardo's hands.

3. She was no Lady, she was his Wife

Myth! **The real Mona Lisa was a Florentine woman named Lisa Giocondo.**

From the custom of nomenclatures at the time, *La Gioconda* suggested that the subject was married to a man named Giocondo.

It would be written in subsequent centuries that Mona Lisa was born in Naples c. 1480 and married in her early twenties. She became the third wife of a Florentine nobleman or merchant known as Francesco di Bartolommeo del Giocondo.

Francesco allegedly commissioned the painting for himself or for his wife. But according to Pallanti, since Leonardo's father was a close friend of del Giocondo, it was equally likely that "(the) portrait of Mona Lisa, done when (she) was aged about 24, was...commissioned by Leonardo's father himself for his friends as he is known to have done on at least one other occasion." This would be one explanation why Leonardo never turned over the finished work to another person but kept it with him almost until the day he died.

Bruno Mottin of the French Museums' Center for Research and Restoration offers scientific evidence that the transparent gauze veil worn by the smiling lady is a *guarnello*, typically used by women while pregnant or just after giving birth. This, and other proof obtained in 2004 that the painting dated from around 1503, the year of birth of the Giocondos' second son, would suggest that Leonardo's model was indeed Francesco's wife. Recent research from Italy purports to show that Lisa Gherardini was a prolific mother of five children, including two daughters who became nuns. However, the case for Lisa has been diminished somewhat by the unconfirmed report that Francesco was old and impotent and would not have allowed his wife to pose for a portrait while carrying a child that was not by him.

Leonardo himself may have indirectly rebutted the belief that Mona Lisa was the lady Giocondo. During the last years of his life, the artist spoke of a portrait "of a certain Florentine lady done from life at the request of the magnificent Giuliano de Medici." Art experts say this portrait was possibly that of Constanza d'Avalos, duchess of Francavilla, a patroness of Leonardo and mistress of Giuliano de Medici. D'Avalos, coincidentally, was also nicknamed 'La Gioconda'. Of course, since there is no certainty that this portrait was the *Mona Lisa*, there is always the assumption that the master was talking about one of the two other portraits he did of women in his time.

At least ten other prominent women of the 16th century, not to mention various courtesans and prostitutes, have been linked to the *Mona Lisa*, including Isabella d'Este, Cecilia Gallerani, Isabela Gualandi and Pacifica Brandano. Maike Vogt-Lüerssen thinks the woman behind the famous smile is Isabella of Aragon, the Duchess of Milan. She bases her deduction on Leonardo's 11 years as the court painter for the Duke of Milan, and on the pattern on Mona Lisa's dark green dress indicating that she was a member of the house of Sforza. Maike concludes that the *Mona Lisa* was the first official portrait of Isabella as the new Duchess of Milan and was done in 1489 instead of 1503.

4. The Lady shows her Hand

Myth! The most masterfully rendered part of the *Mona Lisa* is her smile.

Most lay people regard the beguiling smile on the *Mona Lisa* as a singular stroke that only a master of the human form like Da Vinci could have fashioned. To them, it's the 'most perfect' part of the painting hands down (no pun intended).

On the other hand, experts believe the real mark of perfection in the *Mona Lisa* is not her smile, nor even her face, but the right hand she lays across her waist and on her left hand. It is opined that not one of Leonardo's imitators, past and present, has been able to approximate the soft and exquisite quality of that quietly positioned appendage.

We are advised nonetheless not to confuse the sense of perfection with which Leonardo imbued certain parts of his masterpiece—e.g., the hand, the gaze, and the smile—with his sense of the beautiful. The *Mona Lisa* as a whole is arguably Leonardo's 'most perfect' work, yet most critics believe his most beautiful painting of a woman's face is that of the angel in the *Madonna of the Rocks*.

5. Cherchez l'Homme!

Myth! Leonardo originally intended the *Mona Lisa* to be his self-portrait.

Going beyond the gender barrier in their pursuit of the real Mona Lisa, some art historians state that Leonardo's mysterious poser was the same male model he used for St. John the Baptist, which shows an uncanny resemblance to La Gioconda. Other anonymous statements link the *Mona Lisa* to an image of Francesco del Giocondo himself. All these serve to introduce the controversial idea that the *Mona Lisa* is the portrait of a man.

The most surprising postulation yet is that the *Mona Lisa* might have been a self-portrait of the artist. Dr. Lillian Schwartz of Bell Labs posits this theory based on the results of a digital analysis of the facial features of Leonardo's face and that of the famous painting. When merging the mirror image of a Leonardo self-portrait with an image of the *Mona Lisa* using a computer, the features of the faces align perfectly. Cynics throw water on the theory, saying the congruence of the two images can be explained by other reasons, namely, (1) both portraits were painted by the same person using the same style; (2) the drawing on which the comparison is based may not really be a self-portrait; (3) as Sigmund Freud surmised, the *Mona Lisa* depicts the artist's mother Caterina, accounting for the resemblance between artist and subject, and further explaining why Leonardo kept the portrait with him wherever he traveled until his death; and (4) the resemblance is purely accidental. Wikipedia adds that, being "an artist with a great interest in the human form, Leonardo would have spent a great deal of time studying and drawing the human face, and the face most often accessible to him was his own, making it likely that he would have the most experience with drawing his own features. The similarity in the features of the people depicted in the *Mona Lisa* and *St. John the Baptist* may have resulted from Leonardo's familiarity with his own facial features, causing him to draw other faces in a similar light."

6. Italian Cosmetic Job

Myth! A notable imperfection in the *Mona Lisa* is the lack of eyebrows on her face.

Mona Lisa's face is criticized for being marred by an imperfection, caused by Leonardo's alleged failure to paint eyebrows on his subject. Fortunately, art historians assure us that Mona Lisa was painted as she would have appeared in those days—with no eyebrows. Renaissance fashion in Florence called for ladies to shave them off, as they were considered unsightly. Some sources say that, for modern viewers, the missing eyebrows are a plus as they add to the slightly semi-abstract quality of the face.

However, there are others who venture that Mona Lisa's missing eyebrows may not have been deliberate on Leonardo's part. To test the possibility, Pascal Cotte, a French engineer and inventor, focused a high-definition camera on the painting in October 2007. Blown 24 times by an ultra-high resolution, Mona Lisa's face revealed a single brushstroke of a single hair above the left brow. Cotte says this suggests Leonardo painted the requisite eyebrows, as he had on his other portraits of women, but they were eroded by time or have been inadvertently erased by a poor attempt to clean the painting. There is historical support for Cotte in Vasari's writing, in which the Renaissance critic praises Leonardo's beautiful sitter for her elegant eyelashes and realistically painted eyebrows. Ironically, because Vasari's comments are at odds with what appears (or does not appear) in Leonardo's painting, the writer has been accused of either fabricating his description of the *Mona Lisa*, which apparently he had not seen in person, or confusing it with another painting.

7. Making Eyes all the Time

Myth! The *Mona Lisa* has eyes that will follow you everywhere.

97

Expect a guide at the Louvre to say that Mona Lisa's mouth and hand are not the only points of interest in the painting. Watch out for her eyes as well, because they have a knack of following you as you move around the room. Her gaze seems to be fixed on the observer wherever they are, as if to invite them to engage in some silent communication with her.

The trick, however, is not unique to the *Mona Lisa*, nor is it limited to the works of the masters. Any portrait that rests on a flat surface and has only two dimensions will give the same result. The eyes of a subject in such a portrait will give the illusion that they are looking at you from every angle, because they are just so many points fixed on a plane and will be precisely the same points seen at any angle they are viewed from. If the eyes are pictured or drawn as looking directly at you when you are in front, they will be seen looking at you when you move to either side; and if the eyes are represented as looking in some other direction, you cannot place yourself in a position so they will appear to look at you.

The same experience may be obtained from viewing motion pictures. The audience at the extreme left side of the theater sees exactly the same scenes and the same positions of the characters as those on the extreme right side see them. In real life, it is the third dimension—depth—that discloses new lines and hides others when the viewer shifts locations, thereby offering a new perspective.

8. Her Life on the Rocks

Myth! **The *Mona Lisa* was originally wider in dimension.**

The *Mona Lisa* is said to have become smaller through tampering, not when it was stolen from the Louvre in 1911, as some might think, but long before that. It appears that, unlike Rembrandt's Night Watch, which was also reduced in size at some point but which essentially remained as it was before, Leonardo's lady was substantially affected by the alteration. When it left the artist's hands, it had columns on both sides, which made plain that the subject was seated on a balcony and not among the rocks, as is now seen. Part of the panel comprising the columns at both sides have been cut away for some undetermined reason, causing even Walter Pater, the writer-critic who gave the most famous description of the *Mona* Lisa, to make an error. It is claimed that, while the elimination of the columns has highlighted the mystery of the background and contributed to the allure of the painting, the result is one that Leonardo never intended.

Art historians like Martin Kemp insist the painting has not been altered, however, and that the columns depicted in alleged copies of the original were added by the copyists themselves. This view has been confirmed in 2004-05 by an international team of 39 specialists who, after undertaking the most thorough scientific examination of the *Mona Lisa*, discovered beneath the frame (the current one was fitted to the *Mona Lisa* in 2004) a 'reserve' around all four edges of the panel. A reserve is an area of bare wood surrounding the painted or 'gessoed' portion of the portrait. That this is a genuine reserve and did not result from the removal of the paint or 'gesso' is demonstrated by the raised edge of the painting caused by a buildup from brush strokes at the border of the gesso area. The reserve portion, which was likely to have been as much as 20 mm originally, looks as if it has been trimmed to fit a frame; however at no point has any of Leonardo's actual paint been trimmed. The experts concluded that the columns in early copies must have been inventions of those artists, or else copies of another (unknown) studio version of the *Mona Lisa*.

9. The Lady shows her Worth

Myth! The *Mona Lisa* is the most valuable painting in the world.

The *Mona Lisa* is widely perceived as Leonardo's greatest work, but not many critics agree. Those who are enraptured at the outset eventually grow weary of it, some even finding the subject "faintly repulsive." More lasting respect is paid to *The Last Supper*, which is seen as a complex psychological panorama compressed in very limited space.

Nonetheless, the marketability of *The Last Supper* is inhibited by its relative size and the absolute fixity of its location, whereas that of the portable *Mona Lisa* is deemed limitless. In fact, the lady has a financial worth matched only by its fame, as attested to by Guinness, which lists the painting as the most valuable in the world based on an assessment of $100 million in 1962. The honor is of dubious merit, however, since the appraisal was made for an insurance coverage that was never taken. As a practical matter, those that have gone through public auction—e.g., Van Gogh's *Irises*, which sold for $53.9 million in 1987—are financially more valuable because of their proven market performance.

Actually, the *Mona Lisa*'s theoretical value of $100 million has already been surpassed in terms of realized cash by three other paintings, the *Adele Bloch-Bauer I* by Gustav Klimt, which was sold for $135 million (£73 million), the *Woman III* by Willem de Kooning, which sold for $137.5 million in November 2006, and *No. 5, 1948* by Jackson Pollock, which sold for a record $140 million also in November 2006. But the lady still has the last word: although these figures are greater than the amount suggested for the *Mona Lisa*, the comparison does not account for monetary changes due to economic factors—$100 million in 1962 is approximately $670 million in 2006 when adjusted for inflation using the US Consumer Price Index.

And the billionaire connoisseur who is lucky enough to snag the *Mona Lisa* at $670 million will be getting himself a bargain— the original plus the three 'copies' layered underneath for the price of one!

10. The Lady has a Medium

Myth! The *Mona Lisa* is an oil painting on canvas.

Some of those who have not seen the *Mona Lisa* on exhibit expect it to be shown some day hanging side by side with the *Last Supper*. In their minds, they see both artworks as large pieces of canvas even more richly detailed than the prints that hang from their bedroom walls.

Of course, we can never hope to see *The Last Supper* hanging beside the *Mona Lisa*; the former happens to be a fresco of the Biblical event painted on an entire wall of a building. On the other hand, though the *Mona Lisa* can be readily hung like an easel painting, it is not one. Rather, it is a piece of work on a wooden board measuring less than 2 feet by 2 feet. As described by a critic, "The painting is not large in its dimensions but impresses the viewer as monumental, an effect achieved by Leonardo's placement of the figure in relation to the background."

What may have given rise to the false notion that canvas was the medium Leonardo used for the *Mona Lisa* is the fact that some versions of the famous work were painted on this material. *La Gioconda* is one of the most replicated art pieces in the world, and the best copies were those made by Leonardo's own students and contemporaries. The clone found in the Vernon collection in the US is the most controversial because it is believed by its owners to have been by Da Vinci in imitation of himself, and is valued at millions of dollars.

Incidentally, while the real *Mona Lisa* is undoubtedly the one that can be seen hanging proudly in the Louvre, it is not in the strictest sense the original. In the process of producing the piece, Leonardo painted four versions in succession, all co-existing with and inseparable from each other. Modern x-ray studies have shown that under the visible facade of the 'Louvre oeuvre' are three more layers, each painted over by Leonardo because he wasn't satisfied. The *Mona Lisa* that smiles mystically at the viewer these days is the maestro's fourth and final rendering of the lady from Naples.

Even that last layer doesn't show everything, as there are some details that stay hidden and could only be discovered through scientific probing. For instance, a reflectography made in 2006 has revealed that Mona Lisa's hair is actually attached at the back of the head to a bonnet or pinned back into a chignon and covered with a veil bordered with a somber rolled hem. Until then, what could be seen by the naked eye was her hair hanging loosely down on her shoulders. In the 16th century, this free style was customary with unmarried young women or prostitutes—an evident contradiction with Mona Lisa's alleged status as a married woman.

11. The Lying Apostles

Myth! Jesus and the apostles were seated at a long table during the Last Supper.

Sticklers for truth in art like to point out that Leonardo made a mistake when he depicted Jesus and the twelve apostles sitting straight at the Last Supper. When the Jews celebrated Seder, they sat in a reclining position on their left side throughout both the service and the meal to show their freedom from slavery. The Jews in those days copied the Roman practice of dining at a rectangular table called the *triclinium*. Three sides of the table had low couches on which guests could recline while eating.

Leonardo's advocates bring up two points in defense of their champion. First, there is no real consensus among historians that the Last Supper was in celebration of Seder. The view that it was an ordinary dinner made significant by Christ's anticipation of his passion seems as valid as any other. Second, Leonardo may not have been true to tradition, but he was at least essentially faithful to artistic conventions. Since early Christian times and especially during the Renaissance, artistic representations of the Last Supper have indicated one of two dramatic moments: one was Christ's statement that a disciple would betray him, and the other was Christ's institution of the sacrament of Holy Communion. As a rule, those intending to depict the latter put the figures in a reclining position. In Leonardo's painting, however, the figures are all seated because the subject matter is the impending betrayal of Christ by Judas.

The old boy defense put up by Leonardo's friends might be good enough for them and for artists in general, but it definitely isn't for Biblicists and historians. A careful look at each of the four Gospels reveals that in three of them, Jesus was "reclining at the table" during the Last Supper, proof that Leonardo didn't just break tradition, he also quite unforgivably broke the Biblical footing of that tradition when he painted his masterpiece.

12. Maker's Dozen

Myth! Leonardo's *The Last Supper* suggests there were more than twelve persons in the room with Jesus.

The persons present at the Last Supper, aside from Jesus, numbered twelve. This is a 'gospel truth' expressed in three of the Books ("he reclined at table with the twelve disciples" and "Jesus came with the Twelve"), dousing the speculation that others in the room were deliberately hidden from view or were outside Leonardo's perspective. There were not more than a dozen in Jesus' coterie before he died; he had especially appointed them as preachers of the faith, calling them apostles as opposed to ordinary disciples who were mere followers or learners. Contrary to Dan Brown's contention in his fictionalized book *The Da Vinci Code*, Leonardo could not have deduced that one of the apostles was a woman; the name and distinctive personality that the Synoptic Gospels assign to each of Jesus' close associates are clearly indicative of the male gender. Wikipedia and others demolish the idea that Leonardo inserted a female figure in the painting in the belief that *John* 13:33 of the New Testament ("Now one of his disciples, he whom Jesus loved, was reclining at Jesus' bosom") alludes to a woman. Their conclusion: no amount of theorizing based on revisionist or apocryphal versions of the Holy Book can support the hypothesis—or any literary plot advancing it—that John, who was one of the original five apostles, was actually Mary Magdalene.

Because of its association with the apostles, the number 12 has gained a mystic significance for the faithful and for a few unbelievers as well. Jesus himself beatified the digit by promising the apostles that at the Last Judgment they would sit upon twelve thrones and judge the twelve tribes of Israel. Actually, 12 turned out to be a mere transitory number within a range that also included 11 and 13. When Judas hanged himself for indirectly causing Jesus' death, the apostles were reduced to eleven, and the number was temporarily restored to twelve when Matthias replaced Judas. The number finally settled at thirteen with the appearance of the converted Pharisee Paul, also called the Apostle of the Gentiles.

13. Thirteen at Dinner

Myth! The superstition intimated in Leonardo's painting of the Last Supper is about the number 13.

Leonardo's depiction of Jesus with the twelve apostles in the first Passion scene raises the number 12 to a high level of mysticism. By dramatizing two presences that have both been regarded by analysts as the 'thirteenth' in the tableau—Judas as a harbinger of misfortune and Jesus its victim—the painting gives the impression that it has something to do with the origin of the superstition about the number 13.

This is giving Leonardo more credit than he deserves. A moment's thought should tell us that *The Last Supper*, even if it were meant to proclaim the unluckiness of thirteen at dinner, cannot be more than a derivative for what is sometimes called triskaidekaphobia. The earliest source of the tradition is obviously the New Testament, considering that Leonardo's creation is simply a depiction of the event as it is originally described in that book. In fact, it was in consequence of this Biblical description that the idea of thirteen as an unlucky number prevailed in early Christian times, presaging the Renaissance by more than a thousand years. The superstition may have since become an inherent feature in Leonardo's and other artist's renditions of the Last Supper, but it definitely did not originate from any of these works.

The only superstition Leonardo is known to have purposely shown in his painting has to do with the figure of Judas. Scholars point out that in the pre-restoration version of *The Last Supper*, the renegade apostle can be seen spilling the table salt to indicate that a great evil was about to be perpetrated against Jesus. This minor flourish, however, is hardly detectable in the present version of the painting, but no matter. As in the case of the number 13, Leonardo did not originate the belief regarding the spilling of salt, as this goes way back to the days of ancient Rome. Salt used to serve as the Roman soldiers' salary (accounting for the phrase 'salt money'), and spilling salt means simply wasting money and bringing bad luck on the person doing so. There are many other theories about the origin and significance of the superstition, and all but a few center on this old Roman view of the matter.

104

14. A Brooder in the Brood

Myth! In *The Last Supper*, **Leonardo isolated Judas from the apostles by placing him on the other side of the table.**

A saving grace for Leonardo showing that he indeed favored realistic appearances is the way he located Judas at the dining table in relation to the other disciples. Even before Leonardo's time, the practice was to depict Judas as physically isolated from his associates, which usually meant placing Christ and the 11 faithful disciples on one side of the table and Judas all by himself on the other. Leonardo's conception was different. He decided to seat Judas on the same side of the table as the others but cut him off psychologically with the subtle use of shadows, facial expressions, gestures and symbols. Leonardo achieved a stronger effect of isolation by portraying the traitorous apostle spiritually alone a dark, staring figure who, while nervously clutching a moneybag, leans away from Christ and upsets the salt while doing so.

15. Holy Graffiti!

Myth! **Leonardo painted** *The Last Supper* **on a large piece of canvas.**

The Last Supper is not painted on canvas but on a wall in the monastery of Santa Maria delle Grazie in Milan, and is called a fresco although it is done in tempera. Leonardo left it unfinished in 1497, and two decades later—according to Vasari in 1556—the dampness had reduced it to a "muddle of blots." Some monks, believing there was no way to salvage the painting, carved a doorway through Christ's legs, and in 1796, Napoleon's callous soldiers desecrated it further by using Christ's head for target practice. The wall almost didn't survive a bomb attack that destroyed the rest of the monastery in World War II.

16. When Last is First

Myth! *The Last Supper* is the most popular work of art based on the number of copies reproduced.

The *Mona Lisa* is the most famous painting on earth, considering the number of people who have seen it. Of course, if popularity were to be measured by the number of copies reproduced and distributed, *The Last Supper*, although the less visible of the two, would beat the lady by a mile. The portrayal of the Lord's last meal has a socio-religious motif that gives it a functional relevance in millions of Christian homes. Nevertheless, devotees of religious trivia will be disappointed to learn that *The Last Supper* is not the most reproduced and widely distributed art in the world. That record is still held by Norman Rockwell's *The Four Freedoms*, prints of which were sent in the tens of millions all over the world during World War II.

17. Rejuvenating an Old Master

Myth! The latest restoration of *The Last Supper* has brought it to the near quality of the original.

Today, Leonardo's painting is so heavily restored that only the outline and a few brush strokes are traceable to him. It is practically the work of lesser artists, mostly from the 17th and 18th centuries, who painted over Leonardo's assemblage in a style that tried—but failed—to ape the master. Thus, in the present painting, St. Peter has a villainously low forehead, clearly a misrepresentation of the figure that Leonardo showed with the head tilted back in foreshortening. What was once the profile of St. Andrew has been turned into a three-quarter view of the same disciple, while the head of St. James the Less is clearly no longer Leonardo's but by an unknown hand. It is not surprising that the mishmash of colors resulting from the alternating abuse and restoration has produced ghost images of disciples and other mysterious entities that people think they see from hard copy prints of the painting or on the Internet.

The knife that some say was used by St. Peter to cut off a servant's ear at Gethsemane was held by a disembodied hand in the early version of the painting. Later artists attached the hand awkwardly to the arm of the apostle, as can now be seen in the restored work. It is relevant to note that John is the only Gospeller who cites St. Peter as the knife wielder in the ear-cutting incident, while the three other Gospels believe the culprit was not an apostle at all but "one in the crowd" or "a bystander."

The result resembles the original only because of the expert restoration between 1946 and 1954 by Mauro Pellicioli, a master of the art. Efforts to strip off the non-Leonardo paint are continuing, although it is becoming increasingly evident that improvement will only be minimal.

II

Creation And Recreation

On Michelangelo

"Every block of stone has a statue inside it
and it is the task of the sculptor to discover it."

•

Michelangelo

1. Horned Dilemma

Myth! Michelangelo blundered when he sculpted the figure of Moses with a pair of horns.

Michelangelo's masterpiece of sculpture is the colossal figure of Moses in the Church of St. Pietro in Vincoli at Rome. Designed for the tomb of Pope Julius II, it presents a sitting Moses as this venerable holy man is described in the Old Testament.

The work invites curious attention from those who can't believe that anyone, much less Michelangelo, would portray the Biblical patriarch as having a pair of horns growing out of his head. A few surmise that Michelangelo was probably only expressing some hidden meaning from *Exodus*, while others see it as an outright blunder. However, both suggestions fall flat for most historians, who suspect that the great sculptor intentionally shaped Moses' head according to the notion that the Biblical Jews actually had horns. This genetic oddity of the ancient Israelis was generally assumed during the artist's time, when many Renaissance painters besides Michelangelo depicted Moses with horns protruding from his head.

The medieval belief apparently arose from a mistake occurring in the Latin translation of the Hebrew text of the Old Testament, which states: "And when Aaron and all the children of Israel saw Moses, behold, the skin of his face shone; and they were afraid to come nigh him" (*Ex* 34:29-30). The Hebrew word for this kind of shining is *qaran*, which means "rays of light darting out" or "sending forth beams," and for 'horn' is *qeren*. Confused by the similarity, the Vulgate translators came up with the phrase *quod cornuta esset facies sua*, meaning "his face was horned."

The change from 'light' to 'horn' was facilitated by the ancients' regard for horns, such as those on pagan gods, as symbols of power and strength. Horns were basically a symbol of divinity, and a horned head was the most distinguishing feature of a divine being. The devil acquired his pair of horns for being the composite of all the horned gods of paganism.

2. Exemplars of Piety

Myth! Michelangelo gave the highly descriptive name *Piéta* to his sculpture of the Virgin Mary supporting the dead Christ.

Only a few are aware that *Piéta* is not the name of any specific work by Michelangelo, but of a whole theme in Christian art that portrays the Virgin Mary supporting the body of the dead Christ. Of Franco-German origin, the genre was never of any great importance in Italy, although the better-known works in the group today are those of Michelangelo and other Italian masters like Botticelli, Titian, and Perugino. Michelangelo alone has four Piétas, each of which is a masterpiece in its own right, and the best known is the one that can be seen at St. Peter's Basilica in the Vatican.

Many mistakenly regard Michelangelo's *David,* like his *Piéta,* as a unique piece by the artist. Even art connoisseurs are surprised to learn that Michelangelo sculpted two large Davids, one marble and the other bronze. Completed in 1504, the marble statue is now in the Academia, and should not be confused with the one popularly seen in the Piazza della Signoria, which is only a copy. The bronze statue, on the other hand, had been commissioned as a gift to Marechál de Gie of France, and was finished in 1508; its exact whereabouts are unknown, although it is believed to be somewhere in France. A third *David*—a small-scale marble statue recently recovered from the ruins of an Italian building—has been authenticated, despite its severely damaged condition, as a lesser Michelangelo artwork.

3. An Unfinished Statement

Myth 3: The architectural design of St. Peter's Cathedral was the last great project Michelangelo completed.

No one who has been awed by the magnificence of St. Peter's would dare question that this was the last great work of

Michelangelo. Yet there is disconcerting evidence that Michelangelo's contribution during his tenure as architect of the cathedral from 1546 to 1564 was not at all substantial. He stayed with the project from the time he took it on when he was 71 years old until the day he died at age 89. Unfortunately, he left it largely unfinished and with practically no design for the guidance of his successors. When pressed by his friends, he created a complete wooden scale model of the dome, but failed to leave any detailed plans for the rest of the church. And even with a model, the only part of the dome Michelangelo saw fulfilled was the drum, which he based on his final concept of a hemispheric dome with an extended lantern at the peak.

By the time Michelangelo died, he thought he had achieved his aim, for the main structure was within sight of completion. But after his death, architects changed the proportions of the building and even the silhouette of the dome, which became steeper. Giacomo della Porta raised the new dome in 1588-1590, building it not on Michelangelo's drum but on a light drum of travertine that the architect Luigi Vanvitelli (1700-1773) later braced with iron. The interiors of the Basilica, which Michelangelo completely neglected, had to be commissioned to other architects. The most notable of these, Giovanni Lorenzo Bernini (1598-1680), designed both the bronze *baldochino* (canopy) over the papal altar and the papal bronze throne.

4. Signature Art

Myth! **Michelangelo's easel painting of the Holy Family was the only piece of art he signed.**

Since easel paintings are the only works artists customarily sign, it is hastily—and erroneously—inferred that the only piece of art Michelangelo signed was his singular easel painting of the Holy Family. Like many artists of the day, Michelangelo frowned on the idea of affixing one's mark on his work, so that not even *The Holy Family* bears the painter's signature. He thought signing was neither appropriate nor necessary, and that one's distinctive style and quality of work should be sufficient to identify the piece as his own.

111

But Michelangelo did sign an item, although oddly enough, it was neither a painting nor a drawing but a sculpture. This was the *Piéta* (or, more appropriately, *Michelangelo's Piéta*), which the artist created c. 1499 when he was in his mid-twenties. This most widely viewed work of art in St. Peter's Basilica in Rome vividly displays the artist's signature on a ribbon on Mary's chest. It seems the young sculptor deigned to advertise himself this one time, when he still lacked the reputation that would allow him to eschew public recognition in later years. He also probably felt upon seeing his masterpiece that it deserved a distinct mark by way of setting it apart from the *Piétas* of other masters.

5. Horizontal Perspective

Myth! Michelangelo painted the ceiling of the Sistine Chapel while lying on his back.

The wondrous and complicated panorama on the ceiling of the Sistine Chapel has made many a viewer ask how the great Michelangelo did it. The usual answer: he painted the whole thing lying down on a platform close to the ceiling, as this seemed to be the only convenient way to gain a perspective.

While quite logical, the belief is false, according to proof that Michelangelo himself provided. The artist wrote a sonnet—his most famous—describing the difficulty he endured on the job, and on the same page he drew a caricature of himself standing up painting on the ceiling. The historian Vasari tells us that he worked on a scaffold high above the floor, his beard pointing to heaven and his face splattered with "a rich mosaic" of paint. He pursued the project for four years almost unaided, doing 5,800 square feet of surface, and painting more than 300 giant figures even though the original plan had called for only 12. No doubt he had the necessary infrastructure to help him paint on difficult locations in the Chapel, but it is equally certain he did all of this work standing up.

112

6. Multiple Dimensions

Myth! Michelangelo's greatness lies mainly in his sculpture.

It is a fallacy to think that Michelangelo's genius can only be appreciated through his sculpture, or that he didn't leave much legacy in other areas of artistic endeavor. Michelangelo, for one, produced a lot of paintings, most of which have survived, and the only reason they are never seen in a museum is that they are painted on walls and ceilings. His work on the Sistine Chapel under the mercurial sponsorship of the warrior pope Julius II, and the *Last Judgment* he executed above the altar of the same Chapel for Pope Paul III twenty-five years later, are transcendent masterpieces that rival or even overshadow his sculptural achievements. The only known work of this master done on an easel is *The Holy Family*, a painting of Mary, Joseph, and Jesus commissioned by Doni Strozzi upon his marriage to Maddalena Strozzi around 1503.

The fact is equally well known that Michelangelo could draw as brilliantly as he could sculpt or paint. For each of his projects, the conscientious Michelangelo would produce dozens of sketches, often drawing from live models or clay or wax figures. It was claimed that he burnt all those drawings before he died in 1564, so anxious was he that his works "give no other appearance than that of perfection." But that claim has since been withdrawn with the discovery of at least 630 drawings that unquestionably reveal the hand of the great Renaissance artist.

7. End in View

Myth! Michelangelo's *The Last Judgment* is typical of the artist's orthodox works.

A quarter of a century after completing his painting on the ceiling of the Sistine Chapel, Michelangelo was commissioned by Pope Paul III to paint another mural above the Chapel's altar. The result was *The Last Judgment*, a masterpiece that critics say outranks his earlier work in the Sistine Chapel in maturity and originality.

There are many unorthodox depictions worth noting in this magnificent fresco. Christ has no beard, angels have no wings, and mythological figures like Charon on the river Styx mingle with Christian ones. This is not to mention the artist's using a false perspective, by drawing the figures on the lower part of the painting proportionately smaller than those above. As a final note of irony, Michelangelo leaves a personal touch, which is clearly out of character: a caricature of his own likeness on a flayed skin held by St. Bartholomew, seated at the lower left of Christ.

Of the few orthodox features that *The Last Judgment* had, one was even changed after Michelangelo died. The figures had been originally nude, but as seen now, they are technically no longer in this state. Eighteen years after the work was finished, the overzealous Pope Paul IV—to placate counterreformation prudes who found the nakedness offensive—ordered Michelangelo's good friend, the artist Daniele da Volterra, to cover the figures with loin clothes. It proved just as embarrassing to Volterra, who was thereafter mocked with the title of *Il Brachettone* (the Breeches Maker) by the Roman populace.

III

Masters Of Art

On Famous Painters

"Painting is the grandchild of nature. It is related to God."

•

Rembrandt

1. Lending an Ear

Myth! Van Gogh cut off his ear and presented it to a lady he was wooing.

Actually, the famous expressionist artist only sliced off a portion of his left ear lobe, and this has led to erroneous stories of a more serious injury. Some writers would like to blame the myth on Hollywood, but in *Lust for Life*, there was really no indication that van Gogh cut off the entire auricle.

The event followed two months of hard work, immoderate drinking, and an argument the day before with his friend and fellow painter Paul Gauguin. Van Gogh's deteriorating emotional state precipitated the self-mutilation on December 23, 1888. Although just a small part of the lobe was cut off, it is true that he wrapped it in paper and mailed it to a local prostitute.

Van Gogh's greatness at the easel belies the fact that he spent most of his life not as a painter but as an art dealer, schoolteacher and preacher. He devoted no more than ten years to painting, during which he completed hundreds of works and revolutionized art. Although many are now worth millions of dollars, he sold just one painting during his lifetime. An art critic once observed that today you would need a money magnet to afford a van Gogh.

Van Gogh was eccentric, but history has painted him worse. Recent research reveals that the artist was actually an active worker who was in control of his reasoning ability, as attested by 796 letters he wrote to his family and friends between 1884 and his suicide in 1890, at age thirty-seven. Unfortunately, he was handicapped during much of his productive life by a disabling inner-ear disorder called Meniere's disease, which left him with severe tinnitus (ringing in the ears), chronic vertigo and depression. Modern biographers take a more forgiving view of van Gogh's irrational behavior, saying it was perhaps his own way of mitigating the physical pain. Or else it was a reaction to what he felt was a wretched existence living as a preacher, evangelist and peripatetic missionary among the impoverished coal miners in the region of southwest Belgium.

2. Day into Night

Myth! **Rembrandt painted a group of nocturnal city defenders live and called the classic piece *Night Watch*.**

Of the various works of Rembrandt that have come under critical appraisal, few have elicited as much controversy as *Night Watch*. Some have considered the subject it portrays colorless and dull, while others have gone as far as to call the entire painting a symbol of failure for the Dutch master. Many, though generally sympathetic, have simply refused to recognize it as a fine example of the influence of classicism in late Renaissance art.

Night Watch is not the real title of Rembrandt's controversial painting. The name given it by the artist on its completion in 1642 was *The Shooting Company of Captain Frans Banning Cocq and Lieutenant Willem van Ruytenburch*. The term *Night Watch* came to be used only late in the 18th century when, after being covered by boiled oil and varnish, the picture lost its sheen. Once cleaned of the varnish in 1946-47, it revealed a brilliantly colored work showing Cocq and Ruytenburch in the foreground. It immediately became obvious that the words 'Night' and 'Watch' were both wrong. The civic guards depicted in the picture were now seen not as nocturnal city defenders but as participants in some civilian day affair that included even children, perhaps a sports fest or a parade. It is said that when the sheen returned, journalists promptly changed the title to *Day Watch*.

What further heightened the fallacy that it was a night scene were the multiple shadows that suggested the presence of several artificial light sources in the painting. Actually, the effect was caused by Rembrandt's inconsistent (but, according to critics, aesthetic) placement of the sun's shadows. One who looks at the painting carefully will note that, while the shadow cast by the captain's hand on the lieutenant's coat puts the sun at an angle of about 45 degrees to the left, the shadow of the captain's extended leg indicates a different angle altogether.

An airlines advertisement once offered an invitation for tourists to visit Holland and see *Night Watch*, "Rembrandt's spectacular 'failure' (that caused him to be) hooted...down the road to bankruptcy." The 'fact' has been bruited about since the 19th century that the painting was poorly received and marked the artist's downfall from favor. It is not clear just what in the picture caused the sudden, dramatic downturn in Rembrandt's fortunes and forced him thereafter to live the life of a rejected artist. New evidence has revealed that no critic during Rembrandt's lifetime 'hooted' it, and that the picture was actually held in high esteem. Captain Banning Cocq was so happy he had a watercolor made for his personal album, and the painting was proudly hung in several prominent locations in Amsterdam. It seems *Night Watch* even put Rembrandt's career at the summit—he received about 1,600 guilders for the painting, and four years later the Prince of Orange paid him 2,400 for two lesser works. After attaining this height, Rembrandt went down in popularity, but it was not as abruptly or as extensively as is sometimes suggested. Moreover, the decline was not due to any fault or failure of Rembrandt's making, but to the gradual shifting of Dutch tastes to the style of new Flemish painters like van Dyck.

#	3. Op Art

Myth! In Rembrandt's *The Anatomy Lesson*, a group of medical observers and a lecturer are grouped around a skeleton.

Calling Rembrandt's 1632 work *The Anatomy Lesson* is misleading, since it is not the only notable painting with that name. There were other 16th-century Dutch painters who found an intriguing theme in the anatomy lessons given by the surgeons' guild of Amsterdam. The lectures were sometimes conducted before a large paying audience, but the preference of Rembrandt and his contemporaries was for the kind performed privately before the medical profession. Thomas de Keyser, for instance, painted *The Anatomy Lesson of Dr. Sebastiaen Egbertz,* which shows five medical observers and a lecturer grouped around a skeleton. This work is generally considered inferior to Rembrandt's version, which shows seven such observers watching a doctor dissect a corpse. Rembrandt's apt title is *The Anatomy Lesson of Dr. Tulp.*

It is claimed Rembrandt didn't sign his first name on *The Anatomy Lesson of Dr. Tulp,* but he did. This most creative and influential of all Dutch artists of the 17th century signed Rembrandt on nearly all of his canvases. The claim arises from the mistaken belief that Rembrandt was his last name, not his first. Many are surprised to learn that his full name was Rembrandt Harmenszoon van Rijn (or van Ryn). If Rembrandt had been Picasso, he would have had trouble choosing which of a dozen names to sign on his works. Picasso's full name is Pablo Diego Jose Francisco de Paula Juan Nepomuceno Maria de los Remedios Cipriano de la Santisima Trinidad Ruiz y Picasso.

4. Portrait of the Artist as a Whistler

Myth! *Whistler's Mother* **shows a white-capped woman sitting moodily in a rocking chair beside a wall picture, a loving tribute by the artist to his mother.**

The nineteenth-century US artist James Whistler was first and last an etcher, but it is his works in between as a painter that made him famous. He called them "Arrangements" and "Harmonies" in various colors, such as *Arrangement in Grey* for his self-portrait and Arrangement *in Black and White* for the portrait of a young girl.

Thus, it is a fallacy to call this artist's most famous painting *Whistler's Mother* (or, at other times, *A Portrait of My Mother*). The title, though widely used, is actually a common parody resulting from the painting's long years of overexposure. The piece is considered a realistic portrait of Whistler's mother, Anna McNeill Whistler; the artist, who was not as close as his brother was to their mother, intended it purely as an objective study—an "Arrangement" in gray and black—rather than an emotional work. This is why many reference books give it the name *Arrangement in Grey and Black*, though this is still a mistake because there are two "Arrangements" in grey and black, the other being the portrait of Thomas Carlyle. The only correct title is the one Whistler chose from the portrait's inception, which is *Arrangement in Grey and Black # 1: The Artist's Mother.*

The painting depicts Mrs. Whistler in profile, capped in off-white and dressed in black and seated on a straight chair. But because of the dark tone of the picture and the general posture of the subject, many become visually confused and think she is sitting in a rocking chair. It has not helped that the portrait, like many other popular and widely reproduced masterpieces, is now seldom scrutinized so that many of its details have become practically invisible.

5. After Death Experience

Myth! Guido Reni's *Portrait of Beatrice Cenci* was painted live, but Grant Wood's *American Gothic* was not.

Beatrice Cenci was a 22-year-old Roman lady who was beheaded in 1599 as an accessory to the murder of her villainously cruel father. Nicknamed the Beautiful Parricide, she was condemned to death along with two of her brothers by Pope Urban VIII despite public pleas for leniency. Her cruel fate, seen particularly by anticlerics as a martyrdom suffered at the hands of the Church, has become a romantic theme for numerous poems, dramas, and novels (e.g. Shelley's 1819 *The Cenci*, and the latest, Alberto Moravia's 1958 *Beatrice Cenci*). It is said that the soulful eyes on the famous portrait of Beatrice hanging in the Barberini Palace in Rome give away the fact that the Italian painter Guido Reni painted her live on the eve of her execution. But historians begging to differ insist this is improbable, because Reni began to paint seriously only in the early 1600s and did not open a studio in Rome until 1601.

Unlike Reni's *Cenci*, Grant Wood's famous painting of an elderly couple in front of their Indiana farmhouse looks totally like a product of the mind but was actually painted live. This the artist himself attested, in essence a confession that his style, plus the fact that the subjects and the setting were fake, was what gave the portrait a synthetic effect. Wood couldn't get suitable characters from a real farm, so he decided to work with his own resources. He posed his sister and their family dentist in front of a structure that had once served as a bordello. The finished product has become the most parodied major work of art by an American master, a development critics say was encouraged by Wood himself when he called his tableau *American Gothic*.

120

6. Dollar Portrait

Myth! **The most celebrated painting by an American artist is a finished portrait of George Washington by Gilbert Stuart.**

Of the nearly 1,000 portraits done by the American painter Gilbert Stuart, the one that stands out for reasons not readily obvious is the unfinished portrait of George Washington (1796) at the Boston Museum of Fine Arts. Those who have gazed admiringly at The Athenaeum, as the work is called, are probably not aware that it has no finished version, and that the artist left it in that imperfect condition deliberately. Martha Washington had commissioned Stuart to do the portrait, but when it was finally delivered to her, the background and Washington's body were still undone. Stuart had stopped before completing the picture and had retained the original for as long as he could make copies for sale, hoping to capitalize on the deceased President's popularity. He wanted to be able to tell Martha truthfully, whenever she asked for the portrait, that it was incomplete. The work remained in Stuart's studio unfinished until his death in 1828, and so far as is known, there has been no effort to have it completed by any other artist afterwards.

The 1796 Athenaeum, the second of three portraits Stuart made of America's first president, is oftentimes confused with the third, called the Lansdowne. A common observation is that the former seems to be a work in preparation and the Lansdowne its finished version, especially since the distinctive 'clenched facial expression' brought on by Washington's new set of false teeth appears in both paintings.

Despite its imperfect state, The Athenaeum holds the enviable position of being the most celebrated and famous painting by Stuart and, for that matter, by an American artist. This is less because of its quality than of the fact that it was the model for old George's likeness on the ubiquitous dollar bill.

7. Painting by the Book

Myth! Reuben's *The Adoration of the Magi* recreates a famous Biblical scene.

Peter Paul Rubens' painting entitled *The Adoration of the Magi* is a famous portrayal of the wise men adoring Jesus at the manger. It is unfortunate that, despite its impeccable quality as a work of art, this Renaissance piece has perpetuated the fallacy that the Magi were the ones who visited the manger to see the newborn God-child. *Matt* 2:11 says, "On coming to the house, they (the Magi) saw the child with his mother Mary, and they bowed down and worshipped him." And *Luke* 2:16 says, "So they (the shepherds) hurried off, and found Mary and Joseph, and the baby, who was lying in the manger." These are clear statements from the Gospels that what the Magi visited was a house (or, sometimes, inn), and those who came to Jesus in the manger were the shepherds. Rubens' scene is a composite of two separate events—the visitation of the infant Jesus in the manger by the shepherds, as described by Luke, and the adoration of the child Jesus at the house or inn by the Magi, according to Matthew. Evidently, Rubens chose to paint not from the description in the New Testament but from his own recollection of popular lore.

8. Sign of the Greek

Myth! Because he was originally Greek, the Spanish painter of the masterful *Toledo in a Storm* signed his work "El Greco".

El Greco was a man of multiple nationalities—Greek, Cretan, Spanish and Venetian—but a citizen of only one country. He was born on the island of Crete when it was still part of Venice, and lived there until his middle twenties. After Crete was ceded to Greece, he acquired the sobriquet El Greco, or "The Greek," in Italy, where he studied under Titian. "El Greco" is not Spanish, as one might think, but Venetian.

He based himself in Spain starting from his middle years, and eventually flourished as one of Spain's greatest painters. However, because Crete during his youth was a Venetian possession, El Greco considered himself primarily a citizen of Venice.

This painter's affection for Spain can be seen from many of his classic paintings, notably *Toledo In A Storm*, but none of them bears the signature El Greco. Contrary to what some art books imply, this sixteenth-century painter never signed the sobriquet on his works. Born Doménikos Theotokópoulos, he put this name on all his paintings, writing it in Greek characters, sometimes followed by Kres for "Cretan," his original nationality.

IV

Black And White In Color

On Colors

"The pain passes, but the beauty remains."

•

Auguste Renoir

1. Color It Black

Myth! **Black is a color.**

Auguste Renoir dubbed black "the queen of all colors," voicing his artistic preference based on two misconceptions common in his profession. One is that black is the presence of color and white the absence of it. Sir Isaac Newton faced fierce opposition when he debunked this fallacy three centuries ago, proving in his famous work on 'the celebrated phenomenon of colors' that it's the other way around—white is the composite of all colors, whereas black is totally devoid of them.

According to Newton's doctrine, white is the color of white light, which combines all the colors of the spectrum. White light is everywhere except in pitch-dark places, imparting its combination of colors to any object exposed to it through the process of *reflection* and *absorption*. Depending on the reflective character of its surface, the object absorbs some of the colors from the light source while reflecting others. The reflected color (or mixture of colors) becomes the color of the object, as this is what is transmitted to, and perceived by, the eye of the observer. If the object reflects all the constituent colors of white light, the eye sees white; if it absorbs all, the effect is black. Color as an aspect of light does not include black at all, black being neither a hue nor a degree of lightness but the total absence of it.

2. Pigments of the Imagination

Myth! **The pigments an artist uses are what impart color to his work.**

The second misconception underlying Renoir's impression of black as a color is that the pigments on the artist's easel are a source of color. On the contrary, they are only objects that absorb or reflect the colors of light in varying configurations. The black pigment is especially not a color because, by absorbing all the colors from the light source, it leaves nothing to be reflected from it. Thus, when the artist combines pigments, say black with white, he is not really mixing colors but several *malleable* objects each containing proportions of molecules that absorb or reflect light; the result is a reapportionment of the molecules to form a new hue or color, such as gray. In the laboratory, black being a non-color does not appear in the spectrum, but on the easel, it is a pigment that can be mixed with another color to produce a new shade or intensity of that color.

3. Primal Senses

Myth! The three primary colors on an artist's easel are red, green and blue.

The quarrel between science and art becomes even more serious and complicated in their treatment of primary colors. Primary colors are so-called because of two distinguishing characteristics, namely, (a) when combined with each other, they will produce another color, a non-primary one; and (b) they themselves cannot be produced from any combination of colors. A third characteristic not often mentioned because somewhat confusing is that a primary crossed with a non-primary will result in a color not belonging to the spectrum.

From the acronym RGB on a television monitor, we assume that the three primary colors are red, green and blue. Scientifically speaking, we are correct: all the colors that we see on the TV screen are derived from a beam of red, blue and green light, either alone or overlapping with each other. To the artist, however, the third primary color that cannot be created from any combination of pigments is yellow, not green, and it is a mixture of red (magenta), blue (cyan) and yellow in proper proportions that will produce any other color (including green) on the easel.

If you don't see it yet, try overlapping a beam of red light with another of green to get yellow. Now, try mixing red and green paints, and all you'll have is a dirty black. The answer to this riddle is in the totally different way colors are achieved with light as opposed to pigments. The differences are analogous to addition and subtraction in mathematics. Adding, in varying degrees of intensity, different amounts of the three primary components of light from the spectrum creates all the colors in the television picture tube. Pigment colors are different. As an object and not a light beam, a pigment achieves its distinctive color from its own set of molecules some of which absorb, or subtract, certain parts of the spectrum and others reflect, or add, the parts that remain. For some reason, while yellow and blue pigments sometimes make green, no exact proportions of molecules can be obtained from any mixture of red, green or blue pigments to obtain yellow.

4. Shades of Hades

Myth! Brown and gray are shades of black.

Because of the action of black on other pigments, many mistakenly regard certain hues, such as brown and gray, as shades of black rather than as colors. Actually, in both the artistic and the scientific world, brown can be obtained only by mixing or overlapping certain primary colors, of which black is not one. What appears to be brown as a result of black being reduced to a lower degree of lightness or saturation (as in 'brownout' or 'brown' skin) enjoys no kinship with the true brown that is produced on the artist's easel by combining the red and yellow pigments.

A case in point is the word 'brownout' as used in some English-speaking countries, in reference to the oftentimes official practice of saving energy by turning off the electricity in limited areas on a scheduled basis. Through this action, the whiteness of the remaining electric lights suffuses the environment and the resulting darkness is less intense. If the occurrence is longer or more extensive, it becomes a blackout. No one seems to realize that there is no such word or idea as a brownout in any existing lexicon, and that, while a power failure in a small community would appear to be of a lesser degree than one affecting a whole city like New York, both are blackouts nevertheless.

Those who assume that black and white are the constituent colors of a blackout suggest that the term for what is otherwise called a brownout, where white light is still available, should be 'grayout'. Others believe that the proper term should be 'greyout', and that black and white mixed on the easel is 'grey' rather than 'gray'. During most of the twentieth century, the basis of the difference has been primarily geographical—gray is American, grey British—and a matter of spelling preference in the rest of the English-speaking world. However, when polled more than a hundred years ago by the English Oxford Dictionary, the English public expressed the belief that the two words represent subtly different colors, gray being a bit darker because of an additional tinge of red or brown. Naturally, this raises a chuckle from the scientist, since in his book, gray or grey has nothing to do with black (and, consequently, with a blackout) and can only be brought about by combining equal amounts of the primary colors red, green and blue. In short, outside the artist's canvas, no gray area exists between black and white except an entire array of colors called the spectrum.

5. Color it Dead

Myth! **Black is the universal symbol of mourning.**

Wearing black to mourn the dead is a familiar practice in most of the Western World. What there is about black that makes it adaptable for a morbid purpose is not evident, except perhaps the idea that death is the doorway to the dark unknown, and nothing can bring on a blacker mood.

In any case, it is a fallacy to suppose that black's association with death or sadness is unique or that it is universally recognized. In more than half the world, black is eschewed as a symbol of mourning in favor of real colors, such as brown in Ethiopia and Iran, yellow in Egypt and Burma, sky blue in Syria and Armenia, and red and violet among the Gypsies and the Turks. Indeed, if there were a universal symbol for mourning, it would be white, this being the funereal color of more than a billion Chinese, not to mention other Asians. Even in the West, white used to be preferred, as in Ancient Rome, Greece, and England. It is said that Henry VIII wore white for Anne Boleyn's funeral, but whether it was to mourn or to rejoice we do not know. The most publicized historical incident in this regard involves Mary, Queen of Scots, who insisted on wearing her favorite color—white—when she

128

married Francis Dauphin of France. This was rather odd, because white during her time was the traditional color of mourning for French queens. Her husband died shortly afterward, and so did she, although not before white became established as a bridal color. Mary's piquant behavior broke a tradition to begin another, and earned for her the sobriquet 'White Queen'.

6. Dreamscape

Myth! One always dreams in black and white.

Federico Fellini once said that he made his film *8 1/2* in black and white because "dreams are never in color." How Fellini could be so sure only this great director knew. It is hard to recall the details of a dream, and harder still to remember the color and texture of each component image, even if it stays fresh in your memory. Although there is a sense of shape and movement, no one is obviously aware of each dream object as vividly as he would be when awake, and the result is likely to be a monochromatic haze.

However, scientific tests have provided evidence that visual images in dreams are as often in color as those in real life. While color is better seen than dreamed about, one conclusion is that it does occur in mental visions and can be evoked by prodding the subconscious. Patients have shown under psychoanalysis that they can distinguish the colors of objects that appear in their dreams. Many artists have successfully produced colored art through dream transcription, i.e., painting what they see in their dreams while in an induced state of sleep. It is believed black-and-white or monochromatic dreams occur only when the mind intends to convey a psychological meaning from the lack of color.

7. Southern Blackface

Myth! The Black Hills of South Dakota is just that— black hills located in South Dakota.

The Black Hills of South Dakota are famous not for their colored topography but because they have some of the best tourist attractions in the region—Mount Rushmore, Custer State Park, and the Black Hills Passion Play, to name a few. In fact, no part of the promontories can be considered black or blackish to any notable extent. Why the word 'black' appears prominently in the name is not clear, and some reference books can only suggest that this might be because the rounded hilltops and well-forested slopes present a dark appearance from a distance.

Ironically, it is not only 'black' but also every other word in the name 'Black Hills of South Dakota' that is misleading. The hills, for one, are really mountains that rise approximately 3,000 feet above the Great Plains. The highest, Harney Peak, is 7,242 feet, higher than any elevation in the Appalachian or the Ozark ranges, and several others exceed 6,000 feet above sea level. And contrary to what the name implies, the mountain range extends well beyond South Dakota and into the neighboring state of Wyoming.

---

8. Flower Perfect

Myth! White can be seen in its purest form on the lily flower.

'Lily-white' is an expression meant to convey a pure-white color. The suggestion is that the white one sees on the lily flower is uncorrupted white, which is of course not true. A lily can be of various colors, but even the white kind is not totally unblemished.

There is, in fact, some doubt that a lily-white object can exist at all except in the laboratory. Scientifically, purity of white is achievable only by a surface that can reflect all the colors of light, without allowing any color wavelength to be absorbed. This is theoretically possible, but unlikely to occur in the real world. For one thing, the light source itself may have an imbalance in its color constituency. Man-made light usually has a dominant color which, when reflected, tarnishes the white. For another thing, the surface texture of the object, though fully reflective, may not be able to reflect certain colors as strongly as would prevent any

130

absorption. Because of these anomalies, the only lily-white item in the world is the white light that comes from nature.

9. Green Passions

Myth! Green is the color of jealousy or envy.

Many people think the statement, "Jealousy is a green-eyed monster," is simply a rephrasing of the term 'green with envy'. This is fallacious, for two reasons, the first being that jealousy and envy are not the same thing. To quote from Wikipedia: "'Envy' and 'jealousy' are often used interchangeably, but in correct usage they stand for two different distinct emotions. In proper usage, jealousy is the fear of losing something that one possesses to another person (a loved one in the prototypical form), while envy is the pain or frustration caused by another person having something that one does not have oneself. Envy typically involves two people, and jealousy typically involves three people. Envy and jealousy result from different situations and are distinct emotional experiences."

Secondly, in the two expressions, the word 'green' is not used in the same way for both jealousy and envy. In 'green with envy', green does not describe envy but the sick feeling that goes with it. The color has always been a symbol for sickness, as suggested by the phrase 'green around the gills' and by cartoons in which sick persons are depicted with green-tinted faces. The emotion that is traditionally colored green is jealousy, the notion being probably older than Shakespeare, who coined the phrase "green-ey'd monster" in Othello (Act 3, scene 3). The metaphor likens jealousy to a cat—a green-eyed monster in the real sense—that teases and torments its victim before finally destroying it.

The disquieting element in jealousy is enough to suggest that there is something wrong with the theory that green is the most restful color of the spectrum. We are sometimes advised to look at something green to calm our nerves, as this produces in us a more secure feeling because our ancestors lived in forests and jungles. It is true that artists frequently use specific colors to achieve a desired emotional impact, e.g., "greens are cool and soothing, and tend to recede; while reds are hot and exciting, and bright red

131

jumps forward." Except in this sense, however, there is no physiological basis for the notion that green is distinctly comforting, and some people may indeed equally find violet or even bright Chinese red to be restful. People love to assign a color match for almost everything in their daily lives, but the feeling is highly individualistic and there is no consensus on the proper color.

10. Dark Waters

Myth! The Black Sea is named for its blackish waters and the black rocks on its shores.

Some believe this oval-shaped sea shared by the former Soviet Union, Turkey, Bulgaria and Romania is called black because of the black rocks that dot its shores. Others say a myth has something to do with it—a kingdom at the eastern tip (now Georgia), reputed to be the site of the legendary Golden Fleece, was once inhabited by a black race. Both conjectures are false. The real reason is mood, not color, and is provided by the sea's Turkish side, which is notorious for the dense fogs, violent storms and generally hostile weather that prevail over its waters. The Turks coined the name *Kara Dengiz,* or Black Sea, as an appropriate reference to this often bleak, dark and forbidding atmosphere. In winter particularly, heavy fogs and stormy clouds obscure the sun and lend a dark aspect to the entire sea.

However, this is only one country's view. On the whole, "the Black Sea climate is mild, with cool summers, warm autumns, short winters, and prolonged springs, with the southern Crimea and the southeastern shores enjoying the best conditions." The average January air temperature in the central portion is only about 46° F, while spring air temperature everywhere ranges from 61° to 75° F. The Black Sea is a sophisticated year-round transportation artery, and a major recreational and recuperative center and tourist destination. The first to recognize the misconception about this body of water were the early Greeks, who had originally named it *Pontus Axenus*, meaning not hospitable, but quickly changed this to *Pontus Euxinus*, meaning hospitable.

11. Managing the White Pieces

Myth! **The classical Greeks did most of their sculpture in white.**

Illustrations, art pieces, relics, and literature all promote the idea that sculptures during Hellenic days had only one color, which was white. Experts on classical Greek say this is not true. The ancients loved painting their statues, particularly of fully clothed persons, in all kinds of colors, including gold and ivory. The practice, which often required the artist to leave the painting of the composition to others who were specialized for it, was carried on until the time of Michelangelo.

The polychromatic objects of art turned into white relics mainly because their original colors faded over time. Fortunately, we have an idea of what the completed statues looked like when they left the hands of their creators. Modern techniques can now determine the kind of finish these art pieces used to have, and have in fact proved that most were literally awash with colors.

12. Bullish Tendency

Myth! **The color red unduly excites a bull and goads it into action.**

The belief that what goads the bull into action in the ring is the color red has gone well with bullfight-loving nations. The Spanish, for one, use a generous amount of red in the *muletas* (capes) of their toreadors and the pennants of their *banderilleros* apparently because of their belief in this notion

This belief is fallacious. Bulls being color blind like all other cattle, movement is a much more significant element than color in bullfighting. The brightness of any color in motion, rather than a particular color *per se*, is what excites and maddens the bull. The color red has been adopted especially for the *muleta* only because it produces a more colorful spectacle even while it minimizes the sight of blood, to which some spectators are sensitive. It has been noted that the bull charges the yellow side of the cape just as readily as it does the red. Of course, while bulls have no vision for color, their remarkable memory allows them to distinguish movements, for which reason they are never used in the *corrida* a second time.

However, the expression "to see red," which is apparently based on the popular but erroneous view of a bullfight, has turned out to be more than a metaphor. Extreme anger can make a human, though not a bull, see red. Under certain conditions a state of rage can cause the eyes to become suffused with blood, causing the person to see things through a red haze.

Incidentally, the Britannica tells us that a bullfighter is a torero, never a toreador. The error is apparent in Bizet's opera Carmen, which features the familiar rousing tune "March of the Toreadors."

13. Meet Roy G. Biv

Myth! **The rainbow always displays seven colors.**

All that people should know to remember the seven colors of the rainbow is the name Roy G. Biv, which is the acronym for red, orange, yellow, green, blue, indigo, and violet. However, it is not quite true that rainbows show only these colors, or that they show the seven all the time.

Primary rainbows show the seven colors properly arranged, but there are also secondary rainbows, too faint to be seen, whose colors are exactly reversed. Some rare manifestations consist of only one color, i.e., an all-purple or all-red hue, or plain white. The purple ones can be seen before or at sunrise; high clouds that scatter the blue and violet light, which raindrops reflect back to the observer, usually form them. An all-red rainbow, on the other hand, is seen only at sunset, when the sun is low in the sky, because the shorter blue, green and yellow wavelengths have been dispersed during their relatively long trip through the atmosphere. White rainbows can appear either in daylight or in moonlight, although the one seen by moonlight is not white at all but only seems so.

Rainbows, like raindrops and soap bubbles, show varied hues but have no color of their own, whereas white light appears colorless yet is chock full of colors. One will also find odd that a rainbow, which is not a material thing but only a light sensation in the eye of the beholder, can be reflected in a large body of water. The scientific explanation is simply that the rays of light producing the rainbow in one's sight can be reflected after leaving the drop but before reaching the eye.

14. Proof of Life

Myth! The color of blood is red.

'Blue blood' originated from an old belief, common among medieval Spaniards, that the blood of Spanish aristocrats whose race had suffered no Moorish admixture was blue-colored, as suggested by their blue veins. This may be something to be laughed at today, but what most people don't realize is that it is fallacious only half of the time. Science has duly established that human blood is not always red, at least not inside the body. It is, in fact, naturally blue, but turns red under certain conditions in half of our circulatory system.

In other words, there is more literal truth in the phrase "blue blood" than in the expression "blood red." The blood that travels through the veins towards the lungs and the heart is blue with a tinge of purple. It becomes red when, after being pumped out of the heart, it flows through the pulmonary artery and to the lungs, where the hemoglobin in the red blood cells combines with oxygen to produce the red color. Blood from the veins also turns red when exposed to the oxygen in the air, which is what happens when a person bleeds. Once the oxygen has been released throughout the body, blood picks up carbon dioxide and other wastes from the body's cells and again assumes a bluish hue as it is returned to the heart. There is no better proof of this than bruises that turn "black and blue" after a severe beating. The blow breaks the tiny oxygen-supplying blood vessels under the skin, and the blood as seen through the skin seeps into the surrounding areas where it can no longer get oxygen.

15. Legally Blonde

Myth! Caucasians are the likeliest to produce blue-eyed and pink-fingered babies.

That newborn baby is worth a second look, if you are not Caucasian. Seeing a pair of clear blue eyes and ten little pink fingers may mean it's time to consult the hospital authorities (no, not a divorce lawyer). There's a chance somebody made an inadvertent switch and put the wrong baby in the crib.

Well, not really. Popular belief to the contrary, no race has a monopoly on blue-eyed babies. All races have them, and in fact, they have them not just some of the time but also all the time. We often use the cliché "baby-blue eyes" without being aware of its literal truth, i.e., that all babies regardless of race do have blue eyes. The color of one's eyes is dependent partly on the color of the pigments in the iris and partly on the way light influences those pigments. When there are no such pigments, as in the case of babies of any race, the resulting color is always blue.

It is also quite likely for babies of any race to have pink fingers, but this is not the reason for the etymology of the word "pinkie." Most people assume that the term originated from some child talk about baby's little fingers and their characteristic pink color. In fact, it is derived from the Old Dutch word *pinkje*, meaning little finger, or at least from the obsolete English word "pink," meaning small.

Speaking of blue and pink, the first is said to be the traditional color for boys and the second for girls. This has not been a long-lived tradition, though. It used to be just the reverse, when pink was the male color and blue the female, and it still is in some cultures. "Before World War II, blue signified 'delicate and dainty,' and pink represented 'a stronger, more decided color'...Colors have extraordinary power, but the meaning of those colors is subject to change, as are styles and cuts of clothing." (*Gender Shock*, Phyllis Burke, p.141).

16. Panic Button

Myth! The US president pushes a red button to signal the launching of nuclear missiles.

Movies have conditioned us into thinking that there is a red button near the President's desk in the Oval Office that will electronically trigger the release of US missiles toward certain pre-determined targets. Common sense dictates such a contraption is too dangerous to exist in a nuclear war setting. What the President most likely has is a telephone of some standard color, possibly black. While no red button plays a role in the excellent Hollywood send-off *Dr. Strangelove: or How I Learned to Stop Worrying and Love the Bomb* (1964), this and another film, *Fail-Safe*, also released in 1964, show in some detail the procedure for activating an order to release nuclear missiles on a target. However, we will never be sure to what extent Hollywood imagination has been able to guess what is essentially a military secret.

According to popular sources of this kind of information, the president is accompanied at all times by an Air Force warrant officer carrying a thin black satchel containing the Emergency War Order (EWO) authentication codes. To launch a nuclear attack, the president calls up CINCSAC (commander in chief, Strategic Air Command, Omaha, Nebraska), uses the codes to establish that he is indeed the president, and gives his orders. Having verified the president's orders, CINCSAC activates the Single Integrated Operational Plan, a command-sequencing computer that electronically issues EWOs to the pertinent parties. After each land-based missile command center confirms its orders, two crewmembers must simultaneously turn brass keys at control consoles some distance apart, casting one "launch vote." The crew in another command center some miles away does the same thing, and the two votes together launch 10-50 ICBMs.

17. Hot Styles are Cool (and Vice Versa)

Myth! Light-colored clothing is generally cooler than dark-colored ones.

The belief that light-colored clothing is generally cooler than dark-colored ones is exaggerated. Assuming the materials used are the same, the difference in warmth between black and white clothing under ordinary circumstances is marginal. That white material reflects more light than does dark material is a scientific truth, but the effect on one's comfort will probably be felt only in bright sunlight. In hot, humid days when there is no sun, the color of clothing is not as important as, say, texture, which determines capability to soak up perspiration, or design, to promote the circulation of air throughout the body.

This is obviously the case even among animals, where the only difference is in the color of their body hair or fur. Denizens of the coldest regions of earth, such as polar bears, feel as much warmth under their white fur as do the black bears under theirs. For horses, however, experts say the principle that light colors are cooler may be true: black horses are indeed affected by the heat of the direct sun more than white ones.

There may be some psychological benefit from wearing light clothes if the wearer sincerely believes he is more comfortable that way. However, authorities have advised that where one's objective is health rather than comfort, what matters is the weave and not the color. Closely woven fabric, though not as comfortable as open-weave cloth, is best for spending a summer day outdoors because it is the only kind that can prevent or minimize the transmission of dangerous ultra-violet rays to the skin.

V

According To Doyle

On Sherlock Holmes

"As a rule, said Holmes, the more bizarre a thing is
the less mysterious it proves to be."

•

Arthur Conan Doyle

1. First on the Crime Scene?

Myth! Doyle's Sherlock Holmes stories introduced the detective mystery genre.

A Scot created Sherlock Holmes and the English launched the Golden Age of detective fiction, but neither fact makes the modern detective story British. Edgar Allan Poe, an American, is generally regarded as having invented this type of writing when he wrote 'The Murders in the Rue Morgue' in 1841, and even Watson doffs his hat to Poe's C. Auguste Daupin as the first detective in Holmes' own style ('A Study in Scarlet'). The critic Richard Alewyn and a few others have their own candidate in E.T.A. Hoffmann, the German romantic who wrote 'Das Fraülein von Scuderi' in 1818, twenty-three years before Poe produced his own tour de force. According to Alewyn (*The Origin of the Detective Novel*, 1974), Hoffmann's story about a series of murders and jewel thefts in Louis XIV's Paris contained all the elements of the detective novel, plus the extraordinarily frequent, though not obligatory, element of the locked room.

Sadly, Poe may not even make it as the father of the American detective story, a title already claimed for Ellery Queen by connoisseurs of the genre. Queen, it is said, gave the art a truly American flavor even while Poe failed to leave the slightest trace of Americanism (not even the word 'detective', for instance) in his stories. Poe's mysteries, unlike Queen's, were all set in the Continent, which is probably another reason people are inclined to think Europe, not America, is the whodunit's home ground.

Coming back to Holmes, it can be said, at least, that he was the world's first forensic investigator, a distinction capped by an honorary fellowship he received from the Royal Society of Chemistry in 2002—the only fictional character so honored. Holmes' success at his brand of deduction is believed to be due to "his mastery of both a huge body of particular knowledge of things like footprints, cigar ashes, and poisons, which he uses to make relatively simple deductive inferences...he then proceeds to find one explanation that is clearly the best at explaining the evidence." He accumulates his information from tracking and observation, "skills that have little to do with deduction per se, but

140

everything to do with providing the premises for particular Holmesian deductions."

2. Needling Questions

Myth! Dr. Watson finally cured Holmes of his habit of sniffing cocaine.

Holmes and Watson admitted to each other all their known shortcomings before agreeing to share quarters at 221B Baker Street. But it seems Holmes deliberately held back on one—his affection for cocaine. Watson would later describe Holmes, in the only Doyle story mentioning his addiction (*The Sign of Four*), as "alternating from week to week between cocaine and ambition—the drowsiness of the drug and the fierce energy of his own keen nature." The doctor eventually weans the detective from the drug in a non-Doyle tour de force, the 1974 novel *The Seven Percent Solution* by Nicholas Meyer. This psychological study of Holmes' tormented past and the reason he lapsed into the cocaine habit ends with the sleuth being cured of his hang-ups with professional help from Sigmund Freud.

"Quick, Watson, the needle!" rings familiar, as it readily points to Holmes' cocaine addiction and his dependence on Dr. Watson to administer the drug. The phrase corroborates as well the suggestion in *The Sign of Four* that Holmes is one of the few-recorded addicts that did not sniff cocaine but had it injected in them. However, one will be sorely disappointed to find that the quotation is not in any of the 60 stories by Arthur Conan Doyle or in any of the clone fiction that abounds about Holmes. And except for the final line in the 1939 *The Hound of the Baskervilles* ("Oh, Watson, the needle"), nothing close to it can be heard in any of the Holmes films, including Billy Wilder's 1970 *The Private Life of Sherlock Holmes* and the 1976 Herbert Ross adaptation of Nicholas Meyer's story. According to a film reviewer, the scene was criticized as too risqué by 1939 audiences, and "caused the film's producers to make a conscious decision to omit any additional mention of Holmes' recreational drug use in future outings."

3. Gumshoe in Steele Trappings

Myth! Doyle created the deerstalker cap and the Inverness cape as original parts of Holmes' fashion image.

The deerstalker cap and the Inverness cape, two of the items most associated with the Holmes persona, did not originate with Doyle. The first was the idea of the well-known Strand Magazine illustrator Sidney Paget, while the second was the brainchild of Frederick Dorr Steele, the artist who illustrated the Doyle stories after Paget died. Following the introduction of these items on the stage by American actor William Gillette, they were integrated into the image that soon achieved familiarity worldwide. Gillette added his own flourish by having his character smoke a curved meerschaum pipe in lieu of the calabash pipe the literary Holmes brandishes in his stories. It is Gillette with cap, cape and pipe that became the basis for Steele's final illustration of Holmes as well as Basil Rathbone's later appearance in the dedicated films.

The famous detective dons the deerstalker in the two 1939 period movies, *The Adventures of Sherlock Holmes* and *The Hound of the Baskervilles*, but beginning with the 1942 *Sherlock Holmes and the Voice of Terror*, he replaces it with a modern hat at the insistence of Dr. Watson. The Inverness, a sleeveless coat with a shoulder cape serving as protection to the arms and upper body, suffers the same fate in the later movies when Rathbone discards it in favor of a heavier overcoat.

4. The Hounds of Baker Street

Myth! Doyle invented the line, "The game's afoot," to signal the start or the climax of a Sherlock Holmes investigation.

It seems like Holmes is forever hurrying up the plodding Watson with "Come, Watson, come! The game is afoot," especially when the detective is hot on the trail of a clue or of the villain himself. The utterance has attained an even higher level of association with the showing of the Spielberg-produced movie *Young Sherlock Holmes* (1985), in which the phrase 'the game is afoot' is repeated several times by the teen-aged protagonist as if to declare an intention to make it his favorite expression in future adulthood. However, Doyle probably had no such purpose, since he used the line only casually in 'The Adventure of the Abbey Grange' and, as far as is known, not anywhere else. Doyle for certain couldn't have invented it, as the words were already common among the hunting gentry in England at that time. In fact, more than 200 years before Doyle, Shakespeare had committed one of his principal characters to saying prior to a hunt, "The game's afoot: Follow your spirit, and upon this charge, cry 'God for Harry, England, and Saint George!'" (*King Henry V*, Act 3, Scene I).

---

5. Rules of Deception

Myth! 'An exception proves the rule' is one of several proverbs Doyle originated for Sherlock Holmes.

Contrary to some people's belief, Arthur Conan Doyle did not coin the expression, "An exception proves the rule," and Sherlock Holmes certainly never mouthed it. The proverb existed centuries before Doyle was born, its age betrayed by the peculiarity of its phrasing. In the old days, 'prove' meant 'to test or challenge', and in that sense the maxim was comprehensible, but with the present connotation of 'prove', which is 'to show to be true', the line is self-contradictory if not entirely meaningless.

An alternative theory is that the original line, which was in Old English, read, "The exception probes the rule," and this also made sense. It is said the fellow who translated it into its more modern form made the mistake of changing the 'b' to 'v', an error that has stayed through the centuries and become more or less permanent.

However the proverb may have originated, its false attribution to Doyle is probably because one of the Holmes novels contains a similar-sounding line. In *The Sign of Four*, Holmes tells Watson, "I never make an exception. An exception disproves the rule." Doyle no doubt intended the aphorism to be a twist on the original, but what it has done, in effect, is restate in modern terms what the original has always meant.

6. Eliminate to Illuminate

Myth! **Dorothy Sayers devised her famous 'dictum by inference' in honor of Sherlock Holmes.**

The usual fallacy involving a Holmes quotation occurs when a line not found in any of the stories and novels sounds so much like Holmes and is credited to the detective. Where the utterance is indeed by Holmes but is attributed to another, a very rare reverse fallacy results. This latter type is best exemplified by a quote that guides the thinking of most classical fictional detectives. Called the 'dictum-by-inference', it states that, "When you have eliminated all the impossibilities, then, whatever remains, however improbable, must be the truth." Howard Haycraft and many others trace the saying's origin to Dorothy L. Sayers, creator of the popular Lord Peter Wimsey, although Miss Sayers is supposed to have said it not in a fictional work but in one of her treatises on the subject of mystery writing.

The quotation does appear in an essay by Miss Sayers, but what her admirers failed to take into account is that she was only paraphrasing Sherlock Holmes when she wrote it. In the short story 'The Beryl Coronet', where the original line is spoken, the great detective explains a point to Watson by remarking, "It is an old maxim of mine that when you have excluded the impossible, whatever remains, however improbable, must be the truth." One thing that can be said for Miss Sayers, however, is that she was mouthing Holmes in the spirit of criticism, quite unlike the few who utter Holmes as though it were their own wisdom.

7. Welcome to the Doyle House

Myth! **The only factual circumstance about Sherlock Holmes is his Baker Street address.**

144

Sherlock Holmes' address in London has acquired a cult following of its own, thanks to the vivid description of the detective's lodgings in the stories. The apartment, located at 221B Baker Street, is the only Holmes trapping that people have endowed with a previous existence. Many indeed believe it still exists, albeit in a regenerated form, e.g., as a private museum to house Doyle's Sherlock Holmes memorabilia.

British authorities attest to the countless queries that continue to be sent to Doyle, and sometimes even to Holmes and Watson, at this address, while foreign and local tourists have not stopped scouring Baker Street in search of 221B. Loyal members of hundreds of Sherlock Holmes clubs visit, photograph and map the area searching for clues to bolster their positions in the prolonged debates over the residence, and cases have been made out for several sites, particularly the present No. 111 Baker Street. No one seems ready to admit that 'the house where Sherlock Holmes lives' is a mere literary concoction, prompting one writer to observe that, as a practical matter, 221B Baker St. today is "where the dead letter files are kept in the London post office."

8. Art of the Double Doyle

Myth! Doyle is the unchallenged creator of the original Holmesian body of work.

The universal belief that Arthur Conan Doyle wrote the authentic Sherlock Holmes stories has been shaken to its roots by the findings of the highly respected science writer, Martin Gardner. In *Science Good, Bad and Bogus*, Gardner suggests that a real-life Watson wrote the stories and Doyle, who was allowed to take the credit as author, merely edited them. According to Gardner, "Doyle had no interest in—indeed, he had contempt for—the stories he pretended were his own. But as soon as they became great popular successes, bringing him an income needed for other projects, he let them continue to appear under his own name, touching them up here and there, but editing them so hastily that many of Watson's contradictions...were allowed to remain." One such contradiction, tending to show Doyle's lack of intimacy with the subject, involves the location of a wound Dr. Watson received when he participated as an assistant surgeon at the Battle of Maiwand in the second Afghan War. In the first novel, *A Study in Scarlet* (1887), Watson discloses that the wound is in his shoulder, but three years later, in *The Sign of Four* (1890), Watson changes his mind and points to his leg.

Gardner thinks the best evidence that Doyle did not write the famous stories is "the enormous contrast between the mentality and philosophical outlook" of Doyle, on the one hand, and his two characters, on the other. Both Holmes and Watson have an abiding respect for rationality, science and common sense, whereas Doyle had none. Doyle spent the last twelve years of his life lecturing, debating and writing for the cause of spiritualism, and expressing opinions on the occult that were so far removed from the rationalizing process Sherlock Holmes used in his cases. A man who would believe in fairies and dematerialization, Gardner concludes, could never have constructed, as figments of his imagination, the coldly rational Holmes or his admiring Dr. Watson.

Apropos of the suspicion that the Holmes stories are not what we think they are, another school of thought theorizes that the same person wrote all the stories but he wrote some while in an altered state of mind. Among its adherents is Ronald Knox, a Catholic priest who knows his Sherlock Holmes as much as he does his Church canons. In his 'Studies in the Literature of Sherlock Holmes', Father Knox quotes critics who find three popular works—*A Study in Scarlet*, 'The Gloria Scott', and *The Return of Sherlock Holmes*—deviating in many parts from the usual Holmesian pattern. For instance, contrary to what we learn from the other tales, Holmes is described in *A Study in Scarlet* and 'The Gloria Scott' as having had less than two years of College and no stint at the University, and with practically no knowledge of literature and philosophy. In the *Return* stories, the inconsistencies are so numerous and varied that Knox has to sort them out into "(a) those suggested by changes in the character and methods of Holmes, (b) those resting on impossibilities in the narrative itself, (c) inconsistencies found by comparison with the previous narrative."

Knox finds that, while Holmes is consistently logical throughout, the interrelationships of the stories are not. Nevertheless, he believes all the stories are the works of the same

146

hand, and the 'spurious' adventures merely "the lucubrations of (the author's) own unaided invention." But in writing them, Holmes' creator, perhaps pressured by the demands of his publishers and an insatiable public, sometimes deviated from the general pattern that he himself established for the entire cycle.

9. Say it Again, Basil

Myth! Sherlock Holmes' favorite expression is, "Elementary, my dear Watson."

The line most associated with Sherlock Holmes—"Elementary, my dear Watson"—appears nowhere in any of the conversations between Holmes and Watson in the four novels and fifty-six short stories featuring the sleuth. What Holmes says is, "Elementary," often in response to Watson's expression of wonderment when the detective makes a shrewd and well-elucidated deduction. One typical exchange is, "'Excellent!' I cried. 'Elementary', said he" ('The Crooked Man'). Holmes also says, "My dear Watson," as in 'The Blue Carbuncle', and sometimes, "My dear Doctor" or "My dear fellow," but never in combination with "Elementary."

The false phrase came into vogue to form part of Holmesian apocrypha after Sir Arthur Conan Doyle stopped writing about his creation in 1927. It was carried over into film adaptations and broadcast versions, and really caught on when Basil Rathbone, Hollywood's definitive Sherlock Holmes, made it one of his most memorable lines on screen.

10. In his Own Image

Myth! Doyle patterned Sherlock Holmes after himself.

It's almost unbelievable that Arthur Conan Doyle (assuming it was he who wrote the Holmes stories) would impart his personality to any character other than his master creation,

147

Sherlock Holmes. But Gilbert Chesterton was the first of several to surmise that it was Dr. Watson, not Holmes or his brother Mycroft, whom Doyle patterned after himself. Martin Gardner (*ibid*) denies that Watson was a mere product of Doyle's imagination, but notes that "Doyle and Watson were both medical men, slow thinkers, good writers, and sensitive to the poetry of London;" they were also similar in physical appearance, each with a beefy frame and sporting a walrus mustache.

In fact, Holmes has a greater resemblance to Dr. Joseph Bell, who had been Doyle's patron when he worked as an apprentice at the Royal Infirmary at Edinburgh. Doyle, it is said, was impressed with Bell's reputation as 'the champion of the theory of deductive methodology in the diagnosis of diseases', and decided to bestow a similar talent on Holmes, making it his character's main resource in the detection of crime.

Some of Doyle's traits can be found in Holmes— ruggedness, a fondness for sports of all kinds, preference for the underdog, lack of malice, and a strong fighting spirit. But this is only to be expected, since Doyle's own personality was shaped earlier under Bell's tutelage. Most Holmes aficionados conclude that Doyle, in a manner of speaking, gave a bit of himself to both Watson and Holmes, with most of it to Watson.

11. Whose Name is it, Anyway?

Myth! Doyle named his detective after Oliver Wendell Holmes.

A school of thought led by the Holmesian critic Vincent Starrett ('The Private Life of Sherlock Holmes', 1933) once claimed that Doyle surnamed his immortal detective after the American poet and physician Oliver Wendell Holmes. The claim was based entirely on a line in Doyle's book of reminiscences, *Through the Magic Door* (London, 1907), in which, speaking of Oliver Wendell Holmes, he wrote: "Never have I so known and loved a man whom I had never seen." Later, Starrett admitted that the two gentlemen might never have corresponded, much less met, and there was no evidence that Oliver Wendell Holmes had read any of Doyle's stories ('American Notes & Queries', June, 1941).

148

There is an apocryphal bit about Doyle alleging in an English newspaper interview that he had "made thirty runs against a bowler named Sherlock and thereafter had a kindly feeling for the name." Doyle, however, fails to mention anything about the origin of the famous name in his autobiography, *Memories and Adventures*, and so does John Dickson Carr, who wrote extensively about Doyle's life.

Other biographers, possibly more imaginative than enterprising, say that Doyle had wanted to call his detective Ormond Sacker, then Sherrinford Holmes, and this latter "was nearly adopted when Doyle came across a rather strange Irish Christian name: Sherlock."

VI

Murder On Her Mind

On Agatha Christie and her Characters

"It is the brain, the little gray cells on which one must rely.
One must seek the truth within--not without."

•

Agatha Christie

1. A Mysterious Affair with Style

Myth! Agatha Christie simulated an amnesia attack as part of a plot she was hatching against her husband.

Most Agatha Christie fans know that her greatest mystery was the one that happened in real life—to herself. She was still basking in the glory of her successful first book, *A Mysterious Affair at Styles*, when she suddenly disappeared from her home in Berkshire. Launching a 10-day nation-wide search that employed 15,000 volunteers, the authorities finally found her registered under another name at a Yorkshire health spa, acting like the South African tourist she claimed to be.

What the same fans may not know is that, although the doctors diagnosed her condition as temporary amnesia, possibly brought on by the stress of her marital problems, there was some suspicion that her story was a ploy to conceal a case of attempted murder. According to this theory, proposed in the biographical novel by Kathleen Tynan, the murder victim was to be her husband, whose philandering was giving her sleepless nights, and her idea, worthy of a Hercule Poirot plot, was to have the state do it legally for her. On December 3, 1926, she pushed her car into a quarry, leaving the ignition switch off and her fur coat inside, to suggest that she had been driven there by someone and that she hadn't left the car voluntarily. She registered at the spa under another name and waited for the police to arrest her husband for her murder, planning to feign amnesia after he was hanged.

Before anyone could take action, a fan recognized Mrs. Christie and she was forced to reappear. Fortunately, the theory didn't hold, and Agatha Christie went on to write some more detective fiction, many of them the best in the genre.

2. Rx for Murder

Myth! All of Agatha Christie's plot devices are original.

151

Agatha Christie was not known for writing style or for character development, but in creating plot she was superb and almost without parallel. She produced one ingenious poser after another during her golden years, many of them breaking ground and becoming hallowed standards in the genre.

However, it may come as both a surprise and a disappointment to many Christie fans that her two stories most cited for their inventiveness—*The Murder of Roger Ackroyd* (1926) and *Cards on the Table* (1936)—did not set any precedent at all. In *Roger Ackroyd*, the book that made her famous, she used the highly controversial device of the criminal himself narrating the story, not realizing that variations of this technique had been employed long before she even thought of using it. Christie herself had adapted the ploy earlier in a lesser novel, *The Man in the Brown Suit*, where part of the story is presented in the form of the murderer's diary.

In *Cards on the Table*, Christie has Poirot deducing the identity of the murderer from the way he plays bridge—a method previously used by Christie's American contemporary, S.S. Van Dine, in *The "Canary" Murder Case* (1927), albeit the game was not bridge but poker. Well ahead of Britain or the US in the use of bridge as a device or prop in a detective story is France, whose Stanislas-André Steeman wrote *L'assassin habite au 21*, in which the detective discovers the solution to the murder while playing the game.

---

3. As Plain as Miss Jane

Myth! Agatha Christie patterned her character Miss Marple after herself.

Most see Dame Agatha's likeness in her favorite character, Miss Marple, particularly as Margaret Rutherford portrays her in the movies, and draw the conclusion that the resemblance is intended. But Miss Marple first appeared at the age of sixty-five to seventy in 1930, when her creator was only forty, and her passions in life are gossip, knitting, and seeing the worst side of human nature, none of which appealed to the younger Agatha.

The better view is that the spinster busybody was patterned after the author's grandmother, while Agatha herself was Mrs. Ariadne Oliver, a minor character in some of her books. Like Agatha, Mrs. Oliver is a quiet and shy writer made famous by her fictional foreign detective, and she is often made to speak Christie's personal thoughts. As Mrs. Christie admitted, however, Mrs. Oliver is the author's parody not of her private self but of what she believed her fans thought of her. Moreover, there is no physical resemblance between the two, as one cannot picture Agatha 'with disheveled gray hair carrying bags of apples and being very disorganized and dithery'.

In some respects, Agatha was even more Hercule Poirot than she was Ariadne Oliver. Like her Belgian detective, the extroverted Agatha loved adventure and travel, preferably by luxury train because of a tendency to seasickness. It is also quite undeniable that those 'little gray cells' Poirot uses to unravel ingenious and startling plots are the same cells Christie used to construct them. Ironically, while Agatha Christie, for all her accomplishments in the real world, failed to make it to the obit page of the New York Times, Hercule Poirot on his death in *Curtain* (1975) became the only fictional character ever to be so honored on the front page of that venerable newspaper.

4. Dead man's Mirror

Myth! None of Agatha Christie's works has achieved the realism of a true crime story.

As in most excellent works in the genre, both the mechanics of the crime and the character of the perpetrator in each of Dame Agatha's mysteries are pure figments of the writer's mind. Unlike a standard crime story, which is essentially fact-based and usually presented in a reportorial manner, the puzzle elements in Christie's fiction are given over to a deductive rather than a forensic explanation. Very few of Agatha's work make even the slightest reference to a historical or real event, except perhaps by way of developing a plot element like motive. The best example of such an exception is *Murder on the Orient Express*, which occurs

153

against the backdrop of a famous kidnapping incident eerily similar to the Lindbergh case.

Few people know that, while none of Agatha's work has mimicked reality, at least one has given rise to reality, though probably not deliberately. We refer to the Christie novel *The Pale Horse*, for which the corresponding real-life event is the 1971 Bovingdon Murders. In that year, five employees at Hadland's photographic equipment works in the factory town of Bovingdon, Hertfordshire, England, died from what was at first thought to be a virus. An eminent forensic specialist remembered the Christie story, and told the detectives that the symptoms they had described could be traced to thallium, a poison that had never been used in Britain. The authorities assured a discomfited Dame Agatha that the murderer hadn't read her work, and that it was a clear case of a literary creation presaging—no doubt by sheer coincidence—a real happening occurring 10 years later.

5. Warning Miranda

Myth! Agatha Christie reiterated the famous Miranda warning against self-incrimination in her novel *At Bertrand's Hotel.*

The Miranda warning is one given by law enforcers in the US to criminal suspects before they are asked questions relating to the commission of a crime. The exact wording may vary from state to state and from situation to situation, but its main component is usually the line, "You have the right to remain silent. If you give up that right, anything you say can and will be used against you in a court of law." The warning was mandated by the 1966 United States Supreme Court decision in the case of *Miranda v. Arizona* as a means of protecting a criminal suspect's Fifth Amendment right to avoid coercive self-incrimination.

When applied in the UK, the Miranda warning is referred to as 'caution' and is often heard from Scotland Yard inspectors confronting suspects in the movies or on television. It is repeated in print in *At Bertrand's Hotel* (1965), a popular Agatha Christie mystery featuring Miss Marple. Dame Agatha does not mention it for affirmation, however, but precisely to tell us that it is not the

154

same one spoken in real life by British lawmen. In Chapter 24 of the novel, a police officer and a suspect engage in the following exchange:

"I have already warned you, Mr. Malinowski."

"The famous policeman's warning! Anything you say will be taken down and used against you at your trial."

"That's not quite the wording," said (Chief Inspector Davy) mildly. "Used, yes. Against, no…"

Sources say the actual wording of the famous British policeman's warning is, "You are not obliged to say anything unless you wish to do so, but what you say may be put into writing and given in evidence." Variations are sometimes used to fit other conditions, as when the suspect is asked to write or perform an act instead of speak, but in all cases, the stock phrase 'given in evidence' is requisite and the words 'against you' are omitted. It is believed the police in Britain instruct their men to be careful to avoid the suggestion that the evidence would be used only against the speaker, since this might discourage one who is innocent from making a statement that could help clear him of the charge.

However, it is not entirely clear if Dame Agatha's observation is still valid in Britain today. The writer published her novel in 1965, a full year before the US Supreme Court imposed Miranda as a constitutional requirement on American law enforcers. On the other hand, assuming the British have adopted the Miranda ruling in their own jurisdiction, the policeman's warning that Agatha so aptly explains would apparently still apply in case a suspect is not yet in police custody. The Miranda decision, it should be noted, strictly provides that its warning is mandatory only where a criminal suspect is in a 'custodial situation'.

---

6. Murderers Row

Myth! *And Then There Were None*, **in which all the characters are the murderers, is the only one-of-a-kind story Agatha Christie ever wrote.**

In the Christie novel *And Then There Were None*, ten characters are invited to the island home of a mysterious host who does not reveal himself, and each is killed off according to the famous nursery rhyme 'Ten Little Indians'. In the end, the murderer commits suicide in fulfillment of the title of the book. Having no known precursor or successor, the plot—one of the many variations of the 'least likely suspect' theme popular during the golden age of detective fiction—is a one-of-a-kind of which Agatha is the sole proprietor. Unfortunately, Christie has tolerated numerous corruptions in the scripts of the stage and film versions, sometimes eschewing the twist at the end of the story and always sacrificing the plot's uniqueness for the sake of commercial adaptability. The change allows one or two characters to survive, usually a man and a woman who are romantically inclined to each other. These variations, some authorized and others not, have cluttered up what used to be the exclusive field of the original.

At the other end of the character spectrum is the novel *Murder on the Orient Express*, which is set in a moving train from Paris to Istanbul. Along the way, a snowdrift bogs down the train, giving Hercule Poirot an opportunity to solve the murder. The detective's tour de force nets him the entire passenger list as the murderers, with the exception of the train director who acts as Hercule's foil. It's another of Christie's one-of-a-kind, although critics see the concept of all the suspects turning out to be the murderers as just a reverse treatment of *And Then Were None*, in which all the suspects turn up as victims. Also, the *Orient Express* poser is set against the historical backdrop of the Lindbergh kidnapping case, which somehow makes it less than a complete product of Christie's imagination.

VII

Culture Vultures

On Literary Lions and Lionesses

"An author values a compliment even when it comes
from a source of doubtful competency."

•

Mark Twain

1. Gertie was no Dinosaur

Myth! The poet Gertrude Stein is remembered for the offbeat line, "A rose is a rose is a rose."

Gertrude Stein was a raconteur, an art patron, and a writer whose works are notable for their unconventional forms and radical innovations. It is said that this stalwart of the avant-garde eventually adopted the line, "A rose is a rose is a rose," as her own, although this was not what she wrote originally.

In the poem "Sacred Emily," what appeared is the ranting and almost unintelligible line, "Rose is a rose is a rose is a rose." Popular revisionists obviously thought the words would be more coherent if "an a were added to the beginning and a blossom pruned from the end." In both renditions, the repetition of the word 'rose' makes little sense, yet seems consistent with what she felt. According to Robert Hendrickson (*American Literary Anecdotes*, 1990), Stein once wrote, "You can love a name and if you love a name then saying that name any number of times only makes you love it more." In her prose she had no use for nouns, but poetry, she thought, was "really loving the name of anything." Still, there was no clue whether the word 'rose' referred to the flower or someone named Rose. Those favoring the person point out that Stein had a high regard for the English painter Sir Francis Rose, whose paintings she collected.

Stein wrote another similarly curious line, "There is no there there." Again she uses a word—an article—three times in a clever reference, some say, either to America or to her hometown of Oakland, California. Critics suspect she may have been alluding to her childhood home in Oakland rather than to the city itself; she was apparently alarmed that the address had completely disappeared while she was away.

2. Generation X'd

Myth! Ernest Hemingway coined the phrase "lost generation."

Ernest Hemingway, a war veteran of sorts, was the main spokesman of the 'lost generation'. He was reputedly the first to use the term, which described the young men of the cultivated upper and middle classes who lost their lives in World War 1. But writing in the unpublished preface and later on the flyleaf of *The Sun Also Rises* (1926), Hemingway credited the coinage to Gertrude Stein. He would later explain in *A Moveable Feast* that he first got hold of the expression when Stein told him disapprovingly that his was a "lost generation" because it was drinking itself to death.

In a rare display of humility, Stein denied Hemingway's attribution to her. The words, she claimed, were originally those of Monsieur Pernollet, a French garage owner and proprietor of the hotel in Belley where she and Alice B. Toklas were staying in 1924. According to Stein, Pernollet uttered the phrase almost spontaneously while rebuking his young mechanic for the shoddy repair of her car, telling him that, like all the young men who served in the First World War, he came from the "lost generation."

---

3. The Sweaty Smell of Success

Myth! The typical hero in a Horatio Alger story is a poor boy who becomes exceedingly wealthy in later life.

Most people take for granted that all of Horatio Alger's heroes became immensely rich. In fact, the rags-to-riches theme so often associated with Alger is not in any way evident in his stories, and not one Alger character ever got to be so much as a millionaire. His heroes were bootblacks and newsboys who persevered with great virtue, achieving respectability only after paying off mortgages. In monetary terms, their successes were modest—with perhaps a raise from $5 to $10 per week. Actually, Alger never advocated wealth whether as a means or as a goal to achieve happiness, his point being that success was to be won through virtue and industry and should be sufficiently rewarded with respectability and moderate financial success. But he was practical enough to recognize that luck was no less an important factor than perseverance was. In most of Alger's tales, what brings his boys

159

success is a fortuitous meeting with a wealthy businessman who gives them their first big chance for improvement.

Although Alger saw himself as a moral reformer, he was not exactly the personification of the American ideal of morality. Alger was a slave to his pederastic desires for little boys, who became the heroes of his fiction. His homosexual persuasion was revealed while Alger was serving as a minister of the Unitarian Church before becoming a writer; an 1866 investigation concluded that he and several of his young male parishioners had committed acts "too revolting to relate," forcing him to resign and leave town. Resettling in New York, he wrote some 119 boys' books, at which he became highly successful. Although no such accusations were made against Alger ever again, his life followed a familiar pattern of very close associations with young boys. He gave away his money freely to them, ran a home for wayward boys, never married, and lived out his life with his housekeeper and her young sons. Alger's novels failed to heed the lesson of his own stories, as he died destitute. His parish concealed his secret for more than a century, until its records were made public in the 1970s.

The most definitive book written about Alger—Herbert Mayes' *Alger: A Biography Without a Hero* (1928)—is as spurious as the man himself. It remained for forty years as a standard reference work for both scholars and critics, until in the 1970s Mayes admitted that the book was pure fiction and intended merely to be a spoof on the writer.

---

4. An Intense interest in Tents

Myth! *The Rubaiyat of Omar Khayyam* **is the magnum opus of one of the world's greatest poets.**

The memorable line, "A loaf of bread, a jug of wine, and thou," is quoted by the world's romantics from the Rubaiyat, written by Omar Khayyam, an 11th century Persian. The Rubaiyat is regarded as one of the world's greatest works of poetry, but the author is hardly one of the world's greatest poets. In fact, Omar may not qualify as a poet at all.

Instead, Omar, who was born circa 1050 in Nishapur in what is now Iran, was one of the most notable scientists of his time. As astronomer to the royal court, he helped reform the calendar and worked for the adoption of a new era, called the Jalalian or the Seljuk. As a mathematician, he wrote extensive treatises on algebra, geometry and related subjects.

Like other Arabic scholars who were his contemporaries, Omar's encounter with poetry was limited to the quatrains he composed in his spare time. It would be to Omar's credit, however, that these epigrammatic four-line stanzas, reflecting upon nature and humanity, eventually proved instrumental in defining the West's concept of Persian poetry. Of the 1,000 ascribed to Omar, most if not all have been translated into almost every known language, including English. The *Robáiyat* is an 1859 compilation by the Victorian poet Edward Fitzgerald containing his free translations of a hundred of Omar's verses. FitzGerald was the first to introduce Omar to the West through this version, which many say is a reasonable paraphrase that captures the spirit of the original.

While most literature describe Omar Khayyam as a great Persian poet, historical critiques say his life and circumstances are too unspectacular to deserve such an accolade. Omar is not known to have written anything else poetic, and has become famous in the West only through Fitzgerald's adaptation. For a long while, it was not even certain that Omar is the *Robáiyat*'s composer in spirit, considering that the quatrain is an easy form to use, and the same verse has been attributed to many different authors. Recent research has established that a considerable amount of the quatrains can, indeed, be traced back to the great scientist, who "condensed in them his feelings and thoughts, his skepticism and love, in such an enthralling way that they appeal to every reader." The caveat, however, is that "the imagery he uses is entirely inherited; none of it is original. Some of Omar's contemporaries themselves used the concept to express their mystical wisdom."

Omar Khayyam, who died in 1122, had obscure beginnings. His name means Omar the Tentmaker, encouraging the myth that he was a lowly tentmaker by profession. If he were really so during his youth, it is asked, how could he have later developed a genius for poetry and the sciences?

5. A Hawthorne in his Side

Myth! **Nathaniel Hawthorne wrote some of his fiction in vindication of the Salem witch trials.**

A popular belief that once preyed on the reputation of the famous writer Nathaniel Hawthorne is about an ancestor who was involved as a jurist at the Salem witch trials. The classic American short story "The Devil and Daniel Webster" by Stephen Vincent Benét speaks of Justice John Hathorne, "a jurist of experience" who "presided at certain witch trials once held in Salem." Hawthorne is linked to Hathorne by being born in Salem to a sea captain named Nathaniel Hathorne.

Hawthorne's relationship with Hathorne became an item of public curiosity because of the author's known disdain for Puritan intransigence and its manifestation in the Salem witch trials. His novel *The Scarlet Letter*, written in 1850, was a tragic story about adultery in Puritan New England, but based on its prefatory, 'The Custom House', it was also an indictment of Puritan obsession and spiritual intolerance similar to what plagued Salem in 1692-93. In the following year Hawthorne published another best-selling masterpiece, *The House of the Seven Gables*, a story based on the legend of a curse pronounced on Hawthorne's family by a woman who was condemned to death during the Salem witch trials.

At least one biography of Nathaniel Hawthorne and countless histories and articles agree that Hawthorne had indeed a Puritan grandfather named John Hathorne who participated in the grisly proceedings. Hathorne, according to most accounts, "seems instantly to have adopted an inquisitorial, rather than magisterial, role, assuming the guilt of the parties before they were even asked to plead." This implies he was a judge, a biased one at that, and at the same time a prosecutor examining accused persons prior to their indictment. His actions, which sent nineteen accused 'witches' to their deaths, put him in an untenable position that would not have arisen had he been an enlightened jurist instead of a 'conqueror worm'.

It is believed Hawthorne more than freed himself of Hathorne's curse by modeling one of the most hated characters in *The House of the Seven Gables* after his ancestor. He also added a 'w' to his name, leaving relatively untainted the legacy he was able to build on his own.

6. Twain Spotting

Myth! **Mark Twain got his name from listening to leadsmen operating on the Mississippi river.**

Many are under the false impression that the "Sage of Hannibal" was born in Hannibal, Missouri, a town on the west bank of the Mississippi. It is true that Mark Twain spent his boyhood in Hannibal until age 18 and considered it his hometown, and in addition, his most beloved works—*The Adventures of Huckleberry Finn* and *The Adventures of Tom Sawyer*—were based on the lives of his boyhood friends in Hannibal. The town and the river were no doubt major influences in Twain's life and works, but he was not born within sight of either. Twain moved eastward for the first time to Hannibal with his parents when he was already almost four years old. He first saw the light of day in Florida—not the state, but a small village at the fork of Salt River in nearby Marion County in Missouri.

Another misconception about Mark Twain has to do with his appearance. Most of his pictures and portraits confirm what we have always imagined him to be: hair that looks like white cotton candy, white mustache patterned after the long horns of a steer, and a white suit highlighting a bow tie. But we learn from his biographies that the white suit appeared late in his life, when he was already in his seventies and nearing death. His real sartorial trademark was the black serge he had been wearing for the most part of his career. And his hair? Its normal color was red.

It is said Samuel Langhorne Clemens was inspired to adopt the pen name Mark Twain from listening to leadsmen calling while "heaving the lead" on the Mississippi River. This meant dropping overboard a rope marked along its length to indicate the water's depth with a lead pipe attached to the end. The soundings, of which the most common sequence was "quarter less four, half twain, quarter twain, mark twain," were called out in a rhythmic chant to the pilot to help him navigate on the shallow water, and could be heard, often in fog or darkness, up and down the river.

The myth to this day persists, despite Clemens himself denying that his use of the pen name was based on a direct link with the Mississippi's melodious leadsmen. According to Chapter 50 of his book *Life on the Mississippi* (1883), he had appropriated the name after the death of its original owner, Captain Isaiah Sellers, an old riverboat pilot who wrote a column for the New Orleans *Daily Picayune.* Apparently, it was Sellers who heard the call "mark twain" (or its variant, "mark on the twine"), and decided to adopt it as a name by which to launch his writing career. Although one writer—Milton Meltzer, in *Mark Twain Himself* (1960)—claims Sellers never actually used the name Mark Twain, Clemens obviously thought he had.

7. Mad about Alice

Myth! Lewis Carroll was a professional writer of juvenile fiction.

Lewis Carroll was a shy, stammering clergyman who was ordained an Anglican deacon although he never took priest's orders. His celebrated work, *Alice in Wonderland*, became almost a children's bible and gave him the reputation of being primarily a writer of juvenile literature.

In fact, Carroll, whose real name was Charles Lutwidge Dodgson, was not primarily a writer of anything but pamphlets and textbooks. These were usually on mathematics and logic, the two subjects he was mainly occupied in teaching at Oxford. Carroll did dabble in writing juvenile literature, but only because he liked little girls, employing the hobby, along with photography, for their amusement. *Alice in Wonderland*, possibly the most famous of children's books, was written for Carroll's favorite, young Alice Liddell, daughter of Dean Henry George Liddell (co-author of the standard Greek-English Dictionary *Liddell & Scott's Greek Lexicon*). In photography, he was one of England's best amateurs, and the greatest in the 19th century to specialize on children.

Carroll is assumed to be the inventor of the expression "mad as a hatter." Actually, he had nothing to do with it, although he practically gave life to the expression when he called one of his

164

characters the Mad Hatter. The cliché had been used earlier in 1836 by Nova Scotia-born Thomas Haliburton (*The Clockmaker),* and in 1850 by William Makepeace Thackeray (*Pendennis*). If the simile was ever inspired by anyone, this was either Robert Crab, a real 17th century mad hatter, or William Henry Miller, a hat maker who was elected to the British parliament in 1830. Apparently, hatters in those days frequently contracted chronic mercury poisoning from handling mercury in treating wool for conversion into felt. The poison works on the nervous system and results in various psychotic disorders that put the victim on the verge of madness. However, some wordsmiths offer etymological proof that the expression long preceded hat making as an organized trade and mercury as a commercial item. The words, they say, were originally "mad as an atter," *atter* being Anglo-Saxon for adder, a snake, and "mad" meaning injurious or poisonous.

8. Wooly Retorts from a Dotty Lady

Myth! Dorothy Parker originated the phrases "Pearls before swine" and "The gamut of emotion from A to B."

Dorothy Parker was a luminary of the 1930s, a member of the famous Algonquin Round Table that included Robert Benchley and Alexander Woollcott. Typifying her sarcastic wit, Dorothy's putdowns have found a permanent place in American literary humor.

Some of the greatest of those putdowns, however, have turned out to be the naughty inventions of others. Arguably the best involved an equally famous personality, Clare Booth Luce, who found herself one day vying for elevator space with Dorothy. Feigning courtesy for a friend, Clare stepped back and remarked, "Age before beauty." Whereupon, Dorothy responded, "Pearls before swine." The myth is explored at some length in Keyes' *Nice Guys Finish Seventh* (1991), which reveals that Luce denied the encounter. "The genesis of *this* legend might have been an Alexander Woollcott short story called 'The Pearl,' whose heroine explains that she got her name 'because I'm cast before swine.'"

165

Then, there's the *Life* review by Parker in which she reported on Katharine Hepburn's acting in the stage production *The Lake*. Most everybody was impressed with the rising star's performance, but the feisty critic was not. Katharine herself admits in her autobiography that Dorothy's reaction was, "Go to the Martin Beck (Theater) and see K.H. run the gamut of emotion from A to B." Alexander Woollcott had earlier mentioned the *Life* report, but Keyes says, "There is no such review in *Life* or any other magazine Parker wrote for at the time. According to Hepburn biographer Garry Carey, Parker made such a remark during *The Lake*'s intermission. Carey gave no source."

A famous couplet reads: "I'd rather flunk my Wasserman test / Than read the poems of Edgar Guest." The cutting wit, subtly off-color, devastates the reputation of a literary figure with one swipe. It sounds very much like Dorothy Parker, but she never uttered it. The real source of the short verse remains unknown to this day.

---

9. Just a Jokey Jane

Myth! Lillian Hellman wrote *Pentimiento* based on the life of a close friend who was martyred by the Nazis.

Jane Fonda's image in real life has been that of an idealist rebelling against repression and authoritarianism. On the screen she has played numerous fictional characters of the same bent. We are told that the only time she took on a non-fictional role of this type was when she starred in the award-winning Hollywood film *Julia*, playing the famous playwright and author Lillian Hellman in one of the most dramatic episodes of her life.

In 1973 Hellman (1905-84) published her second book of memoirs entitled *Pentimiento*. In it she described her memorable friendship with Julia, a schoolgirl friend who became an ardent socialist and eventually sacrificed her life in the struggle against Nazism. Julia persuaded Hellman to help her in the dangerous work of freeing prisoners of the Nazis during the war in Europe. In 1977 the dramatic story was adapted into the film *Julia*, with Vanessa Redgrave in the title role and Jane Fonda as Lillian. Lillian later went on TV to add to her story, tearfully recounting how, failing to save Julia, she tried to trace Julia's baby and save her instead.

But in 1984, the year Lillian died, evidence was adduced revealing that Julia was a piece of fiction based upon the life of an American-born woman named Muriel Gardiner (or Buttinger). She had been studying psychiatry in Vienna before the war and working against the Nazis in her spare time, but returned to the US in 1939 and settled in New Jersey. She never had a baby, as Lillian claimed, nor did she ever meet Hellman, who only heard about her from a mutual acquaintance. When *Pentimiento* came out in 1973, Muriel read it and wrote a friendly letter to Hellman, pointing out the uncanny resemblance between her and the playwright's fellow 'patriot', but Hellman never responded.

Vanessa Redgrave gave the title character Julia so much life that she won the Oscar for best supporting actress. In accepting her award, Vanessa tried to follow in Jane's—and Julia's— footsteps by delivering a speech denouncing "the Zionist thugs" who campaigned against her nomination. According to a report, there had been "some not too discreet lobbying against Redgrave's nomination, particularly because of her pro-Arab political sympathies in the Palestinian conflict." The last word, however, came from the playwright Paddy Chayefsky, who castigated Redgrave when it was his turn to take the podium to present the Oscar.

---

10. Zola Power

Myth! **Emile Zola coined the immortal line "J'accuse," which freed the wrongly imprisoned Alfred Dreyfus.**

In 1894 a French artillery officer of Jewish descent, Alfred Dreyfus, was arrested, indicted for treason and tried behind closed doors. Despite the failure of the prosecution to connect him with the only incriminating evidence, an unsigned letter, he was convicted and sent to the infamous Devil's Island. The trumped-up case was apparently to punish Dreyfus for being a Jew and to provide a smoke screen for the real culprit, another French army officer, Charles Esterhazy.

It was the most mendacious military conspiracy in the history of modern France, and the novelist Emile Zola couldn't stomach it. In 1898 Zola wrote an open letter to the French President, concluding it with several paragraphs each introduced by the phrase "J'accuse." The publication of the letter led to Zola's prosecution for libel, and he fled to England, returning to France only when he was amnestied a few months later.

In the excitement of making the acclaimed author a national hero, historians seemed to have neglected Georges Clemenceau, a future two-time French premier, as Zola's fellow in protesting the conviction and the one who actually played the bigger role in freeing Dreyfus from his wrongful imprisonment. Clemenceau's newspapers, La Justice and L'Aurore, published Zola's accusations over and over again, and the journalist would later reveal that it was he who had fed the line "J'accuse" to the novelist. Contrary to popular belief, Zola was never quite able to get Dreyfus off the hook. Although Zola's letter pressured the authorities into reopening the trial, Dreyfus was found guilty again and released only through a pardon. It was not until 1906 that Dreyfus was finally acquitted, after Clemenceau singlehandedly waged a campaign from 1898 to 1905 using his newspapers.

11. A Case for Hard-boiled Yeggs

Myth! Dashiell Hammett's *The Maltese Falcon* introduced the 'hard-boiled' type mystery story.

Dashiell Hammett is generally recognized as having set the vogue for the 'hard-boiled' type of mystery story, if not with his famous novel *The Maltese Falcon* (1930), then with his two previous less admired detective stories in book form published in 1929, *Red Harvest* and *The Dain Curse*. Hammett couldn't have done it, however, because as one well-known anthologist puts it, "by the time the action mystery story first appeared in books it was old stuff."

Hammett's detective stories were first seen in 1923 or 1924 in magazine form, but at least one story of the same hard-boiled type came out as early as 1922 in *Black Mask* magazine. This was Carroll John Daly's "The False Burton Combs" featuring Race Williams, whom many consider as the real forerunner of all the hard-boiled detective characters. Experts believe the wrong attribution to Hammett is due to the confusion between story type, which has to do with the nature of the plot and the behavior of the characters, and writing style, which is the way the author brings these elements to life. Thus, while *The Maltese Falcon* belongs to the hard-boiled type of story, it did not establish it. What it established was Hammett's original and distinctive writing style, which spawned numerous imitators and launched the "Hammett School." People tend to think that the "Hammett School" means also the hard-boiled type, when in fact it is concerned only with style, one of several falling under the story type that Daly had earlier started to develop.

12. Poster Fodder

Myth! The poem *Desiderata* was discovered in Baltimore's Old Saint Paul's Church in 1692.

"Go placidly amid the noise and haste, and remember what peace there may be in silence." So reads the opening line of an inspirational poem "found in Old Saint Paul's Church, Baltimore, in 1692."

Countless people who have read the piece in free verse called *Desiderata* (Latin for "desirable things") believe it is at least 300 years old and anonymous. In fact, it was written in 1927 by an obscure poet from Terre Haute, Indiana, named Max Ehrmann (1872-1945). Bertha K. Ehrmann renewed the copyright in 1954, but this obviously has not deterred the continued reproduction of its lines for commercial and other purposes without the authority of the owner.

In the sixties and seventies, and particularly in the height of the Vietnam peace movement, the verse was popular among counterculture youth for its universalistic wisdom. It was reprinted many times in books and periodicals and on plaques, cards, and posters, almost always with the notation, "Found in Old Saint Paul's Church, Baltimore. Dated 1692." It seems the error arose

169

during Lent in 1956, when Rev. Frederick Ward Kates, rector of Old Saint Paul's, had the poem printed on the cover of a mimeographed booklet of inspirational writings that he distributed to his parishioners. Quite innocently, he had included on the same cover the name of the parish and the date of its founding: "Old Saint Paul's Church, Baltimore, 1692." According to Rev. Kates, someone must have reprinted *Desiderata* along with the notation from the booklet, not knowing that the date referred to the church's own founding and had nothing to do with the poem.

Some justice has been obtained for the Ehrmann estate ever since a federal court ruled in 1973 that anyone reprinting *Desiderata* owed royalty fees to the copyright owner.

13. Does it have 'Encyclopedigree'?

Myth! The Encyclopædia Britannica is British.

The Encyclopædia Britannica remains the leading general reference work in the English language. In the digital age, it has begun to expand into electronic publishing, with a popular CD-ROM that's also plugged into a web site on the Internet. By going multimedia, this "venerable British institution" appears well on the way to shedding its tradition-bound image.

Some encyclopedias are concerned exclusively or chiefly with subjects "that are treated as relevant to or from the point of view of a particular nation or culture." This orientation can be seen in titles like Collins Australian Encyclopedia, Great Soviet Encyclopedia, Canadian Encyclopedia, The Greater Encyclopedia of China, Japonica, Encyclopedia Africana, and (on line) Encyclopædia Arabica.

People should be careful not to include the Encyclopædia Britannica in the foregoing enumeration. The title of the largest encyclopedia in the world, though also suggestively nationalistic, is a misnomer. The Britannica's 32 volumes are devoted not just to people and things British, but also to almost everything in the planet deserving of mention. The closest this 'British institution' got to being British was when three Scotsmen—the printer Colin Macfarquhar, the illustrator Andrew Bell and the editor William Smellie—founded the publication in Scotland in 1768, giving credit for the initial work issued in Edinburgh to "a Society of Gentlemen in Scotland."

At no time in the twentieth century has the Britannica been owned and managed by other than Americans. The publication left Edinburgh in 1901, when the American Horace E. Hooper acquired a major interest and ownership passed permanently to the United States. In 1920, Hooper sold the enterprise to the Chicago mail-order house Sears, Roebuck and Company, which donated it to the University of Chicago in 1943. Britannica reached a zenith in 1974, when Mortimer Adler, who had assumed the chair of the board of editors, mustered enough resources to produce the magnificent 15th edition, called Britannica 3. Bolstered by a list of more than four thousand contributors from more than 100 countries, this new image changed forever the once popular (and misleading) description of the Britannica as "that most distinguished example of British scholarship."

And what about the second largest encyclopedia in the world, which happens to sport a similarly misleading title? The 30-volume Encyclopedia Americana has never been a domain of information that's exclusively American. Although there was some cultural bias at its inception, this was German and not American. The Americana's original compiler was German-American publicist and educator Francis Lieber, who built on the earlier work of another German, the famous lexicographer Friedrich Arnold Brockhaus. The latter had written one of the most useful and successful of nineteenth-century reference works, the *Konversations-Lexikon*, published between 1796 and 1808. Known much later as *Der grosse Brockhaus* (The Great Brockhaus), the tenth edition became the foundation of the first Encyclopedia Americana published by Lieber in 1829.

---

14. His own Worst Enemy

Myth! **Robert Louis Stevenson's characters Dr. Jekyll and Mr. Hyde are manifestations of a split personality disorder.**

"Schizophrenia" is a combination of the Greek words *schiz*, to split, and *phren*, mind, and means "split mind." Early psychologists referred to schizophrenia as the split personality (or multiple personality) disorder, a condition occurring not only in life but also in literature. Later scientists would realize that, in spite of the etymology, schizophrenia is quite different from split-personality disorder and one should not subsume the other.

A writer tells us: "So common is the impression that 'schi' or 'chiz' means 'split' that even casually we speak of a divided attitude toward something as a 'schizoid' approach. Because of this similarity in derivation to the word 'schism', schizophrenia is commonly assumed to be the clinical description of a person who displays radically divided behavior suggesting the presence in his or her psychological makeup of two or more distinct 'personalities'." Thus, the character with 17 personalities played so ably by Sally Field in the TV film *Sybil* (1976), and the alternating *Three Faces of Eve* (1957) portrayed by Joanne Woodward in the movie of that name, are seen as typical schizophrenic types.

But—according to the same writer—this characterization of schizophrenia is false. When the ailment occurs, there is no personality split to speak of but a psychotic disorder characterized by acute melancholy, delusions, catatonia, hallucinations, delirium, paranoia, and a range of other symptoms which, taken together, effectively prohibit the schizophrenic from participating in "normal" society. The mistake arises because it used to be thought that the confusion a schizophrenic feels is the result of portions of the psyche splitting off; these "portions may then dominate the psychic life of the subject for a time and lead an independent existence even though these may be contrary and contradictory to the personality as a whole." Although there are many sub-varieties of schizophrenia, its most consistent characteristics are apathy or indifference to reality and social relationships, and dissociation of thoughts and ideas from normal emotions. None of these is a symptom of split-personality disorder, sometimes erroneously called the Jekyll-Hyde syndrome, a somewhat less serious condition in which "the same individual at different times appears to be in possession of entirely different mental content, disposition and character. In split personality, "one of the different phases shows complete ignorance of the other, an ignorance which may be reciprocal." Since Norman and his "mother" in Hitchcock's *Psycho* (1960) are perfectly aware of each other's existence, they are not split personalities but delusional aspects of the same schizoid individual.

172

Split personality is usually regarded as a neurosis, schizophrenia a psychosis. Nevertheless, experts admit that the lines between psychosis and neurosis are fuzzy, so that "one diagnostician's dissociative reaction may be another's schizoid fit." The irony is that "given the strangeness of the sickness, a person with schizophrenia might be the first to admit to having a split personality."

15. Homo is the Hero

Myth! Lawrence of Arabia had an unpleasant experience with a sadistic homosexual bey.

It seems only natural that many stories should be made up about the late T. E. Lawrence, since this enigmatic man spent much of his life in the Arabian Desert away from the scrutiny of Western eyes. One such story is a strange incident at Deraa that Lawrence himself related in his book, *Seven Pillars of Wisdom* (1926). He described how Syrian soldiers chanced upon him in the village one day and brought him to the Bey. He was about to be raped by the Ottoman in the latter's bedroom when he fought back and kicked him in the groin. Unable to elicit an admission that the adventurer was as homosexual as he was, the Bey ordered his soldiers to take him out and beat him up.

Lawrence's denial that he was gay is implicit in this account, but his other admissions raise the suspicion that he was. For instance, he confessed that he never had sex with a woman, repeatedly saying he never wanted to because it's "dirty." In a letter to a friend, he contradicted himself by revealing that he actually allowed the Bey to bugger him "to earn five minutes respite" from the pain his torturers were inflicting on him. Obviously, it wasn't respite he hankered for but sexual satisfaction to cap the torture; Lawrence is known to be a masochist who welcomed the idea of pain primarily through whipping.

Nonetheless, critics say both versions of Lawrence's encounter at Deraa are incoherent and conflict with the facts regarding the Bey, as established by the Arab historian Suleiman Mousa, by Phillip Knightly and Colin Simpson in their book *The Secret Lives of Lawrence of Arabia*, and by Desmond Stewart in his biography

173

of the Briton. "Given Lawrence's sado-masochistic predilection," one writer observes, "the story is little more than sexual fantasy: to this extent it is a valuable insight into the character of Lawrence, but as an historical event it is sheer fabrication."

16. Never these Twins shall Meet

Myth! The original Siamese Twins were full-fledged Thai nationals who were given their nickname by Mark Twain.

It is not entirely correct to say that Chang and Eng Bunker, physically conjoined from their births in 1811 to their deaths in 1874, were Siamese, or that it was Mark Twain who coined the term 'Siamese twins' for them. The handicapped pair were born in Siam, now Thailand, which was apparently the only reason they were called Siamese twins, but apart from being at least three-fourth Chinese, they spent much of their life in the US as American citizens. After settling in North Carolina before the Civil War, they discarded the Siamese names In and Chan in favor of the Chinese equivalents Eng and Chang, and appended the surname Bunker. The soon-to-become prosperous slaveholders married American twin sisters and fathered 21 children.

We can safely assume it was P.T. Barnum who invented the nickname 'Siamese Twins' when he hired the Bunkers and used it effectively to advertise the two on the carnival and sideshow circuit during the mid-1800s. Some recall Mark Twain also using the word 'Siamese' in describing physically conjoined twins, but there is evidence this came in the heels of the Barnum phrase. The humorist wrote "Those Extraordinary Twins," a supposedly fictional account of a 'Siamese' pair of Italian-Americans named Luigi and Angelo, but the descriptions of Luigi, a heavy drinker, and Angelo, a teetotaler, made it all too obvious that they were modeled after the real Chang and Eng, who had the same predilections. Incidentally, one would be hard put to find Siamese twins even in Thailand today—the occurrence of this rare phenomenon is estimated to range from 1 in 50,000 to 1 in 100,000 births, with only 25 percent surviving.

174

17. John woos Priscilla as Miles' Stand-in?

Myth! Longfellow's narrative poem "The Courtship of Miles Standish" is an accurate rendition of a romantic episode in Plymouth history.

Miles Standish (1584-1656) was the military leader of Plymouth who, in 1627, led his own group and bought out the original London investors in that colony. Legend puts him and a young scholar named John Alden in a love triangle where both vie for the affections of an orphaned girl named Priscilla Mullins. Alden and Mullins were true-to-life figures as much as Standish was, but there is no historical evidence to back the story that Standish had Alden act as intermediary in his pursuit of Mullin's hand, only to have Mullins fall for Alden. It was Henry Wadsworth Longfellow who, in his narrative poem *The Courtship of Miles Standish* (1858), perpetuated the image of a shy and inarticulate Standish asking the literate Alden to press his suit to marry Priscilla. Priscilla refuses Standish but accepts Alden, saying, "Speak for yourself, John," and the two live happily ever after.

Historians believe Longfellow's portrayal may have been unfair, considering that Standish was a brave and wily leader who, with little resources, was able to protect the Plymouth colony throughout its gestation. As early as the Mayflower voyage, Standish had convinced the Pilgrims of his competence, and in Plymouth itself, he showed the perspicacity to befriend the Indians but without hesitating to lead several expeditions against hostile tribes. Despite a few problem years, he helped produce nearly fifty years of peace that led to the English domination of North America. While all this may not prove he had ways with women, it is adequate to show he was far from being unable to "speak for himself."

VIII

Malappropriate Language

On Malapropism

"Don't pay any attention to the critics–
don't even ignore them."

•

Samuel Goldwyn

1. Their Slips showed

Myth! **Richard Sheridan's Mrs. Malaprop was the first to use malapropisms in daily speech.**

The eponymous word 'malapropism' has been allowed to enter popular usage in reference to any form of erroneous speech or *lapsus lingua* in the belief that Mrs. Malaprop was the first known promoter of fractured English. This is a misconception on two counts. First, a slip of the tongue is a malapropism only if it conforms to a certain pattern, i.e., the erroneous word sounds similar to the intended word, and the two words are both recognizable but entirely different from each other. Second, Mrs. Malaprop was not the first fictional character to appear on the (literary) scene and gain a reputation for the use of bungled speech. Mrs. Slipslop, a lady's maid in Henry Fielding's *The History of the Adventures of Joseph Andrews and of his Friend Mr. Abraham Adams* (1742), made her mark earlier with invented words like 'confidous' for 'confident', 'genteelest' for 'gentlest', 'necessitous' for 'necessary' and 'delemy' for 'dilemma'. Unlike Mrs. Malapropos, whose errors are structured, Mrs. Slipslop, true to her name, employs a mishmash of recognizable and unrecognizable words that try pretentiously to pass for English.

Interestingly, some dictionaries define 'slipslop' not in the sense that Mrs. Slipslop uses it but as 'trivial conversation or writing', i.e., language that, while inadequate in substance, is still correct in form. In contrast, malapropism is correctly described in the same dictionaries as "the ludicrous misuse of a word by confusion with one that sounds similar." Thus, phrases like 'abseil across the English channel' (Cilla Black), 'cardial arrest' (Eve Pollard), 'plummeted to the top' (Alan Weeks), 'unleased a hornet's nest' (Valerie Singleton) and 'pull a miracle out of the fire' (Fred Trueman) are popularly regarded as malapropisms but are actually slipslops.

Reports disclose that the politicians guiltiest of slipslops and malapropisms include Ronald Reagan, George W. Bush and Dan Quayle. Among the sports figures, Yogi Berra, who once said, "It's so crowded, nobody goes there anymore", is a real standout. Berra is equally known for saying: "I'll believe in color television when I see it in black and white."

177

2. Goldwyn's Follies

Myth! Sam Goldwyn admitted authorship of many known malapropisms before he died.

The Hollywood producer Samuel Goldwyn, known for a number of classic films of the 30s and 40s, was famous—or infamous—for both slipslops and malapropisms. Verbal whoppers, like "Include me out" and "Quick as a flashlight," are called 'Goldwynisms' because their suspected source is Goldwyn.

Just before he died, Goldwyn reportedly said, "I never thought I'd live to see the day." It appeared to be another unintended gem from the master of misspeak, but it was actually a prepared slipslop from Clifton Fadiman. What Goldwyn officially issued from his deathbed was a denial that he ever uttered a Goldwynism in his life. Most people did not agree, and even today, many believe (wrongly) that the unintelligible malapropism 'Goldwyn Pictures Griddle the Earth' is a Goldwynism direct from his studio's logo.

After his death, his wife withdrew Sam's denial and admitted that he had indeed been the author, consciously or not, of the following lines: (1) "I was on the brink of a great abscess;" (2) "I don't care if my pictures don't make a dime, so long as everyone comes to see them;" (3) "I had a monumental idea this morning, but I didn't like it;" (4) "In this business it's dog eat dog, and nobody's going to eat me." A Goldwyn obituary also claimed the statement, "Our comedies are not to be laughed at," was a genuine utterance from the movie producer.

Sometimes Goldwyn, at other times movie director Michael Curtiz (of *Casablanca* fame), gets the blame for the following dubious quotes: (1) "Don't worry, we'll make them Americans" (when told the film script was about lesbians); (2) "We can get all the Indians we need at the reservoir"; (3) "I read part of it all the way through" (after reviewing a script). Confirmed Curtiz goofs are: (1) "The next time I send a damn fool for something, I go myself", and (2) "When I see the pictures you play in that theater it makes the hair stand on the edge of my seat".

178

3. The Boner Collection

Myth! Goldwyn coined the line, "In two words, im possible!"

Ralph Keyes, in his book *Nice Guys Finish Seventh* (1993), uncovers the true sources of a number of classic Goldwynisms. Charlie Chaplin was the first to popularize the line, "In two words: im possible!," adapting it from an old music-hall gag. The leftist playwright Lillian Hellman was the source of the expression, "Anyone who would go to a psychiatrist ought to have his head examined." The writer George Oppenheimer was responsible for "It rolls off my back like a duck." "Quick as a flashlight" was producer Irving Fein's gem, and "Gentlemen, include me out" was probably from the pen of the controversial scriptwriter and director George Kaufman. This last was a member of the celebrated Algonquin Round Table, an informal luncheon gathering of writers, critics, actors and wits and from which emanated many of the quotable quotes of the 1920s. Of the fake Goldwynisms above, however, only the fourth is a malapropism.

The following gaffs have some structural similarity to confirmed Goldwynisms, but are much too clever or contrived to have been committed by the movie impresario: (1) "I'm willing to admit that I may not always be right. But I'm never wrong;" (2) "I want a movie that starts with an earthquake and works up to a climax;" (3) "Let's have some new clichés;" (4) "If you can't give me your word of honor, will you give me your promise?;" (5) "If I could drop dead right now, I'd be the happiest man;" (6) "These days, every director bites the hand that laid the golden egg;" (7) "I've been laid up with intentional flu"; (8) "For this part I want a lady, somebody that's couth;" (9) "We've passed a lot of water since then;" (10) "You're partly one hundred per cent right;" (11) "It's more than magnificent; it's mediocre;" (12) "I'll give you a definite maybe;" (13) "I don't think anybody should write his autobiography until after he's dead;" (14) "You've got to take the bull by the teeth;" (15) "Let's bring it up to date with some snappy 19th century dialogue;" (16) "Look, Orson, if you will just say yes to doing a picture with me, I'll give you a blanket check right now." The only malapropisms in this group of mostly slipslops are nos. 7 and 16.

4. The Owl behind the Howler

Myth! The line, "A verbal contract isn't worth the paper it's written on," is illogical and clearly a malapropism.

According to film historian Norman Zierold, Goldwyn also said, "A verbal contract isn't worth the paper it's written on." At first blush, the statement may be worth a laugh, but technically it is not a Goldwynism as there is absolutely nothing wrong with it. Although 'verbal' is popularly used in reference to spoken words, it is defined in most dictionaries as "of, in, or having to do with words of any kind." This includes spoken words as well as written ones. 'Verbal' is often taken to mean 'oral', which is the opposite of 'written', but in fact, oral and written words are simply specific kinds of words that are both verbal. In its correct sense, 'verbal' distinguishes concrete thoughts, ideas or actions from those that are abstract.

5. A Queer old Dean

Myth! Spoonerism is another form of malapropism.

Not all structured boners are malapropisms. A Spoonerism is mangled speech, usually not premeditated, in which corresponding consonants, vowels, or morphemes are switched. It is named after the Reverend William Archibald Spooner (1844–1930), Warden of New College, Oxford, who, according to many, was notoriously prone to this kind of miscommunication.

Spoonerisms are often used intentionally as a play on words and in that sense do not qualify as slips of the tongue. Variations often occur unintentionally, however, such as when the nuclei and codas, rather than the onsets, of syllables, are interchanged. The terms 'kniferism' and 'forkerism' were coined by Douglas Hofstadter for these types of Spoonerism, and are best exemplified by the gaff committed by veteran newscaster (and Timex watch pitchman) John Cameron Swayze on a radio show when, in referring to a fellow journalist as a "noted woman columnist," he accidentally said "noted woolen communist."

A church deacon could only have uttered the most famous Spoonerism: "This pie is occupewed, may I sew you to another sheet"? But critics say it's too deliberate to have come from Spooner. Moreover, the one time Warden of New College, Oxford, disclaimed any connection with Spoonerisms, saying, "I don't think that I have ever intentionally made a Spoonerism in my life, and in fact, I don't remember ever having made one. I know that it is very sad to destroy the illusions of England in this way, but this is a thing that is true." The statement is part of an interview with the London Evening Standard of 22 July 1924.

The venerable dean may have been right. The Oxford Dictionary of Quotations (3rd edition, 1979) lists only one substantiated gem from Spooner—"The weight of rages will press hard upon the employer." The cleverness, timing and relevance of the mistake, unintended as it was, must have so impressed the critics and those who heard it that, thereafter, any tongue twisting of a similar nature, whether manufactured or not, was placed squarely on Spooner's lap. It is not surprising, therefore, that the following mythical Spoonerisms were credited at one time or other to Spooner: (1) "It's kistomary to cuss the bride;" (2) "My students are constantly hissing my mystery lectures;" (3) "A blushing crow;" (4) "He rode off in his well-boiled icicle;" (5) "Those girls are sin twisters."

IX

Slices Of Shakey's

On Shakespeare and his Works

"A fool thinks himself to be wise,
but a wise man knows himself to be a fool."

•

William Shakespeare

1. A Poet by any Other Name

Myth! **Shakespeare is the most published name in the world.**

The three known spellings of the Bard's name are Shakespeare (on the tombs of his wife and daughter), Shakspeare (on his own monument), and Shagspere (on his marriage license). Historians believe more spellings are just waiting to be discovered. It is difficult to determine which spelling he preferred; anent his seven unquestionably genuine signatures in existence, an 1869 book by J. R. Wise entitled *Autograph of William Shakespeare* lists the 4000 different ways they can be read. This peculiarity has helped promote the suspicion that several playwrights writing under similar names are the real authors of Shakespeare's works.

'Shakespeare' itself may just be a pseudonym, formed by combining the 46th word of the 46th Psalm, 'shake', with the 46th word from the end of the Psalm, 'spear'. It is alleged that the Bard lent a hand in preparing the King James Version of the Bible, which was published when he was 46 years old. By way of celebrating his role, he adopted a name culled by applying the number of his age to the Book of Psalms. However, like most other myths numerologists love to propagate as fact, this story has no real basis.

It is nevertheless part of the conventional wisdom about the Bard that he signed the name Shakespeare on all his published works. On this premise, and counting the times the famous tragedies, comedies and verses have been printed and reprinted, it makes sense that the name Shakespeare has been touted as the most published in the world. It's a record worthy of Guinness, even barring materials featuring Shakespeare independently of his works. Any reckoning would exclude the many forgeries executed in Shakespeare's name, but it's difficult not to consider the millions of bills and posters, many of them containing facsimiles of the Bard's signature, that have been used to advertise his plays since the early days of the Globe Theater and Old Vic. Spelled Shakespeare, the name has been published more often than those of such prolific producers as playwright Lope de Vega, who claimed to have written 2,200 plays, 500 of them surviving, and

183

the writer Alexander Dumas *père*, whose works fill more than 1,500 volumes.

But in the widest sense that 'published' is used, it is believed Shakespeare can't hold a candle to the legendary graffito-signing Kilroy. No catchphrase has equaled the popularity and ubiquity of 'Kilroy was here' ever since it was found written on walls and on almost every other available surface during World War ll. While Kilroy is apparently just a common pseudonym for millions of anonymous wall scribblers, journalists have turned up evidence that the craze started with a single person—James J. Kilroy, a politician and a shipyard inspector for Bethlehem Steel Company in Quincy, Massachusetts. In 1941, Kilroy began chalking the words 'Kilroy was here' on thousands of ships and crates of equipment to indicate that he had gone over them, thereby preventing unnecessary double-checking by overtime inspectors. From Quincy the phrase traveled to military bases all over the world, and amused Gls replicated the words without knowing or caring what they meant.

2. A Life in Three Acts

Myth! **Shakespeare was born in Stratford-on-Avon, composed his own epitaph, and died on the same day as Miguel de Cervantes.**

Be prepared for some interesting trivia about Shakespeare from tour guides that ply the London area. A favorite is that the Bard was born in Stratford-on-Avon, the English municipal borough that would eventually become—thanks to his memory—a modern tourist center. Some have no idea where he died but are certain he died on the same day as the famous Spanish novelist Miguel de Cervantes. Apparently, his burial site is somewhere near London and marked by an epitaph that the Bard himself composed. Shakespeare's works remain preferred reading for most Britons, except for one or two plays that may have been turnoffs because of their evident bias against certain prominent groups.

It turns out much of the information about the Bard that comes from unofficial sources is misleading. Shakespeare died in what is popularly known as Stratford-on-Avon, where he was born, but sticklers for tradition—and these include modern-day residents of Shakespeare's hometown—prefer to call it Stratford-upon-Avon. He and the great Spanish writer Miguel de Cervantes died on the same date—April 23, 1616—but not on the same day. Shakespeare's demise in England under the Julian calendar was ten days after Cervantes passed away in Spain under the Gregorian calendar. Unlike Spain in 1582, non-Catholic countries were initially averse to the Gregorian system because it was a Catholic invention, and the British Empire would not convert to it until 1752.

Shakespeare is honored by an epitaph on his gravestone at Holy Trinity Church in Stratford, which reads: "GOOD FRIENDS FOR IESUS SAKE FORBEARE / TO DIGG THE DUST ENCLOSED HERE! / BLESTE BE YE MAN THAT SPARES THES STONES, / AND CURST BE HE THAT MOUES MY BONES." Contrary to popular belief, there is no evidence that Shakespeare himself composed it.

---

3. Of Shylocks and Shysters

Myth! **Shakespeare harbored a bias against Jews and lawyers.**

It is said that Shakespeare, in his plays *The Merchant of Venice* and *Henry VI, Part 2,* shows his bias against two groups, one ethnic and the other professional. In the first, he pictures Shylock as an avaricious Jewish moneylender, an apparent stereotyping of Jewish financiers in medieval times. Incidentally, the title character of the play is not Shylock, as some people think, but Antonio, who borrows money from Shylock to help his friend Bassanio. Antonio agrees to surrender a pound of flesh if he defaults on the loan, and Shylock later tries to exact it. The Bard's defenders caution it's only a play, and that, in reality, most moneylenders during this period, despite being Jewish, were not as mean or as greedy as the character that has been presented. A sympathetic historian notes: "They had to smile to keep their customers happy because of the stiff competition."

In *Henry VI, Part 2,* a character is made to exclaim, "Let's kill all the lawyers," a line that's been tagged to reflect Shakespeare's

185

personal contempt for the legal profession. Fortunately for the Bard, there is some doubt he wrote the play. Even if he did, he seems to have sufficiently recovered when he glorified Portia's lawyering in *The Merchant of Venice*, the same play for which he has been accused of anti-Semitism. Because of the remark, Shakespeare has been suspected of authoring the similar and equally popular expression, "Woe unto you, lawyers!" But the phrase is nowhere in the Bard's works and can only be found in *Luke* 11:52 of the New Testament. The complete quotation, Jesus' reprimand to a certain class of sinners, is, "Woe unto you, lawyers! For ye have taken away the key of knowledge: ye entered not in yourselves, and them that were entering in ye hindered."

4. Fingers are All you Need at Shakey's

Myth! In Shakespeare's plays, dinner etiquette is promoted through the use of fork, spoon and knife.

Shakespeare's works record a wide range of contemporary customs and practices, yet none of his plays mentions such common eating utensils as fork, spoon and knife. The obvious reason is that they were relatively unknown in Shakespeare's time—and the dire implication is that the Bard wrote in elegant fashion but dined by scooping up the food with his bare hands!

It seems Europeans ate with their fingers (and only sometimes with knives and spoons) until the sixteenth century, and were not bothered that a number of ancient civilizations, like the Egyptians, the Greeks and the Romans, had much more dignified table manners. *Panati's Extraordinary Origins of Everyday Things*, quoting from an etiquette book of the 1530s, maintains that upper class Elizabethans used the Roman 'three-finger rule', i.e., "when dining in good society, one should be mindful that...it is most refined to use only three fingers of the hand, not five. This is one of the marks of distinction between the upper and lower classes." Still, Elizabethans loved fine linen and wouldn't be seen at the dining table without napkins, which were set at every place for the homeowners and their guests. To wipe their hands on after the meal, no doubt.

186

5. Not to the Manner Born

Myth! **Shakespeare was a man of the masses.**

At least one biography draws a picture of the Bard as a poor, virtually uneducated rustic who fled from Stratford to London to escape prosecution for poaching on the lands of Sir Thomas Lucy. 'Commoner son of a glove maker', 'stable boy', and 'village bumpkin' were some of the epithets the lad had to endure. The uncomplimentary labels may have been justified in a sense; considered a hacker in his profession, Shakespeare was paid not more than £8 apiece for his plays, and since he wrote fewer than 40 plays, his income from writing during his 20 years in the theater was less than £20 a year.

The truth is something else, however. Shakespeare's father John was a respected, relatively wealthy man who held several municipal offices and who married into an equally distinguished Catholic family. Young William was given an intensive grammar school education, which included not only Latin and Greek but also a generous dose of the classics. His decision to go to London may have been prompted by financial difficulties but never by threats of prosecution.

Although William probably earned the better part of his pay from acting, the consistently high quality of his plays attests to the serious attention he paid to his playwriting. It may be true he received only £8 for each play, but this was the highest price available to a playwright in those days. In addition, he engaged in many business activities, including the acquisition of substantial holdings of real estate around Stratford. According to one biographer, his income from all sources was the equivalent of about $50,000 a year after 1599.

6. Ham Maybe, but Bacon Never

Myth! **A lot of technical knowledge went into the writing of Shakespeare's plays.**

The complexity and sophistication of Shakespeare's plays have given the impression that a vast amount of technical and special knowledge went into their writing. The lingering suspicion—and consequently the rumor that would not die—is that one or several literary worthies, among them Christopher Marlowe and Sir Walter Raleigh, may have been the real creators of Shakespeare's works. Mark Twain himself laid his bets on Sir Francis Bacon as the genuine author in the belief that no ordinary actor *cum* playwright who lacked formal education could have written such fantastically literate scripts.

The Sage of Hannibal not only assumed Shakespeare lacked the right amount of education (which he did not), but also that he had no special gift for the task (which he had). Twain was rightly impressed with both the quantity and quality of knowledge that went into Shakespeare's writings—about the law, the military, maritime affairs, geography and history, for instance. However, he failed to discern that it was all common sense, and Shakespeare quite obviously had a lot of it. The plays were neither so special nor technical as would be beyond the scope of a fairly intelligent man. Ironically, Twain himself had been a country bumpkin and a school dropout at age 11, yet he wrote classics effortlessly using no more than his native genius. Indeed, anyone like Twain, with a good level of experience in theater arts and practical in other respects, would have been more qualified to write the plays than Bacon. Sir Francis was, without question, a great man, but his cast of mind was scientific, logical and philosophical, and he was not a poet or playwright.

7. Shakespeare for Dummies

Myth! **Shakespeare's plays are considered highbrow fare in America today.**

The common perception is that Shakespeare used more words than most Americans know and can hope to know, and this is why his plays have never hit it big in the US. Critics say any effort to bring Shakespeare to the masses is bound to fail unless there is a corresponding effort to raise the level of comprehension for his works. They claim putting Shakespeare on every school's curriculum or on a wide range of public media won't get the same mileage as, say, producing a simplified version of each of his tragedies and comedies using everyday language. Following this tack, some screen writers have modernized Shakespeare's dialogues in the hope of advancing the play's plot, but many more have hesitated on the ground that bowdlerization degrades rather than promotes art.

The assertion that Shakespeare used more words than are currently known by Americans is misleading if not outright false. English, which has grown enormously since Elizabethan times, lists up to 800,000 words, the largest vocabulary of any language today. Shakespeare used only about twenty thousand different words in his works, none of which has, as far as is known, become obsolete. The average vocabulary of the modern American—about 2,000 English words in everyday speech—is only one-tenth that of Shakespeare. Still, writers and others of more than average literacy avail of a lexicon far in excess of that used by the great playwright. An intelligent person with a college education but not necessarily of a literary bent may use as many as 60,000 words.

It is nevertheless not correct to say that in the US, only aficionados, highbrows and purists devoted to the old theater ever cared for Shakespeare. At one time, Shakespeare was more in demand in America than in Britain. The experts say that from 1750 until nearly the end of the nineteenth century, Shakespeare was the most popular playwright to every social class in America.

8. Rivals in Arms Deal

Myth! The exchange of weapons between Hamlet and Laertes is accidental and not tactical.

In most modern productions of Hamlet, the exchange of weapons between Hamlet and Laertes—who carries a weapon both poisoned and sharpened—is made to appear as the inadvertent result of a scuffle. Critics say that by making this final, climactic scene turn upon a mere accident, the element of poetic justice in the plot is diminished, and Hamlet becomes less than a hero who has control of his destiny. In other versions, Hamlet forces the exchange by stepping on the sharp weapon that he has

189

knocked from Laertes' hand and presenting his own blunt weapon to his opponent. As intended by the Bard, however, the reason for the maneuver is tactical, as it almost always was in a real life duel. To 'change rapiers' was a well-known technique in Shakespeare's day, and was employed deliberately to disarm an opponent, although it usually ended up with both fencers disarming each other. After stepping back, each side shifted the weapon taken from his opponent from left hand to right, and continued the match. The result was effectively an exchange of weapons, which is precisely the objective that Hamlet has in mind in the dueling scene in order to force Laertes to yield the sharp and poisoned blade to him.

9. Romeo Bleeds

Myth! Shakespeare invented the characters Romeo, Macbeth and Hamlet.

Unlike what most people believe, Shakespeare did not invent many of his characters, and neither did anyone else. Take the case of Romeo and Juliet. The theme of two young lovers meeting a tragic fate in their effort to surmount familial barriers may be as old as the Greek classics, but it's not at all fictional. Romeo and his paramour lived in Verona, Italy, and died in the year 1303, victims of their parents' senseless rivalry. Similar stories appear in Masuccio's *Novellino* (1476) and before that in *Ephesiaca* by the third- or fourth-century writer Xenophon of Ephesus. The Bard himself based his play on Arthur Brooke's long narrative poem 'The Tragicall Historye of Romeus and Juliet' (1562), which was in turn derived from a 1535 Italian story by Luigi da Porto through a 1559 French version by Pierre Boisteau. The tragedy is remarkable for being "a rare example of love's constancie" between an adolescent boy and a pubescent girl. In act 1, scene 2, Juliet's father says she "hath not seen the change of fourteen years," meaning she was only thirteen, and Romeo was probably not more than one or two years older.

Two prominent personalities in Shakespeare's royal menagerie—Macbeth and Hamlet—are so complicated that they are often mistaken as fictional. Actually, Macbeth was a real

Scottish king who was good and strong enough to survive on the throne for 17 years, from 1040 to 1057, "which is more than 25 other occupants of that precarious hot spot can claim." Historical authorities believe he was not the henpecked social climber and conniving usurper the Bard painted him to be. He had as good a claim, if not better, to the throne of Scotland as Duncan had, and he did not murder Duncan in real life for it; the latter died in open combat on the battlefield in the year 1040.

Similarly, Hamlet was a real figure in Pierre de Belleforest's *Histoires Tragiques* (1570), a translation of *Historica Danica* (1514) by the Danish historian Saxo Grammaticus. It is not clear to what extent Shakespeare rewrote Hamlet's story, but he apparently saw a need to inject some local ambience into it to ensure acceptance by an Elizabethan audience. Critics believe the Bard made Hamlet's family Catholic despite the Danes' adherence to paganism during the period setting of the play in order to justify the ghost of Hamlet's father as something spiritual rather than magical or illusory. In one scene, the ghost tells Hamlet that he is "(d)oom'd for a certain term to walk the night, and for the day confined to fast in fires, till the foul crimes done in my days of nature, are burnt and purged away." This is a clear statement of the Catholic belief in purgatory as a place of absolution, and is totally remote from a pagan's notion of the hereafter.

10. Regarding Henry

Myth! Shakespeare wrote all the plays about a king named Henry.

There are several kings named Henry that became subjects of popular plays, all of them attributed to Shakespeare. But most bibliopoles believe the Bard only wrote some of them. The only plays that Shakespeare can call entirely his own are *Henry IV*, presented in two parts, and *Henry V*. The longest story is that of Henry VI, which is told in three parts, but it is highly doubtful Shakespeare penned any of it. The Bard was, for the most part, alone in writing his plays, although scholars believe his last two plays, *Henry VIII* and *Two Noble Kinsmen*, were co-written with

191

younger playwright John Fletcher, a little-known English dramatist of the period. The figure of Henry II has never been featured in a legitimate Shakespearean work, although he has appeared in a play that was once credited to Shakespeare but is now known to be a forgery by William Henry Ireland (1777-1835).

Speaking of forgeries, there is a ninety-line poem called "Shall I Die" which, to this date, has not been ruled as either a genuine or a fake Shakespearean work. Scholar Gary Taylor unearthed the 'new' poem in November 1985, claiming that the poem is Shakespeare's, written about the time of *Romeo and Juliet* (1594-95). Most other scholars disagree, saying the poetry is much too weak, "a second-rate hack work," "a clunker." A typical line goes: "Shall I fend? Shall I send? Shall I shew, and not rue my proceeding?" It does look like a mess, but if authentic, Time surmises, "the work would be the first notable addition to the canon in more than three centuries."

11. Last Seen with Rosencrantz & Guildenstern

Myth! Yorick and the Witch of Endor are characters in Shakespeare's plays.

How well we remember ourselves when, as young aspirants for the high school drama club, we would hold a fish bowl in one hand, and, gazing at it, exclaim, "Alas, poor Yorick, I knew him well!" It was good enough for quick rehearsals, but not for an English test that asked exactly what Hamlet tells Horatio when a clown shows him a disinterred skull. The skull belongs to Yorick, a Dane who, according to Laurence Sterne, in his 1760 novel *Tristram Shandy*, emigrated to England to become the English king's court jester. The flesh-and-blood Yorick never appears in the play, but Hamlet imagines him when he was still alive, and, contemplating the skull, notes how repulsive is the common destiny of man, whether king or court jester. The actual line Hamlet utters is, "Alas, poor Yorick; I knew him, Horatio" (5:I).

Though 'Witch of Endor' sounds Shakespearean, it is not mentioned in any of the Bard's works. Neither does it appear in the Bible, except that in some English editions it is used in the

192

heading for Chapter 28 of *Samuel*. The closest reference in Biblical text is to a medium—not a witch—described as "a woman that hath a familiar spirit at Endor." She brought up the prophet Samuel from the dead upon the request of Saul, who wished to inquire about the fateful battle in which he was to lose his life. Her function was not exactly that of a witch, who is supposed to hold communion with the devil and other evil spirits, but rather that of a spiritualistic medium who claims to have power to convey messages from the dead to the living.

In the play *Two Gentlemen From Verona*, it's not the characters but the place that creates the anomaly of the title. Verona provides the setting for the first act by way of introducing the main characters, particularly the two gentlemen, Valentine and Proteus. The rest of the story, from Act II to Act V, happens elsewhere, mostly in Milan. The only other misleading title from Shakespeare is *A Midsummer's Night Dream*, where all of the action takes place in the spring, from April 29 to May 1.

12. English Spoken Here

Myth! Shakespeare wrote his plays in Old English.

Throughout his plays, Shakespeare used words and phrases in the category of 'Ye Olde Gifte Shoppe', which grabs modern readers as being 'Old English'. In fact, phrases like 'Ye Olde Gifte Shoppe', though already extant a century before the Bard, are a form of Modern English, as is the language of the various illuminated manuscript pages (or their imitations) that are often passed off as Old English in Ye Olde Gifte Shoppe. Old English, which Germanic tribes introduced in 450, thrived only until 1100, when the French influence of the Norman Conquest started corrupting it into Middle English. It finally evolved into Modern English with the arrival of printing in the latter 15th century, chronologically confirming that Shakespeare, Chaucer and Mallory never used Old English in their writings. Chaucer wrote in Middle English, Malory in early Modern English, and Shakespeare in Modern English. Old English has become almost non-existent, and the only manuscript of any length that survives is that of *Beowulf*. In speech as well as in writing, the ancient language is so unintelligible that, if revived today, it would be as hard to master as any of the most intractable ones.

In this regard, we say 'King's English' (or 'Queen's English', depending on who's on the throne) for English as it should be spoken today, confident in the belief that Shakespeare coined the term when he used it in *Merry Wives of Windsor* (1, 4). Actually, 'King's English' is much older than the Bard and was already quite common during his time. The phrase "thou clipst the King's English" appeared in Dekker's *Satiro-Mastix* (1602), and Brewster quotes another from Thomas Wilson, in *Arte of Rhetorique* (1553), "if a manne should charge them for counterfeiting the kinges Englishe."

Further on 'Ye Olde Gifte Shoppe', it seems the word 'ye' was a favorite article in Shakespeare's days, and could mean either 'the' or 'you' as one may choose. It is now heard only in Hollywood period pieces, pronounced as 'yee' as though it were an Old English variant of 'the'. In fact, it should sound exactly like 'the', since, historically, the letter y in 'ye' is just a printing form of the combination *th*. In the early days, a runic symbol called 'thorn'—a p superimposed on a b—represented the sound of *th*. When printing came into vogue, the letter y, and much later the modern *th*, replaced the 'thorn'. All that the word 'ye' stands for, when used in those quaint London signs we still see today, is the commonest, most prosaic of English words: 'the'. Like the opening line of Robert Herrick's "To the Virgins, to Make Much of Time," which should read (aloud) as, "Gather *the* rosebuds, while *thee* may."

X

English Waffles And Danish Sophistries

On Shakespeare's Hamlet

"We ape, we mimic, we mock. We act."

•

Laurence Olivier

1. Two Danish Tarts

Myth! Hamlet tells Ophelia to retire to a convent to dampen her libido, and later castigates his queen mother for pretending to be virtuous.

In the famous scene in which Hamlet rejects Ophelia (3:1, 90 ff), he tells her, "Get thee to a nunnery!" The usual interpretation of this is that Hamlet is asking Ophelia to keep away from him by staying in a convent. But experts say Shakespeare meant the line to be even more spiteful and abusive than is popularly believed, as a sign of irrationality to reveal Hamlet's state of depression. Thus, they point out, the word "nunnery" as heard from Hamlet's lips is actually Elizabethan slang for 'whorehouse', and the whole line is an out-of-character outburst from the noble Dane ordering his betrothed to indulge her libido by spending time with prostitutes. Other critics don't believe the slang bit at all, but agree nonetheless that the Bard was using the word "nunnery" metaphorically for that purpose.

Hamlet apparently has the same brusque attitude when he asks his mother: "Assume a virtue, if you have it not" (3:4, 160). From a modern point of view, the line is our hero's sarcastic advice to the queen when he sees her cavorting with his uncle while appearing to mourn the untimely passing of her husband (and Hamlet's father) the king. In Hamlet's context, however, 'assume' is not used in the sense of 'pretending to have' but of 'taking on', a meaning still current today, as when one 'assumes' the responsibilities of an office. Far from being sarcastic, Hamlet sincerely wants his mother to be virtuous, that is to say, to make a habit of doing good, rather than to just put on an appearance to hide her turpitude.

2. Protestant Queen

Myth! When "the lady doth protest too much," Hamlet suspects she has something to hide.

That would be so if Hamlet were the speaker, but in fact it is not Hamlet but his mother, Queen Gertrude, who is voicing the complaint. Hamlet asks her how she likes the show (a play within the play) the two of them are watching, and she replies, "The lady doth protest too much, methinks" (3:2, 240). The lady in question is one of the show's principal characters, a queen like herself.

The more popular version, "Methinks the lady doth protest too much," is not only inaccurate, it is also commonly misinterpreted, as if the lady is being blamed for making too many objections because she has something to hide. In fact, Shakespeare's "protest" means "proclaim," "avow" or "declare solemnly," which was the principal connotation of the word during the Bard's time. It was then common to hear expressions like "I protest my loyalty to the crown," the essence of which has been retained today in such phrases as "to protest one's innocence." Contrary to popular belief, the meaning of "protest" as "object" or "oppose" is of relatively modern vintage and is still secondary. Therefore, when Gertrude says the lady "doth protest too much," she means that the lady is affirming something, not denying or objecting to it, but does it too often and perhaps too strongly as to lose credibility and achieve the exact opposite of her intentions.

3. The Ploy's the Thing

Myth! Hamlet descends into madness on learning that her mother and uncle are the murderers of his father.

An example of a popular saying that improves on Shakespeare is, "There's method in his madness." Compare this to *Hamlet* (2:2), where Polonius, suspecting that Hamlet is losing his mind, listens to his diatribe and then makes an aside, "Though this be madness, yet there is method in it." From Hamlet's rambling, Polonius becomes convinced that the Prince is mad, but he recognizes some 'method', that is, a kind of artfulness that one would hardly expect from a crazed mind.

What is not obvious to many readers is that the only genuinely mad character in the play is Ophelia. Although Hamlet exhibits erratic behavior after the ghost makes its shocking revelations, in fact he is only pretending to be mad to protect himself against his

197

uncle's devious intents and to implement a plan to avenge his father's murder. Thus, Hamlet tells his friends Marcellus, Bernardo, and Horatio that he may "put an antic disposition on" (5:1, 172), which is to say, feign madness, and later (3:4, 140 ff.) he tells Queen Gertrude, his mother, the same thing in equally forceful terms.

Hamlet confirms that he is putting up a false pretense when he says, "I am but mad north-northwest; when the wind is southerly I know a hawk from a handsaw" (2:2). Critics say the comparison between a hawk and a handsaw makes no sense, unless 'handsaw' is regarded as a corruption of 'hernshaw', a young heron. On the other hand, 'handsaw' may be what it really is—a workman's tool—if 'hawk' is taken to mean a small square board with a handle underneath, used to hold plaster or mortar. It is not certain, however, if 'hawk' had this secondary meaning in the days of Shakespeare, and for this reason the first interpretation is given greater probability.

4. In a Spectral Manor

Myth! Hamlet admits to his royal bloodline by saying that he is 'to the manor born'.

"To the manor born" is to be born wealthy or of noble blood, but this is different from a similar-sounding expression found in *Hamlet* (1:4). Upon hearing a flourish of drums and trumpets at midnight, Hamlet's friends ask him what it means, and he replies that it is a royal drinking custom, "But to my mind, though I am native here, and to the manner born, it is a custom more honour'd in the breach than the observance." Note that Shakespeare uses the word 'manner', suggesting a habit, custom or practice, and not 'manor', which implies rank, aristocracy or high estate. "To the manner born" is to be accustomed to or practiced in a particular way. Another phrase in Hamlet's statement worth noting— "More honour'd in the breach than the observance"—means, in the modern context, "more often disregarded than adhered to." But the meaning intended by Shakespeare is, "more appropriate for breaching than for observing." That is to say, the custom in question is so unworthy and undesirable that one is better off

198

("honour'd") violating than following it. Put in another way, "the custom is observed too often, denigrating its observers rather than conferring honor on them."

5. Polonaic Wisdom

Myth! **Polonius says that to be witty, one must be brief.**

Instead of just telling the king in simple terms that Hamlet is mad, Polonius goes into a long discourse that ends with the observation: "Therefore, since brevity is the soul of wit, and tediousness the limbs and outward flourishes, I will be brief. Your noble son is mad..." Critics think Polonius' recitation of a long preface to introduce his point that 'brevity is the soul of wit' (2:2, 90) is a nice instance of dramatic irony. The self-contradiction is heightened by the fact that Polonius hardly shows any wit in anything he does or says throughout the entire play.

Actually, Polonius does not use 'wit' in the modern sense of 'acumen' or 'quickness of perception', a meaning not widely known in 17th century England (although the Bard himself used it in *Much Ado About Nothing*: "They never meet but there's a skirmish of wit between them"). 'Wit' derives from the Old English verb witan, 'to know', and was synonymous with 'wisdom', 'perception' or 'insight'. It is as 'wisdom' that wit appears with euphonic clarity in Polonius' proverb, a simple affirmation that a person is unwise if he or she cannot put things succinctly. Polonius is admittedly tedious, but since he does not claim to be wise, he cannot be accused of violating his own precept and engaging in irony.

6. Fine Dining at the Front

Myth! **Hamlet's 'caviare to the general' presupposes something exotic or special for the elite.**

199

Hamlet tells one of the players in the traveling dramatic troupe, which has come to the Danish court to entertain the king: "I heard thee speak me a speech once, but it was never acted . . . for the play, I remember, pleased not the millions; 'twas caviare to the general" (2:2, 414 ff). The phrase "caviare to the general," referring literally to an exotic dish prepared for a commanding officer, is taken by many to mean something fit for a connoisseur. This is essentially the same meaning Shakespeare had in mind, but he approached it in a quite different way. Instead of the redundancy from the words "caviare" and "general" (both are suggestive of the cognoscente), Shakespeare coined the phrase as a contradiction, using the word "general" to refer to the other end of the spectrum, i.e., the general public. Hence, like the more modern "pearls before swine," "caviare to the general" is a connoisseur's item which, when offered to the multitude, proves too exotic for their taste. Hamlet's reference is to a stage play that failed because it was too sophisticated to be appreciated by the public.

---

7. More than Meets the Eye

Myth! Hamlet accuses Horatio of narrow-mindedness when he says, "There are more things in heaven and earth, Horatio, that are dreamt of in your philosophy."

This statement (1:5, 166-67) is one of those in the Shakespearean trove that people love to quote without knowing exactly why. Swaddled in the mystic elegance of the Bard's language, its highly nuanced meaning eludes most. The popular interpretation, which is actually just a suspicion, is that Hamlet is accusing Horatio of being ignorant of "things." In the context of the play, the word "things" is a variable ranging from ghost appearances, the perfidy of loved ones, and creeping madness. It is also not clear if the reference is to things that Hamlet doesn't know and would like answers to, or to those that Hamlet knows and is keeping only to himself.

When taken out of context, the word "things" really get out of hand and could mean anything depending on the genre or setting to which it is adapted. In a Vincent Price horror movie, for instance, it could allude to the supernatural, and in the Star Trek series, to scientific phenomena. Or it could be a label for some philosophical concepts that Hamlet thinks Horatio missed in school. Critics say that by the statement, Hamlet is making fun of Horatio's hidebound beliefs and attitudes, but others claim this is not exactly what the Bard meant. They point out that in Shakespeare's book, "your" is used as a substitute for the definite article "the," and "philosophy" is not somebody's personal belief or credo but the discipline taught in universities. Thus, Hamlet is merely telling Horatio that philosophy as a field of study has its limitations, although by using the Bard's language, he can't help but obscure the point. The quote would probably be better understood if it said, "There are more things in heaven and earth, Horatio, than are dreamt of in philosophy." But, as one critic notes, the syntax won't be there and it won't be Shakespeare.

Film & Music

I

A Failure To Communicate

Quotes from Classic Films

*"Any time you got nothing to do –
and lots of time to do it - come on up."*

•

Mae West

1. Don't Snarl when you Say That

Myth! "You dirty rat!" and "All right, you guys" are James Cagney's favorite expressions from the movies.

Contrary to what some people think, Cagney went from musicals to cops-and-robbers pictures and not the other way around. After turning to gangster roles, the former song-and-dance man became forever typecast as the tough guy who hitches up his pants and says with a nasal growl, "You dirty rat!" This is the line that comedians and impressionists like Frank Gorshin most often mimic when they lampoon the Hollywood actor, and one of several most associated with Cagney. Keyes reports that before receiving the American Film Institute's Life Achievement Award in 1975, Cagney had someone check all of his films to find out if he had really said it because he couldn't remember ever doing so. He later told his audience that he hadn't, "but I thank all of you who have given me credit for it." The nearest Cagney got to expressing the thought was in *Blonde Crazy*, when he called someone "a dirty, double-crossing rat."

The second most lampooned line attributed to Cagney is, "All right, you guys." According to his autobiography, the actor never recalled saying these words either, and it is likely he didn't in any of the many moods he reflected on screen. The expression was a favorite of the Bowery Boys, but must have been mistakenly assigned to Cagney by his imitators because the kids worked closely with him in *Dead End* (1937) and *Angels With Dirty Faces* (1938). "All right, youse guys" is usually paired with the phrase "Listen up, see" or "Put your hands in de air," and may have originated with the early cops and robbers serials aired on radio.

2. Minors' Extravaganza

Myth! Mickey Rooney tells Judy Garland, "Let's put on a show," in *Babes in Arms* (1939).

In *Babes in Arms* (1939), a Busby Berkeley film based on a Rodgers and Hart musical, Mickey Rooney and Judy Garland persuade the other children of retired vaudeville people to stage a show in their hometown to save their elders from financial distress. This quintessential 'putting-on-a-show' movie is everybody's source of the cliché "Let's put on a show." But there isn't one scene in the movie in which the line is spoken, despite all other aspects of plot and dialogue being geared to the central idea of amateurish characters trying to put on a professional show.

The theme is repeated in other Berkeley musicals, notably *Strike Up the Band* (1940) and *Babes on Broadway* (1941), where an enterprising and impetuous Mickey Rooney, assisted by Judy Garland, gathers together his young friends for a big show of their own. The musical documentary *That's Entertainment!* ties together several clips from these films, but in none of them is the line "Let's put on a show" spoken. The documentary does make the point that there is a common intention behind the various scenes presented, and this is obviously what the imaginary phrase expresses so well.

3. When you See this Bogie, just Whistle

Myth! Lauren Bacall tells Humphrey Bogart, "If you want anything, just whistle," in *To Have and Have Not* (1944).

The movie *To Have and Have Not* (1944) marked the acting debut of Lauren Bacall and sparked her celebrated romance with her costar and future husband Humphrey Bogart. She spices her performance in the film by singing two songs, "Am I Blue?" and "How Little We Know." The routine, though apparently out of character, helped put her on a career path that has survived well beyond Bogart's.

Ironically, the belief persists that her musical voice in the film was dubbed. The low, throaty style of the dialogue was hers but the singing appeared to be a feat of lip-synching while she was being filmed from behind. It is claimed someone ghosted for Bacall, most likely the 14-year old Andy Williams, but the hardy actress has consistently maintained that she sang the songs herself, first in a recording studio and then sans voice before the cameras.

Siding with her loyal fans, most film historians say Bacall had no reason to have her voice dubbed because she happens to be a good singer. This was proved by her Tony-awarded performance in 1970 on the Broadway stage in the long-running musical *Applause*, where she belted out several numbers like no other professional vocalist could.

Recalling how the word 'whistle' started the love life of the couple, which lasted through their marriage until Bogart passed away in 1957, most biographies mention a scene in the movie in which Bacall tells Bogart, "If you want anything, just whistle." Classic Hollywood lore tells us that the catchy line boosted Bacall's stardom almost overnight and became so memorable to the couple that when Bogart died, Bacall placed a gold whistle beside his body. However, it should not take a punctilious cineaste to spot the line as a mere paraphrase of the one Bacall actually speaks: "You don't have to say anything, and you don't have to do anything. Not a thing. Oh, maybe just whistle." Some people compound the error by assigning the words to Bogart without bothering to find out that in the film, the actor remains quiet—dumbstruck as it were—while Bacall utters her role-defining line.

4. Celluloid Passport

Myth! *Casablanca* dramatizes the plight of World War II refugees who could not exit that city without letters of transit from General Charles de Gaulle.

The most popular misconception about the movie *Casablanca* (1942) has to do with Ingrid Bergman telling Dooley Wilson's character, "Play it again, Sam," when it should just be "Play it again." We make much of this false dialogue when our attention should be focused on several plot loopholes instead. For instance, during the Second World War, refugees from all over Nazi-dominated Europe and its colonies paid a high premium for anything that could ensure their passage from Hitler's persecution to democracy and freedom. The drama of this desperate quest in wartime Casablanca is captured in the film, which shows sundry characters clamoring for fake passports from Bogie's character Rick as a sinister purveyor of sorts, but the manner of its presentation to the audience is erroneous. The Warner Bros. classic would have us believe that these passports, or so-called letters of transit, were issued by the French Vichy Government to allow travelers to leave Casablanca without a hitch. Actually, despite some of the film's characters, notably the one played by Peter Lorre, killing and dying for the coveted documents, as a historical matter they never existed.

The same movie tells us Charles de Gaulle, leader of the Free French and the avowed opponent of the Nazis and their Vichy cohorts, signed the elusive letters. Common sense dictates it should be Marshal Pétain, since wartime Casablanca was under the puppet government of Vichy France.

The airport climax, when Rick must decide whether Ilsa should stay with him or leave with her husband Victor, is tagged by many as the most crucial part of *Casablanca*. Others argue, however, that the drama of that scene, indeed vital from a strictly romantic perspective, is only secondary to the quiet majesty of an earlier one, when the drunken Nazis sing "Die Wacht am Rhein" in Rick's Cafe Americaine, and Rick nods at the house band to drown them out with "La Marseillaise." The political moment is designed to show Rick taking a militant stand for the first time since Ilsa ditched him, and the simple gesture, marking him the true patriot that he is, presages the act of self-sacrifice that he will later make at the airport.

5. Breaking the Sound Barrier

Myth! The first time Al Jolson used the line, "You ain't heard nothin' yet, folks!," was in *The Jazz Singer* (1927).

The Jazz Singer is popularly honored as the first full-length talking picture, but the distinction is dubious. It is essentially silent, with several sound musical interludes, most of them songs the movie made famous in that era. The dialogue is limited to two short sequences consisting of just 354 words, twenty-seven of which is the famous statement made by an excited Al Jolson. Al was just about to sing a song when he held up his hands and ad-libbed, "Wait a minute. Wait a minute. You ain't heard nothin' yet. Wait a minute, I tell yer…you wanna hear 'Toot Tot Tootsie'? All right, hold on." Jolson apparently didn't realize that the cameras were already rolling and his sentences were being preserved for posterity. The word "folks" is never really spoken, but for some reason is added by Bartlett, Oxford, and Flexner. People also think it was the first time Al Jolson spoke the line, when actually it had long been associated with the singer as the title and part of the lyrics of a song in his repertoire: "You Ain't Heard Nothing Yet."

6. Eye-lashing in a Small Town

Myth! Charles Boyer tells Hedy Lamarr, "Come with me to the Casbah!," as he leads her to the native part of Algiers.

The scene most often talked about in the film *Algiers* is that of Charles Boyer inviting Hedy Lamarr to a mysterious section of the city called the Casbah. Boyer half-embraces the turbaned Lamarr and, in a suave French accent, whispers enticingly, "Come wiz me to ze Casbah!" This recollection is no doubt abetted by Boyer's Gallic personality, Lamarr's exotic appeal, and Hollywood's excellent Algerian sets. But movie buffs know better: the scene is nowhere in the 1938 classic and more properly belongs to an impressionist's act. Boyer is simply one more actor who has been stereotyped by an imaginary quotation.

Thanks to the film and Boyer's mythic line, people think Casbah is specifically the name of the native quarter of Algiers, which serves as the residential, commercial and social center for its Arab populace. Actually, the word Casbah is not peculiar to Algiers, but refers generally to the native ghetto in any city with a substantial Arab population. In fact, Casablanca's Casbah in Morocco has become more widely known than the one in Algiers because of the popularity of the 1942 Bogart-Bergman movie and the postwar Hitchcock movie *The Man Who Knew Too Much*.

7. Three and three from Two

Myth! **"Judy, Judy, Judy" is Cary Grant scolding a teenager, and "Petah, Petah, Petah" is Bette Davis cautioning a lover.**

It does sound like Cary Grant in one of his screwball comedies, and the scene conjured is rather typical of many movie situations involving the actor. Assuming a professorial stance before a young girl, he reproves her with "Judy, Judy, Judy," not for failing to do her homework but for having fallen in love with him. In reality, it is only nightclub comedian Larry Storch doing a send-up of Grant. The actor himself never said the line in any of his films, while off the set, he could have said it just to mock his imitators. According to Keyes, Grant believed it started when somebody introduced Judy Garland to him at a party by thrice repeating her name, "and it caught on, attributed to me."

Cary saying "Judy, Judy, Judy" is like Bette Davis saying "Petah, Petah, Petah" while puffing on a cigarette. Bette's performance will not be seen as well on the screen or elsewhere because it never happened. The actress appeared not once opposite an actor or character named Peter. Many who do not know Arthur Blake invented the parody continue to be impressed by the line as one truly befitting the image of the actress.

8. Is that Mae West or is it Just Silicone?

Myth! **In *She Done Him Wrong* (1933) Mae West tells Cary Grant, "C'mon up and see me sometime."**

This well-stacked Brooklynite was a screen and vaudeville performer whose irreverent wit, mostly double entendres and one-liners, put her male leads to shame. Who can forget Mae in her first film encounter with Cary Grant when, as the unforgettable Diamond Lil, she seduces him with the invitation, "C'mon up and see me sometime"?

Actually, the line Mae throws at the young Cary is, "Why don't you come up some time and see me?," in the 1933 *She Done Him Wrong*. It is in her next movie, *I'm No Angel* (1933), also with Cary Grant, that the inverted but more popular phrase, "C'mon up and see me sometime," is heard. W. C. Fields repeats this as parody when he meets Mae West in the 1939 *My Little Chickadee*. Mae may have also said, "Come up and see me sometime," in the play *Diamond Lil* (1932), but definitely not in the first Mae-Cary film pairing into which it was adapted.

Although Mae had only a minor part when she debuted in the 1932 *Night After Night*, she stole the whole show with a scene in which she ad-libbed her line. "Goodness, what diamonds!" the hatcheck girl exclaims. "Goodness had nothing to do with it, dearie," Mae responds. Some reference books omit the last word "dearie" obviously because Mae herself dropped it when she entitled her autobiography, *Goodness Had Nothing To Do With It*.

"When I'm good I'm very good, but when I'm bad I'm better," is another of Mae's dubious quotes, attributed to her by the Hollywood press to further bolster her public image as a sexpot. Far from being original, it is a paraphrase of Longfellow's famous short verse about a little girl who, "When she was good / She was very, very good, / But when she was bad she was horrid."

9. A Butler did it

Myth! David O. Selznick introduced the word "damn" in the movies through Clark Gable's character in the final scene of *Gone With The Wind* (1939).

When the Hays Office heard Rhett Butler telling Scarlett O'Hara, "Frankly, my dear, I don't give a damn," it raised a storm and wanted the offensive 'damn' out. But the Motion Picture Association could not bear the pressure brought upon it by David Selznick, and passed the controversial word by amending the Production Code.

Many legends have since grown around that dispute. One is that Hays fined Selznick $5,000, and another that Hays had been willing to accept the word 'darn' but not 'damn'. Yet another (from William Safire) is that, as a condition for its approval, the MPA required Clark Gable to place the vocal emphasis on 'give' to draw attention away from 'damn'. Whichever has a basis in fact, Margaret Mitchell's novel readily discloses that the only word Selznick added to the original line was 'frankly' to give it more tang.

'Damn', in any case, was not a groundbreaking word, as many believed, for it had appeared before in popular magazines and mainstream editorials. Previously, Warner had been allowed to use 'damn' in *The Man Without a Country* ("Damn the United States! I never want to hear that name again"). It was spoken by both Leslie Howard and Marie Lohr in *Pygmalion* (1938); Fred Stone in *Alice Adams* (1935); and Emma Dunn in *Blessed Event* (1932). The first screen occurrence of the expletive was probably the three 'damns' that punctuated the early talkie *Glorifying the American Girl* (1929) These notwithstanding, Selznick was not sure he would get the word approved and had *Gone With the Wind* previewed a number of times sporting the line, "My dear, I don't care."

Interestingly, there is some speculation that the controversy could have been avoided had somebody offered the folk etymology that the word 'damn' in such expressions as "I don't give a damn" and "It's not worth a damn" is not an intended profanity. According to William Safire, early linguists believed the word 'damn' as thus used should be spelled 'dam', because the reference is to the *dam* or *dawm*, which is "an Indian coin worth barely the fortieth part of a rupee." Safire mentions another theory holding that 'dam' is "the small clay guard that a tinker—an itinerant mender of household utensils—puts around a hole that is to be sealed with solder, to prevent the solder from running off the rounded surface of the pot until it has cooled. The hot solder dries out the clay, which is then thrown away. Thus there is hardly anything in the world worthless than a tinker's dam."

10. Swedish Message

Myth! Greta Garbo said, "I want to be alone," in real life but not on the big screen.

Although the public has been led to believe that Greta Garbo never said, "I want to be alone," she actually did—on the screen.

211

In *Grand Hotel*, Garbo's second talkie and winner of the 1932 Oscar for best picture, the actress is a lonely ballerina who utters the statement in one of the film's not-too-memorable scenes. She had previously mouthed the line in the 1929 *The Single Standard*, but was even less effective because the film was silent and the words were merely printed on the screen.

The line became relevant only when Garbo started adopting her screen persona in real life and committing herself to a hermit-like existence. She never married, had few friends, and kept her private life strictly to herself. The words, particularly when spoken in a mock Swedish accent ("I vant to be alone"), perfectly matched Garbo's image off the set, and people reported hearing her say them whenever she was beset by her fans or the press. Finally, in exasperation, she told a friend: "I never said, 'I want to be alone'... I only said, 'I want to be let alone.' There is all the difference."

A related anecdote tells about Garbo when she was just a fledgling star receiving a fixed salary from the studio. A film she had just completed came out a hit, giving the actress the courage to approach a studio executive for a raise. When her request was turned down, she reportedly said, "I t'ank I go home." It's an unlikely story, but it remains one of the favorites of Garbo trivia collectors.

11. Choosing Bubbles

Myth! The phrase "Hobson's choice" was lifted from a film title to mean 'no choice at all'.

The Charles Laughton film *Hobson's Choice* (1954) is about a boot-maker who is desperately opposed when his daughter decides to marry one of his employees. The film title appears to be the source of the phrase 'Hobson's choice', a figure of speech meaning 'no choice at all.'

Actually, the etymology of the phrase is not traceable to the movie but to the story of Thomas Hobson (1544-1631), who owned a Cambridge livery stable that hired horses to the students at the university. On seeing that the young men were hard riders, Hobson, afraid for his best horses, which were most in demand, proposed to equalize the burden among all his animals by prohibiting his customers from choosing their steed and insisting that each rider take the first horse in line.

As interpreted by most people, Hobson gave no choice to his customers because there was only one animal to pick from—the first one in line. But this is obviously not correct, as there was one more choice open to them, and that was not to hire a horse at all. When an imperative is presented, accepting it may seem like the only choice, but in fact, it is only a hard choice since rejecting it is clearly another alternative. A real 'no choice' situation leaves no alternative—not even rejection—and forces on the subject the only course of action available.

Nevertheless, some wordsmiths brand the Hobson connection an error and the whole story false. A 1617 quotation makes no mention of Hobson, but of Hodgeson, i.e., "Hodgeson's choise, to take such privilegese as they will geve us, or else goe without."

12. Those Itchy-bitchy Years

Myth! The "seven-year itch" is an original reference to the end of a married couple's romantic period.

The 1955 movie made famous by the classic scene of Marilyn Monroe standing on a subway grating enjoying the breeze that lifts her dress is equally remembered for its title *The Seven Year Itch*. The term is often used in reference to the urge for extramarital affairs that surfaces in men after seven years of marriage, and is also a metaphor consistent with the belief that the chances of a couple divorcing are greater after seven years of marriage. In the movie, this notion is the topic of a paper that Tom Ewell is studying for possible publication by his company, but he soon discovers the condition applying to him when he encounters Marilyn after his wife and boy go away for a summer vacation in Maine.

Surveys have purportedly shown that the seventh year is the turning point in one's married life because it marks the end of the couple's romantic period and begins a risky one during which separation or divorce becomes increasingly possible. However, the more reliable studies reveal this to be a sociological myth, and that a marriage in fact enters a period of greater stability on the seventh year. According to most experts, it is almost proverbial that the longer a relationship lasts, the greater the chances it will remain as strong, if not stronger. In any case, wordsmiths say the real reason for the seven-year itch is arboreal, not domestic—the original phrase describes a rash from poison ivy recurring every year for seven years.

II

The Hitch In Hitchcock

On Hitchcock Films

"For me, the cinema is not a slice of life,
but a piece of cake."

•

Alfred Hitchcock

1. Spy up his Nose

Myth! 'North by Northwest' in the film of the same title means flying north by Northwest Airlines.

In one of Hitchcock's action-paced thrillers, harried ad-man Cary Grant is chased cross-country by spies who think he's a double agent and by the police who suspect he's an assassin. He flies to a place that people say is only vaguely suggested by the film's title and gets entangled with the villains in the famous Mt. Rushmore climax.

Vivid scenes in the 1959 film *North by Northwest* include the chase in the New York premises of the United Nations and the attack by a crop-dusting plane. However, we are told Hitchcock himself liked the Mt. Rushmore finale so much that he wanted to call the film *The Man in Lincoln's Nose*. For irony, he would have added a scene of Cary going into a sneezing fit inside the presidential nostril; unfortunately for film buffs, the park commissioner thumbed the idea down because it might defame the monument. The master eventually chose the enigmatic title 'North by Northwest', slyly suggesting that the MacGuffin lay somewhere in that direction but without admitting that the words had something to do with a location or compass bearing.

One significant scene is of Cary at an airport in Chicago preparing to fly by Northwest Airlines to Rapid City in the north central state of South Dakota, near the Mt. Rushmore National Park. But movie historians say Hitchcock intended 'North by Northwest' to have more than a literal meaning. The phrase is actually a misquotation of Hamlet's "I am but mad north-northwest; when the wind is southerly, I know a hawk from a handsaw." Being 'mad north-northwest' is to feign madness, which is exactly what Cary does in some sequences of the movie to escape his tormentors.

Despite the excellent direction, a few illogical things stick out. The crop dusting scene has no rationale, and nobody really knows what 'secrets' the spies are supposed to be dealing in. There is a memorable gaffe involving a boy who, in one tense scene, covers his ears with his hands before a gun in the background is drawn and fired.

216

2. The Twist at the End of the Stairs

Myth! 'The 39 Steps' in the movie of the same name indicates the flight of steps leading to the gallows.

Done in 1935, this vintage black-and-white thriller by Alfred Hitchcock remains unsurpassed despite two color remakes, one in 1959 and the other in 1978. While the action is sparse for a spy movie, the dialogue is a masterful blending of comedy, romance and suspense in a witty give-and-take between the male and female leads.

However, it is the 1978 remake by Don Sharp that does justice to the novel by John Buchan, who felt particularly aggrieved that Hitchcock used only "the title and ten percent of the book" for his version. Worse, the master completely missed the significance of the term '39 steps', which was explained by Buchan and justified the appearance of the words in the title. The book uses the phrase as a clue to the meeting place from where the spies intend to make good their escape, and refers literally to a flight of steps from a house that leads down to the beach. In the Hitchcock film, it becomes the ubiquitous but irrelevant MacGuffin; though whispered about by the characters with some sense of mystery and foreboding throughout the film, it is revealed at the last minute to be nothing more than the name of a spy organization.

The typical poster that advertised the picture showed a flight of steps leading to the gallows, perhaps to allegorize the predicament in which the hero finds himself after a strange woman is murdered in his apartment. But observers believe the allusion to a scaffold is improper, since there is no place in Europe where a condemned man would be made to mount more than a dozen steps before he is hanged.

According to the IMDB, Hitchcock may have committed a 'deliberate error' in the scene where Professor Jordan suggests Richard Hannay commit suicide. Jordan asks, "What if I leave you alone with this revolver?," when what he is clearly brandishing is a small-caliber semi-automatic pistol. But several gaffs occurring near the beginning of the film are not 'Hitchcockian' at all and were obviously not intended.

217

3. Lowdown on a High Crime

Myth! Hitchcock's *Vertigo* is the titular condition that afflicts the hero and compels him to retire from the police force.

Not a very popular movie when it hit the theaters the first time, many today regard *Vertigo* as Hitchcock's masterpiece and one of the greatest films ever made. Not a few of the best directors in the world include it in the list of the top ten or twenty all-time classics as a paean to Hitchcock's genius for the thriller genre.

Vertigo also happens to be one of Hitchcock's deliberately mistitled works. James Stewart is a retired police detective who is hired by an old school chum in San Francisco to keep an eye on his wife. The hero suffers from a morbid fear of high places, technically called acrophobia, which is the psychological condition that triggers the main twist in the story. Yet, what appears in the title is 'vertigo', referring to an ailment that has little relevance to the plot.

Since Stewart's character seems to suffer from both afflictions, he is careful to explain the difference between the two at the beginning of the film. Vertigo is a feeling of dizziness that usually results from an aberrant condition, such as a disease affecting the inner ear and impairing a person's sense of balance. Acrophobia, on the other hand, is a non-pathological aversion to heights, and is basically psychological, although it may sometimes produce vertigo-like dizziness, as in Stewart's case. Vertigo is an effect whereas acrophobia is a cause, and it is the latter rather than the former that prevents our hero from mounting the stairs leading to the belfry during the critical moments of the movie. Perhaps it is just as well that Hitchcock's film was mislabeled, for not all critics might have been as sympathetic had this great work been given the book's original title *From Among the Dead* or a cult horror name similar to that of Frank Marshall's *Arachnaphobia*.

Like *The 39 Steps* and other Hitchcock movies, *Vertigo* contains some errors that critics believe Hitchcock made deliberately in the spirit of fun. For instance, as Scotty and Judy are driving on a two-lane road to Mission San Juan Bautista, it is obvious Scotty is driving on the 'wrong' side of the road.

Reportedly, when this was pointed out to Hitchcock, he replied, "You drive your way; I'll drive mine."

4. Long Distance Slaying

Myth! In *Dial M for Murder*, the phone is a murder tool; in *Stage Fright*, the stage is the setting of the crime.

Although fashioned in different ways, *Dial M for Murder* (1954) and *Stage Fright* (1950) are reasonably good suspense thrillers with catchy titles.

Critics deem *Dial M for Murder*, based on the mystery play by Frederick Knotts and starring Grace Kelly, inferior to *Rear Window*, the other film Kelly did for Hitchcock in 1954. While the telephone plays a prominent part in the suspense, there is no murder, contrary to what the film's title suggests. The misnomer is abetted by movie posters depicting a woman about to stab her assailant with a pair of scissors—a killing that happens in the film but is not the crime that the ingenious detective solves in the end. Actually, what the scissors inflict is justifiable homicide, and the murder hinted by the title is not consummated. (Viewers on the watch for gaffes should see a metallic object conveniently sticking out of the victim's back before he is stabbed). Still, because of the conspiracy that Ray Milland's character hatches during the first half of the movie, there is a crime and a criminal, and the justice theme is subserved.

The title *Stage Fright* has nothing to do with the queasy feeling that sometimes overcomes theater performers, especially new ones when they make their first appearance on stage. Although the protagonists are theater actors, the plot centers on a domestic crime that has no connection to a stage performance; in fact, it is committed offstage as well as off-screen. Some suggest that the name might have been used to refer to the reaction of a character that flees after catching sight of the police, in allusion to Hitchcock's well-known phobia for armed men in uniforms.

5. "I was Rebecca's Altar Ego"

Myth! Joan Fontaine won an Oscar for portraying the title character in Rebecca.

Joan Fontaine was Oscar-nominated for her shy, naive wife of a Cornish landowner in Alfred Hitchcock's *Rebecca* (1940). Although the role's dynamics did not interest Oscar (Fontaine failed to win the statuette), the actress came back a year later to receive the award for a Rebecca-like role in another Hitchcock film, *Suspicion*.

People who have not seen the film or read the book assume Fontaine played the title character Rebecca. Rebecca is actually Maxim de Winter's first wife, who never appears for the reason that she is already dead when the picture opens. Fontaine's character as the second wife has no first name in the film and is referred to solely as 'the second Mrs. de Winter'. The flourish was from producer David O. Selznick, who felt a first name like the one in the Daphne du Maurier novel would only militate against the screen presence of the mysterious and absent Rebecca.

This effort notwithstanding, it is the creepy housekeeper, Mrs. Danvers, who has become a household word to movie buffs, thanks to the sterling performance of the character actress Judith Anderson. Hitchcock himself deviated from the original story when he caused Rebecca's death by accident instead of murder at the hands of de Winter. These indiscretions paid off, and the master's first American venture became his only work to win the Best Picture Oscar.

III

Celebrity Rolls

On Film and Stage Personalities

"A day without laughter is a day wasted."

•

Charlie Chaplin

1. Pie in your Eye

Myth! Charlie Chaplin invented the comedic routine called the Dance of the Dinner Rolls.

Two sequences most often duplicated in films are Charlie Chaplin's dance of the dinner rolls and the Keystone Kops' pie-throwing routine. Other sequences, like the reverse countdown used in sci-fi movies, appear to have been lifted from real life.

Contrary to popular belief, the actors most associated with two of the greatest comedic sequences ever seen in the movies did not invent them. John Kobal points out that the famous 'dance of the rolls', ingeniously portrayed by Chaplin in *The Gold Rush* (1925) and in this format wildly applauded wherever it was shown, "had been dreamt up and 'performed' before, magnificently in *The Cook* (1918) by Chaplin's former but since 'forgotten' co-star and comedic peer, Roscoe 'Fatty' Arbuckle."

The pie-throwing routine, which is usually credited to Mack Sennett as a concept for execution by his Keystone Kops, was not original with that wacky group. Those who can still remember attest that the silent actress Mabel Normand did not only throw the first movie custard pie at the face of Ben Turpin in a 1915 Keystone Kops comedy, she was also the first to come up with the idea. During a break at the studio, Mabel went to a bakery and bought herself a pie. When she returned, one of the crewmembers started teasing her about it, and just as Mack Sennett was coming in the door, Mabel flung the pie in her assailant's face. The rest, they say, is film history.

According to the eminent sci-fi writer Isaac Asimov, the Germans were the first to use the reverse countdown to time the launching of their rockets. Most people assume this was the basis for the movie version. Actually, it was the other way around: the Germans originated the technique in a movie and applied it only later to real rocket experiments. Fritz Lang was a German movie director, not a rocket scientist, a whole decade before World War II when he used reverse counting to dramatize a space rocket launching scene in *Die Frau im Mond* (1928).

2. A Naked Half-Wit

Myth! **Bette Davis gave the name Oscar to the Academy Award statuette.**

According to the Hollywood grapevine, the Academy Award statuette was named after Betty Davis' husband Oscar. It seems Betty herself made the claim, and rightfully did so. Having lost her flesh-and-bone Oscar, she gained two gold-plated ones in his place.

Of several persons claiming to have given Oscar its name, Bette Davis is the most popular choice. It is said that Bette, gazing at her first statuette for the 1935 *Dangerous*, casually remarked that its backside reminded her of her then husband, Harmon O. Nelson. Says one report: "Since the O. in Harmon O. Nelson stood for Oscar, Oscar it has been ever since."

Sidney Skolsky, another claimant, wrote that he had been irritated by Katherine Hepburn's best actress award for *Morning Glory* (1933), and searching for a name that would "erase the phony dignity," he remembered the popular vaudeville routine that included the comic line, "Will you have a cigar, Oscar?" Many suspect the columnist merely heard the name Oscar from elsewhere but concede that he coined the word on paper in 1934.

However, Margaret Herrick, the Academy's first librarian and later its executive secretary, had most historians backing her when she said she had picked up the statuette on her first day at work and mused: "He looks like my Uncle Oscar." Oscar was Oscar Pierce of Texas, Herrick's second cousin.

Herrick's claim is favored by the fact that there were already *known* references to the statuette as an Oscar before 1934. It is reported that in 1933, Walt Disney even "gave Oscar a new dimension after being used by others as a term of disparagement." Disney, who won best cartoon for *Three Little Pigs* that year, uttered the word in affectionate terms, and only then did Oscar pass into the language with the honored meaning that it has today.

3. The Rat Packer's Way

Myth! Frank Sinatra's singing rocketed him to early popularity without the aid of publicity.

Most any performer who became a celebrity must surely have hired some publicity to launch his or her career. But Frank Sinatra has always been held up as an exception. It was thought that he did not obtain professional services at the start because of his self-complacent belief that his voice could carry him through.

Apparently, this wasn't so. According to a source, the crooner decided to engage the services of publicity agent George Evans to promote a supporting act that he felt was not getting proper attention. Evans hired a dozen young women, trained them to jump, scream and faint, and after dressing them up as bobby-soxers, planted them at Sinatra's performances.

On Oct. 12, 1944, they did one of their routines, and immediately provoked 30,000 fans to act wildly while shrieking, "Frankie, we love you." As Sinatra stood on the stage of Manhattan's Paramount Theater singing what would become his standard repertoire of romantic lyrics, throngs of women denied admission broke store windows, stopped traffic, and generally did mayhem to get a glimpse of Ol' Blue Eyes. Most concede this was the event that made Sinatra, not realizing that, like many other landmarks in American pop culture, it had a fake start.

Sinatra would eventually become an accomplished actor, winning an Oscar for his supporting performance in *From Here to Eternity*. But his tour de force roles that would endear him to President Kennedy and other Camelot residents were in two films that eerily foretold JFK's assassination: *The Manchurian Candidate* (1962) and *Suddenly* (1954). The former later gave rise to the erroneous rumor that Sinatra, who owned the rights, withdrew the film from distribution because of its odd similarity to the killing of his political patron. The real reason, however, is purely commercial: the film had played out and necessitated its hibernation in the market.

4. The Sorcerer's Apprentice

Myth! **Harry Houdini was performing a dangerous escape act in a water cell when he died.**

Houdini's most popular act, called the Chinese Water Torture Cell, consisted of a tank of water in which he would have himself immersed in chains and stock and suspended upside down. Behind a screen blocking the audience's view, Houdini worked—or appeared to work—feverishly, and after a tense interval, he would emerge somewhere on stage dripping wet and free of his bonds. Since the feat had to be executed underwater, it posed a considerable challenge to Houdini's abilities but was not at all dangerous. The tank had hidden plugs in the bottom to let out the water in case of emergency, and the steel frame that encased him had false rivets that could be removed and replaced to free him should it be necessary.

The 1953 movie *Houdini* was a major Hollywood effort to substantiate the rumor that the great conjuror drowned during one of his sessions in the Water Torture Cell. In truth he died only after many successful performances of the act and of other acts far more dangerous, and the cause of death was an appendix that ruptured apparently from a young fan's playful punch to his abdomen. Houdini did break his foot while doing the trick in Albany on October 11, 1926, just a few weeks before his death in Detroit; the proximity between the two events as well as the mystique of the Water Torture Cell were probably what misled *Houdini*'s scripters into thinking that the act had something to do with his death.

The act has been touted by its name as having its roots in an excruciating yet simple form of torture dating back to the beginnings of Chinese civilization. But in fact, there is no known historical antecedent for any such practice. John Swain's *History of Torture* describes a rather exotic method of inflicting pain by water, but establishes no Chinese connection. "One version practiced in the West was squassation," says Swain. "A thin cloth was placed over the face of the supine restrained victim. A trickle of water was directed straight down on the face. The cloth clung to nostrils and lips and conducted water into them. The victim

225

couldn't blow or shake the cloth off because it clung. Usually they became distressed in a short time." The nearest Asian reference is

Manuel Conde's Philippine-made movie *Genghis Khan*, which depicts a form of squassation performed by the early Mongols on their captives. Other than this, there is no direct or indirect proof that the method was originally Chinese, or that the relatively modern Japanese, Korean, Vietnamese and Cambodian forms of water torture, from water hosing to slow drowning, had an ancient Chinese origin. The Chinese appeared to have eschewed the art of water torture because it was not exquisite enough to meet the standards set by their ancestors.

Incidentally, the common noun 'houdini', meaning magician or conjuror, and the verb 'to do a houdini' are popularly believed to be in honor of Harry Houdini. The application of Houdini's name is no doubt sincere but it is based on a couple of fallacies. First, Harry was an escape artist, not a true magician, and second, he was born Erich Weiss in Budapest, Hungary, not Harry Houdini in Appleton, Wisconsin, as he had always claimed. The rightful owner of the name that has become synonymous with 'magician' is Jean Eugene Robert-Houdin, the great 19th-century French magician who founded the modern school of magic and from whom Houdini borrowed his alias and some of his techniques. Robert-Houdin, whose talent lay in making the mundane awesome to behold, was once touted as the only man who could stop his pulse at will despite the claim of his rivals that anyone could do the trick by simply pressing against a 2-inch-thick wad of cloth placed under the armpit

As a teenager, Houdini read the memoirs of Robert-Houdin and immediately resolved to take on his mantle and name. The irony of this devotion is that later on, when Houdini became an even greater celebrity than Houdin, he endeavored to demolish the name of his hero by writing *The Unmasking of Robert-Houdin*. Critics say he did this spiteful act for no real reason other than to feed his ego, and, worse, he was unscrupulous in distorting the facts to fit his case.

5. Wonder Boy

Myth! Sir James Barrie invented the term "The Admirable Crichton."

When we hear the phrase "The Admirable Crichton," our thoughts settle on the literary character wonderfully portrayed by Sir Thomas Urquhart (1611-1660) in his *The Exquisite Jewel*. Others are reminded of the title character of Harrison Ainsworth's novel *The Admirable Crichton* (1837), as well as the fictional butler in Sir James Barrie's 1902 play of the same name.

Urquhart himself revealed that he based his work on a real 16th-century boy wonder who excelled in the arts and sciences and in languages. A son of Robert Crichton, lord advocate of Scotland, he was believed born in 1560 and named James Crichton. He earned his master's degree at the age of 15, and grew up to be an expert swordsman, a poet, an accomplished athlete, a fine horseman and a skilled marksman. Aldus Manutius, an Urquhart contemporary, said that he spoke ten languages, could compose Latin verse on any subject, was a mathematician and theologian, was extravagantly handsome and with the bearing of a soldier. Unfortunately, wrote Urqhart, Crichton was only twenty-two when he was killed in a defenseless position by his own pupil, Prince Vincenzo Gonzaga, son of the Duke of Mantua, out of jealousy for a mistress' affection.

Oddly, not Urquhart, Manutius, Ainsworth or Barrie originated the phrase "The Admirable Crichton." It was borrowed from a Scottish poet, John Johnston, who first applied it in his 1603 work Heroes Scoti. Since that date, the phrase has meant any man of precocious talents, unusual grace and superior accomplishments.

6. All Ears

Myth! Clark Gable inspired Bugs Bunny's ears.

Clark Gable is often mentioned as the inspiration for Bugs Bunny, but for the wrong reason. People think Gable's fabulously big ears had something to do with the shaping of Bugs' own. Actually, Bugs is not meant to look like anything but himself—a cartoon rabbit. The real Gable connection is in Bug's carrot-chomping technique, which was drawn straight from one of the actor's scenes in the 1934 Oscar-winning movie *It Happened One Night.*

Clark is only one of several significant influences in the creation of the rabbit. According to Jerry Lazar ("Hare Roots," *Bugs Bunny's 50th Anniversary Magazine*), various aspects of Bugs' make-up were lifted from real persons, all celebrities. "Bug's signature cry, 'Of course you realize this means war!' came directly from the lips of quipster Groucho Marx." Lazar notes that Bugs' World War II-era Warner Bros. animation directors "stole liberally from street-tough James Cagney and swashbuckling Errol Flynn, with a smattering of Dead End Kids thrown in. To make him funny and smart, they borrowed heavily from Jack Benny's comic timing and Dorothy Parker's put-down witticisms. Bug's pranks and misadventures owe a great debt even to the slapstick routines of early silent-film stars, such as Harold Lloyd, Charlie Chaplin and Buster Keaton." To complete the picture, Lazar surmises that Bugs' coolheadedness under pressure may have been an emulation of the great Humphrey Bogart.

But while Bugs and his public agree totally with Fudd's characterization of him as a "wabbit" despite his long ears, the titles of many of his cartoons (not to mention the pieces written about him, such as Lazar's) employ the word "hare" or its homonyms ('hair,' 'air,' 'heir,' etc.), raising the possibility that he may really be a hare. Some say this may be because "hare" lends itself easily to puns (e.g., "falling hare"), but others insist on the fact that animators throughout Bugs' history have treated the terms 'rabbit' and 'hare' as synonymous. Taxonomically, of course, "they are not synonymous, being somewhat similar but observably different types of lagomorphs. Hares have much longer ears than rabbits, so Bugs might seem to be of the hare family, yet rabbits live in burrows, as Bugs is seen to do." The word "bunny" does not help answer this question, as it is a synonym for both young hares and young rabbits.

Besides the lisping Fudd, Bugs' bête noires include another inarticulate character, the stuttering Porky Pig. Porky, like Bugs, is faced with an identity problem, but is nevertheless famous from his cameo role as the host who closes every Warner *Looney Tunes*

228

and Merrie Melodies with "Th-th-that's all, f-f-folks!" Being old as he is (the pig is the earliest in the Warner animated lot, and was 53 years old when he did a reprise of himself in the 1988 *Who Framed Roger Rabbit?*), Porky should not, technically speaking, be called a pig but a hog. In American farm usage, young swine are pigs, but they become hogs when more than three months old. It is in Canada and Great Britain where no distinction is made and swine of all ages are referred to as pigs. In the same manner, Miss Piggy, who is old enough to be anybody's girl friend despite her youthful pretensions, should be called Miss Hoggy. One thing more: she should not be made to squeal when pleased, since pigs and hogs never squeal with delight. Their squealing, which can reach noise levels up to one hundred fifty decibels, is actually a sign of distress.

7. The Best Year of his Life

Myth! A soldier who had lost both hands in World War II became the first person to win an Oscar without having acted previously in any medium.

Barry Fitzgerald secured two nominations in 1944, one for best actor and the other for best supporting actor, but what's amazing is that both nominations were for the same role in the picture *Going My Way*. Since a double nomination unfairly increases the nominee's Oscar chances for the same performance, the Academy decided to prevent a recurrence by making a rule change immediately after Fitzgerald won the Best Supporting award.

While Fitzgerald is the only actor to win an Oscar based on two nominations for the same role, the only actor to win two Oscars based on one nomination for the same role is Harold Russell. The Academy wanted to be sure that Russell, a disabled veteran who appeared as himself in *The Best Years of Our Lives* (1946), was rewarded for his courage in making a movie despite the loss of both hands in the war. Fearing that he might not win, the governors awarded him an Honorary Oscar "for bringing hope and courage to his fellow veterans." When he came out the winner that same night as best supporting actor, Russell found himself holding two Oscars for a single nomination, a feat that has not been

229

disturbed to this day. It was the reverse of what Emil Jannings and Janet Gaynor had achieved before: one Oscar for several performances in different pictures. Nominated once in the first Academy Awards in 1928, Jannings won best actor for *The Lost Command* and *The Way of All Flesh*, and Gaynor won best actress for *Seventh Heaven, Angel Street,* and *Sunrise.*

The award put Russell in the list as the first non-professional actor to win an Oscar. But strictly speaking, this wasn't his first appearance on screen. He had performed at least once before in an army Signal Corps documentary, which was precisely how director William Wyler spotted him for his acting role. The only person to win an acting Oscar without having acted previously in any medium was Dr. Haing S. Ngor, the Cambodian who was awarded for his supporting role in the 1984 *The Killing Fields.* Ironically, Ngor was murdered in 1996 somewhere in the killing fields of Hollywood.

Russell undoubtedly merited his acting Oscar, but the special Oscar he received for the inspiration he provided to other war veterans was apparently undeserved. For Russell was not exactly a war veteran, and while it is true he lost both hands when they were blown off on D-Day, this was not at one of the invasion points in France but in an explosion at Camp MacKall in North Carolina. Russell, who had never seen real action, was then with the 513th Airborne Division, preparing explosive charges with nitro-starch packages and blasting caps when the accident happened.

Russell eventually sold his Best Actor Oscar to raise funds for the operation and care of his wife.

---

8. Head Turner

Myth! Lana Turner was discovered while sipping soda at Schwab's.

Thanks mainly to fan magazines and press releases, the movie-going public generally believes that a number of female movie stars of Hollywood's Golden Era (from the 1930s to the 1960s) were discovered at the counter of Schwab's Pharmacy on Sunset Boulevard and Laurel St. Schwab's itself lent credence to the myth by claiming that Hollywood characters went there in pursuit of publicity even though their real reason was to play pinball at the back.

Schwab's eventually became the movie colony's most famous drug store, and the prototypical story is that Lana Turner, one of the most glamorous Hollywood actresses of the 40s and 50s, was discovered there in 1936. The 16-year-old Lana, née Julia Turner, was playing hooky from school when she was found dressed in a sweater sipping strawberry malt at the counter. She was immediately hired for a sweatered cameo appearance in Mervyn Le Roy's film, *They Won't Forget* (1937), and the role—that of the murder victim—made her an instant star and tagged her forever as Hollywood's original "Sweater Girl." Leon Schwab, the long-time proprietor of the drugstore, couldn't remember the incident, somehow reinforcing the claim that Lana was really seen at Currie's Ice Cream Parlor in the city, and she wasn't sipping soda but was serving it to customers as an employee. Lana denied all versions, including that of William Wilkerson, publisher of the *Hollywood Reporter*, who attested to his having "discovered" her himself at the Top Hat Malt on Sunset and Highland Avenue, a couple of miles to the east from Schwab's.

IV

Music In A Falsetto Voice

On Anthems and Songs

"The best-laid schemes o' mice an' men
gang aft agley."

•

Robert Burns

1. British Air Apparent

Myth! The tune 'God Save the King' is uniquely British.

Britain has a number of patriotic songs, but the one that's held high as a national anthem is 'God Save the Queen' (or 'the King', depending on who's sitting on the throne). Yet, as endearing as the tune may be to the British, it's not uniquely their own. The music is the current anthem of many other Commonwealth countries, and was once used in the same manner by Germany, Russia and Sweden. A historian notes, "Over the past two centuries, it has been the anthem of Vienna (1782), Prussia (1795), Switzerland (1811), Bavaria, Mecklenburg, Schwerin, and Liechtenstein. All in all, 20 countries, including Britain, have appropriated it as a patriotic song."

One who believes the British ought to be complimented for sharing the song with much of Europe has another think coming. The authorship of both the music and the lyrics of 'God Save the King' is still uncertain, and of the several candidates named, none is British. As one critic puts it, "Nothing is to be owed to Britain, since no one really knows who the author is and the tune is without an original nationality."

Most of the reports agree that the British version was first heard at the Drury Lane and Covent Garden Theatres on several successive nights in September 1745. Though this seems to be the earliest the anthem was played anywhere in Europe, it does not necessarily give the lie to the claim that the tune was originally French. A well-known French historian is said to have written that, during the reign of King Louis XIV, "Jean Baptiste Lully (1632-1687) composed also the music of a song called 'God Save the King', which the English afterwards borrowed and which they made into their National Anthem."

William Chappell, a noted music critic, dissents, saying it was the Englishman Henry Carey (1690-1743) who wrote the words and music of 'God Save the King' for a banquet at Mercer's Hall, Cheapside, in London to celebrate the birthday of King George II. Carey himself never acknowledged this, but after he died in 1743 his son carried on a campaign for recognition and the corresponding pension. In 1814 Richard Clark, organist of

Westminster Abbey, wrote that Carey was indeed the composer, though not the lyricist. After eight years he retracted the statement and gave the credit for the lyrics to Benjamin Johnson (1574-1637) and the music to Dr. John Bull (1562-1628).

There is apparently no official British version of the anthem's origin, but what comes closest is the assertion that the words were written by an unknown lyricist to a tune composed by Thomas Augustine Arne (1710-1778) and sung for the first time in 1745. However, Arne's work, which is displayed in the British Museum, is a mere arrangement and not an original composition. The confusion about Arne's involvement with 'God Save the King' may have been because he composed Britain's other national anthem, 'Rule, Britannia'. The latter first appeared in a masque entitled 'Alfred' and produced in August 1740 at Maidenhead in Cliveden House. James Thomson (1700-1748), author of 'The Season', wrote it, while Arne did the composition at the command of the Prince of Wales, before whom it was performed.

2. Better Sung than Red

Myth! The French Revolution inspired the communist 'Internationale' as well as the anthem 'La Marseillaise.'

The French Revolution may have inspired a lot of things, but not the two best-known European anthems, as claimed. The first, the 'Internationale', is from its name French and not Russian, although it served as the Russian national anthem until 1944. Both the tune and the lyrics were done during peaceful times almost a century after the French upheaval. The original French words, which Eugène Pottier (1816–1887), a woodworker of Lille who would later become a member of the Paris Commune, wrote in 1870, were intended to be sung to the tune of 'La Marseillaise'. But Pierre De Geyter (1848–1932) set the poem to his own music in 1888 and his melody became widely used soon after. It eventually became a symbol of revolution (but not of the French) when European socialists adopted it as a rallying tune, and it has since remained a popular workers' song.

The second tune, the French national anthem 'La Marseillaise', was produced in 1792 during the uprising, but it was to oppose the revolutionary cause rather than to uphold it. The words were laid out "in a fit of patriotic fervor after a public dinner" by a young officer of the royal engineers named Claude Joseph Rouget de Lisle (1760-1836), who had intended it as a marching song for the loyal side under the name 'War Song for the Rhine Army'. But the music was far from original, having been ripped off a composition, *Variazioni sulla Marsigliese per violino e orchestra*, done by the Italian Giovanni Battista Viotti a full eight years before de Lisle adapted it in his quarters at Strasbourg in 1792. The song caught on, and in a few months a party of revolutionaries from Marseilles was singing it with gusto as Barbaroux led them into Paris for the attack on the Tuileries Palace—hence the title 'La Marseillaise.' As an added irony, de Lisle was cashiered and thrown into prison in 1793 and would have been guillotined had he not been saved during the counter-revolution.

3. A-kickin' we will Go

Myth! In the Australian national anthem, 'Waltzing Matilda' is a kangaroo.

To a non-Australian, the name Matilda often evokes the image of a kangaroo dancing—sometimes even jiving—to a waltz. The impression is further heightened when he sees in some parts of the world—not necessarily Australia—trained kangaroos dancing or boxing in animal exhibitions. The perception Down Under is much different, however: 'Matilda' is a bag, pack or knapsack, and 'waltzing Matilda' is a homespun expression for the way one carries or 'humps' his bag or pack as a tramp does. Additionally, there is hardly a kangaroo in the great outback that's called Matilda. The Australian icon is male, and the most popular name given to him is Joey.

Despite the misconception, 'Waltzing Matilda' is the song most identified with Australia, and perhaps the only one to come from there that can be remembered to any degree outside the continent. Contrary to popular belief, however, it is not and has never been that country's national anthem. It is, to be sure, the national song, but the real anthem is the lesser-known 'Advance Australia Fair'.

4. Long, Long Ago

Myth! The poet Robert Burns composed the Scottish song 'Auld Lang Syne'.

'Auld Lang Syne', Scotland's most popular air, is often described as an old Scottish folk tune that the country's most famous poet, Robert Burns, fell in love with and added words to. Burns is said to have written the lyrics as a poem in 1788 and adapted it to the century-old melody in 1796. He stated in a letter that he had never seen the music in print before, and had taken it down only from the singing of an old man. 'Auld Lang Syne' first appeared with Burns' lyrics in *Scots Musical Museum,* a collection of traditional tunes on which the poet worked in the last decade of his life.

Yet there are some references that insist Burns not only wrote the lyrics but also originated the music in one of his moments as a composer. Most critics do not agree. One, a Manchester Guardian correspondent, suspects that the tune is not even of Scottish origin, after hearing it in a religious procession in Corsica where he was told it was 'a very old Corsican tune'. Those who believe the tune is Scottish would give the credit to William Shield, a composer who grew up near the Scottish border and was fond of incorporating traditional airs into his creations. Shield is known to have rendered the tune in imitation of bagpipe music and featured it in his opera *Rosina* in 1783.

There is evidence that two tunes bearing the name 'Auld Lang Syne' existed in the previous century, but neither was acceptable to Burns. It is more probable Burns lifted the air from a melody entitled 'The Duke of Buccleugh's tune', printed in a collection called *Apollo's Banquet* and issued after the middle of the seventeenth century. What is also probable—and embarrassing to Burns fans—is that the poet wasn't wholly original with the lyrics either. The earliest germ of 'Auld Lang Syne' is found in an anonymous poem of the 15th century, which George Bannatyne inserted in 1568 into his well-known manuscript of Scottish poetry, now in the Advocates' Library. The title of the poem 'Auld kindnes Foryett' when translated to modern Scottish is "[Should] auld acquaintance [be] forgot"—the first line of all the subsequent poems on the subject.

Another poem printed in Watson's collection of Scottish verses published in 1711, or several long decades before Burns' work, is entitled 'Old Longsyne', and consists of twelve stanzas of eight lines written throughout in English, with the exception of the term 'Syne' occurring in every stanza. 'Old Longsyne', which shows considerable similarity in its first verse and chorus to that of Burns, has been ascribed to Sir Robert Aytoun, a courtier and well-known poet who followed James the Sixth to England and subsequently became private secretary to the Queen. However, some doubt Aytoun's authorship, since he did not live in rebellious times, the setting mentioned in the verses. According to them, the more plausible author is Francis Sempill of Beltrees, who lived in the middle of the seventeenth century, one of a family that produced poets for four successive generations. While the poem is not in Sempill's style, it is in a manuscript book containing his poems.

Burns' defenders are wont to disregard these charges against 'Auld Lang Syne's originality, saying that, "as Shakspeare has plagiarised 'Romeo and Juliet' from an old Italian tale, and Handel has cribbed the 'Hailstone' chorus from Carissimi's 'Jonah', Burns is in the same list...What all the three named artists touched they embellished—they found dry bones and breathed into them life."

5. Sing a Song of Six Pence

Myth! **The song 'Happy Birthday to You' earns royalties for the songwriter every time it's sung.**

According to the Guinness Book of World Records, it is the most popular song in the English language, and though it has been translated into many languages, it is often sung with the English lyrics even in countries where English is not a primary language. Yet its melody consists of a mere six notes and its lyrics of four words that repeat a number of times in a four-line verse. Originally composed in 1893, both words and music are protected by copyright for a term that extends to 2030. The ditty was valued the first time it changed hands at a minimum $5 million and earns royalties at an average $2 million a year. The copyright hasn't

237

been challenged seriously because the holder is the formidable Warner Chappell, the largest music publisher in the world and a member of the giant AOL Time-Warner media conglomerate.

The song is the simple, ubiquitous and celebratory 'Happy Birthday to You'. It all started when two spinster sisters, Mildred and Patty Smith Hill, teachers from Louisville, Kentucky, wrote the short melody 'Good Morning to You' as a song to welcome young students at the beginning of each school day. The publication of the tune the same year credited the lyrics to Patty and the music to Mildred, but it is not clear if a copyright was obtained under the laws then in effect. What is apparent is that, because of some technicality in the procedure or a failure on the part of the sisters, the song went straight to the public domain as soon as it was published.

The lyrics of 'Happy Birthday to You' would later appear for the first time in 1924 when one Robert Coleman added it to 'Good Morning to You' as its second verse and included the combination in a songbook. Without acknowledging or identifying the authorship of the piece, Coleman published 'Happy Birthday to You' separately from 'Good Morning to You' in *The American Hymnal* in 1933. The Broadway play *Band Wagon* featured the birthday song later that year, catching the attention of a third Hill sister, Jessica, who filed suit for infringement.

The outcome of the suit is unclear, but in 1935, the Clayton F. Summy Company, acting in behalf of the Hill sisters, published under copyright a Preston Ware Orem arrangement of 'Happy Birthday to You'. Obviously, this was in recognition of the principle that public domain material could be altered and made copyrightable provided the alteration is substantial and constructive. But, critics argue, this was hardly the case with the changes wrought on 'Good Morning to You', which involved no more than substituting the words "Happy Birthday" with "Good Morning" and splitting the first note corresponding to the word 'good' to accommodate the two syllables in the word 'happy'. Moreover, there was no indication that the Hills or the Summy Company authored the amended tune with its split note, or that the publication was with notice of copyright under the 1909 U. S. law. For this reason, the 1935 registration may have been flawed, and may explain why Warner has limited its action against perceived violators to sending cease and desist letters in lieu of prosecuting cases of infringement actively.

In any case, it is not correct to say that a royalty must be paid to the Hill sisters every time 'Happy Birthday to You' is sung. Firstly, under the terms governing Warner Chappel's acquisition of Summy (reportedly for $25 million), only half of the proceeds of copyright is to be paid to the sisters through their foundation (apparently a charitable one). Secondly, while royalties are due when the song is performed, recorded, or reproduced in a commercial manner, they are not payable if the use is for a non-profit and/or private purpose. Thirdly, it is believed that if the tune is sung anywhere without the birthday lyrics, or with said lyrics altered, the copyright does not come into play. Lastly, royalty payments are not automatic but are usually negotiated depending on the song's intended use. In the cases cited by Wikipedia, the amount of royalty charged each time the song is sung ranges from $5,000 to $10,000.

---

6. Rest Stop

Myth! The song 'God Rest Ye, Merry Gentlemen' is a warning to Christmas merrymakers against too much drinking.

One remembers well an old rhyming prayer that children used to say at bedside, which went like this: "Now I lay me down to sleep, I pray the Lord my soul to keep; If I should die before I wake, I pray the Lord my soul to take." Adults today have remained comfortable with the words, failing to notice that an error is repeated twice in the four-line stanza. Only a reading of its source, the Book of Common Prayers, reveals that the article 'the' in the phrase 'I pray the Lord' is really the pronoun 'thee'. The correct line, 'I pray thee, Lord, my soul to keep', shows the appeal to the Almighty to be an even more personal one.

Fortunately, the missing letter 'e' has not had much effect on the text of the prayer, unlike in one famous Yuletide song, where a misplaced punctuation has changed the whole meaning of the lyrics. The title of the song, which also appears in parts of the text, is often printed as 'God rest ye, merry gentlemen', with a comma between the words 'ye' and 'merry', implying a pause at this

239

location where there should be none. Thus, the common understanding is that the song is a cautionary salutation to holiday celebrants who have a tendency to get high from much Christmas merrymaking. But with the comma lying properly between 'merry' and 'gentlemen', the line is sung as 'God rest ye merry, gentlemen', and the word 'merry' preserves its old meaning of pleasing or suitable or agreeable (as in Merry Christmas), as opposed to happy, frolicking or lively. 'Merry' is thus made to define 'rest' rather than 'gentlemen', giving the entire line its proper meaning of "May God grant you peace, gentlemen." The phrase 'rest you merry' may sound Irish, but it is really English and dates to the beginning of the fifteenth century.

7. A Handle on Handel

Myth! Handel's famous Christmas oratorio 'The Messiah' was first presented in London before King George at Christmas time.

The belief that George Frederick Handel composed 'The Messiah' as an oratorio for Christmas has unwittingly promoted three misconceptions.

First, the proper title is 'Messiah', not 'The Messiah' as it is often called. Second, the piece was first performed in a music hall in Fishamble Street, Dublin, on April 13, 1742, and not in Covent Garden before the King at Christmas time. Third, while the oratorio has been one of the musical mainstays of the holiday season, it was not composed for a Christmas purpose or for any other celebration.

Handel was asked to write 'Messiah' in 1741 by Dublin's Lord Lieutenant, who wanted to raise money for the city's charities. Feeling desperate because his opera *Deidamia* had been a resounding flop the previous year, the composer approached his task with great resolve—according to him, like a "divine intoxication." The music premiered in 1742 before an awed Dublin audience and became an unprecedented success for the fading composer.

The close association with Christmas came about because of the composition's memorable chorus 'For Unto Us A Child Is

Born'. And its London presentation the following spring, with King George attending, created such an impression that it inspired the myth of the Christmas debut. The king was so moved during the 'Hallelujah Chorus' that he involuntarily stood up, and thereafter it has become traditional for every monarch to do the same during a command performance.

---

8. Out of Time and Place

Myth! John Denver composed 'Take Me Home, Country Roads', to honor his home state of West Virginia.

Now and then, we come across a popular song whose lyrics unabashedly misrepresent the circumstances of its creation. That is to say, the words, though fervent and meaningful, are not true to the time and place in which they were written.

• One can't imagine, for instance, the late John Denver being anywhere else than in the bucolic parts of his home state of West Virginia when he composed the hit song, 'Take Me Home, Country Roads.' In reality, he didn't write the song nor was he anywhere near West Virginia at the time it happened. The writers were musicians Bill Danoff and Taffy Nivert, who, like John, had never been in West Virginia when they made up the song. While driving through the country roads of Maryland on their way to a Nivert family reunion, the two decided to create music to pass the time away. Bill had been impressed by pictures of rural West Virginia, and couldn't help but mention the state in the song as they motored through the countryside along the winding, tree-lined roads. Before the tune fully became 'Take Me Home, Country Roads', Bill and Taffy sang it at a Washington, D.C. folk club in 1970, and it was then that John Denver, who was also performing there, heard it. The three of them stayed up all night finishing it, after which Denver put it on his next RCA album on his way to stardom.

• In 1908, Jack Norworth (1879-1959) was on a NYC subway train when he spotted an advertisement for the old New York Giants club. He scribbled some words on a scrap of paper and, as the legend goes, had his song 'Take Me Out to the Ball Game' in thirty minutes. What he actually wrote were just the words, which

241

he later asked his friend, composer Albert von Tilzer, to set to music. Both succeeded in capturing the spirit of the game in a ditty that soon became baseball's unofficial anthem. The anomaly in this oft-repeated musical anecdote is the little known fact that neither Norworth nor von Tilzer were baseball fans at all, and worse, they had no inkling of how the game was played. In fact, Norworth didn't see his first ball game until 1942, long after the song had become popular, and von Tilzer until 1928. Incidentally, the song did not catch on immediately, at least not until Norworth turned it into a 'Nickelodeon slide show' featuring sing-along lyrics and illustrations shown at movie theaters between films.

• The US Marine Corps copyrighted the song 'The Marines' Hymn' in 1920, although only the words are of military origin. An anonymous Marine wrote it as a poem during the Mexican-American War, probably in 1847, and then, somewhat altered, it was sung for several decades by Marines to an old Spanish folk tune. Meanwhile, Jacques Offenbach created a duet for his comic opera *Genevieve de Brabant*, which he entitled 'Two Men in the Army'. The opera was quickly forgotten after its staging at the Metropolitan Opera House in October 1868, but the tune remained popular in France and America. When new generations of Marines found the marching rhythm of Offenbach's music fitted closely the meter of their popular military poem, the first patriotic song to be based on an opera melody was born. Incidentally, the 'shores of Tripoli' mentioned in the second line of the song is not in Lebanon, as is often thought. While there is a port city named Tripoli in that part of the Mediterranean, the Tripoli referred to is the one in Libya, which, contrary to the belief that it is all desert, has a long coastline lying on the Mediterranean Sea. The phrase is a paean to the naval war waged by the US marines in the early 1800s against Tripoli when it was still independent from Libya, to oppose its demand for increased payment of tribute purportedly for protecting US shipping against the Barbary pirates.

9. Whose Side were they on Anyway?

Myth! A Yalie composed 'The Whiffenpoof Song', and a Johnny Reb wrote the song 'Dixie'.

242

• Whenever and wherever Yale students or alumni get together for some celebration or camaraderie, one will almost surely hear an individual or a group singing the strong but plaintive sound of the Whiffenpoof Song in *a capella* fashion. The song is popular among Elis on and off campus, but it's a special favorite of the Yale fraternal organization Skull and Bones, a secret society that has included some of the most powerful men in America's history, including two or three presidents and CIA directors. The school anthem plays a significant part in Robert De Niro's *The Good Shepherd*, which shows the purported evolution of the CIA from the ranks of the fraternity. The title comes from being the traditional closing number of the century-old (in 2009) Yale Whiffenpoofs, the longest existing collegiate *a cappella* group in the US.

Outside Yale's ivied walls, its most avid interpreter from the 1920s onwards was Yale man Rudy Valee, but Rudy did not compose the song as is generally believed. Die-hard Yalies won't like the idea at all, but the composer is a young man named Guy H. Scull, who happens to be a graduate of that *other* school, Harvard (1898). Scull produced the tune right after his graduation, then had it published in sheet music form in 1909. A Yalie, Meade Minnigoode (Yale 1910), liked the music well enough to provide the lyrics, but here again, the sons of Eli are in for a disappointment. Far from being original, Meade's words borrow heavily from the poem 'Gentlemen Rankers' by Rudyard Kipling. Nonetheless, Vallee's style and dedication would push the song to its heights in 1927, and twenty years later, Bing Crosby would make it a post-war hit. Further commercialization of the Whiffenpoof Song by pop artists like Louis Armstrong, Elvis Presley, Count Basie, Perry Como and the Statler Brothers, as well as through TV programs like 'Baa, Baa, Black Sheep', has not reduced the decibel level of its singing at Yale one bit.

• Five years before the Civil War, when Abraham Lincoln ran for the presidency in 1860, the marching song 'Dixie' was used as a campaign song against him. But he liked the tune so much that on the afternoon he learned of Lee's surrender, he ordered the band to play it on the front lawn of the White House. As it was then the unofficial national anthem of the Confederacy, Abe thought it was of Southern origin and had been acquired by the North as a war trophy. Actually, 'Dixie' was composed by a white Northerner,

243

Daniel Decatur Emmett, who is often erroneously believed to be black because of the kind of music he wrote for blackface minstrel shows. The song started as the number "I Wish I Was in Dixie's Land" on the playbill of one of Emmett's shows, which was staged in New York's Mechanic's Hall on April 4, 1859. A group of peripatetic musicians, Bryant's Minstrels, carried 'the melody to New Orleans in 1860, and soon after it became their signature number. For some years, people whistled the tune only in the South, contrary to Emmet's intention never to use it as an inspirational Southern hymn. Through sheer popularity, 'Dixie' acquired cult status during the war as it was sung on and around battlefields by the Rebels to boost their morale against the North. Emmet came up with the word 'Dixie' in reference to Manhattan farmer Johan Dixie. However, Southern usage confused it with the name of Jeremiah Dixon, one of the founders of the Mason-Dixon Line, and eventually, the term became synonymous with the states below the Mason-Dixon line.

Fantasy & Mythology

I

Animal Farm

On Aesop and his Fables

"We hang the petty thieves and
appoint the great ones to public office."

•

Aesop

1. Ease up on Aesop

Myth! Aesop was a Phrygian slave with a hideous appearance that contrasted with his brilliant sallies of wisdom.

Since very little is known about Aesop, many suspect he is only a legend and his name a conventional representation of the real inventor or inventors of the fable. The Greeks, it is said, liked to ascribe each kind of composition to a real or fictitious "finder out." The *Histories* of Herodotus, written in the second half of the fifth century BC, nevertheless insists that Aesop really did exist as a Phrygian slave belonging to a Samian citizen called Iadmon in the sixth century BC. An Egyptian biography in the year AD 1 added that when he gained his freedom from his master, he went to Babylon as a riddle solver to King Lycurgus. The description of Aesop by later writers is cartoonish and hard to believe. He is alleged to have been "a preternaturally ugly, misshapen little man, whose hideous appearance contrasted strikingly with his brilliant sallies of wisdom. He made everyone laugh not only by the cleverness of his story-telling but by his grotesque manner and his stammering speech."

Modern critics suggest these sources have confused Aesop with another well-known fabulist, Phaedrus, an ugly slave who was born in Macedonia but lived most of his life in Rome and became a freedman of the emperor Augustus.

2. Fabulous Fabulator

Myth! Aesop authored many of the fables we know today.

This may come as a surprise, but none of the fables we know today and assigned by tradition or popular belief to Aesop was written by him at all. A few were found on Egyptian papyri that were 800 to 1000 years older than Aesop's time, which was 6 BC. The larger part of the more than 350 that have come down to us through the ages were written long after Aesop, with the first known collection becoming available 200 years after his death.

Phaedrus, the writer most often mistaken for Aesop, was a freedman of Augustus who, in the reign of Tiberius, translated some of the ancient fables into Latin verse, interspersing them with anecdotes of his own. The fable of the fox and the grapes and of the tortoise and the hare—long traditionally regarded as Aesop's—were actually written by Phaedrus.

Even assuming Aesop was a real person, we do not know if he or any of his contemporaries wrote down his works, since none of the so-called Aesop's fables we are familiar with today can be traced to him. Only Aesop's name and the belief that almost all fables, including newly invented ones, originated from him have endured.

3. Wildcat Strike

Myth! According to Aesop, a 'lion's share' is a major portion of anything.

The common phrase 'lion's share' is a metaphor for a kingly portion or a hefty part of anything. This connotation goes back to ancient times, when Aesop is believed to have composed the story of the lion, the fox and the ass. These three went out hunting together and, using their respective talents, bagged a prey. The lion divided the spoil into three equal portions, presumably one for each of them. But when it came to the actual sharing, he took the first portion as "the king of the beasts" and the second as "a partner in the undertaking." As to the third, he looked at his two sidekicks with a baleful eye and said, "Unless you give it up to me and get out of here fast, you will be very sorry."

In another version, the ass, appointed to do the dividing, apportioned an equal amount as best he could to each of the three. But the lion felt offended, and in a rage set upon the ass and killed him. He then asked the fox to do the dividing himself, and the sly but very scared animal bit off a small piece for himself and left all the rest to the lion.

In an even more deviant version of the fable, the lion and three co-hunters—a heifer, a goat and a sheep—caught a large fat stag.

248

Under the eyes of his companions, he divided the carcass into four equal portions, taking the tastiest part for himself. Then he took another portion, claiming it as his right for being the strongest. Without blinking an eye, he appropriated a third, saying this was due him for being the most valiant. Pointing to the fourth portion, he told the other animals, "This belongs to you, but touch it if you dare!"

We can probably tolerate the idea of the lion, the fox and the ass communicating with each other like humans, as this is an essential feature of this kind of fable, but the three cannot be expected to act in other things against their individual natures. Like "A Case for Patience," their story suffers from certain incongruities with real life, not the least of which is that, being of different types, they can band together to do a common task. Furthermore, it is the lioness rather than the lion that normally does the hunting, whereas an ass, heifer, goat or sheep has neither the tendency nor the ability to hunt for prey no matter how small. The biggest anomaly, of course, is a lion's share being regarded as a share when it comprises the whole thing, with no portion remaining for at least one other. This is different from the currently accepted meaning of the phrase, which assumes that a lion's share, no matter how substantial, is less than the whole. This change of signification was first noted in Edmund Burke's *Reflections on the Revolution in France*, published in 1790.

---

4. Nature of the Beast

Myth! In most of Aesop's fables, animals acting like human beings teach a lesson in morality or prudence.

A fable is traditionally defined as a short story populated by animals acting like human beings and designed to teach a lesson in morality or prudence. This is not necessarily true of Aesop's fables, however. Although animals were the earlier and more popular type of characters in the genre, more than a quarter of the extant fables attributed to Aesop are not about them. Many of these anthropomorphic classics involve only plants or inanimate objects, such as the sea, rivers, the sun and the winds; others had gods, human beings or both, but no animals.

Uncle Remus, who, contrary to his myth, was white and not black, is probably the most consistent in the use of human-like animals, such as Br'er Rabbit, yet not one of his stories is considered a fable. Some say this is because Uncle Remus' tales do not offer a moral lesson, but neither did Aesop's 'fables' when they were first written. Every moral ending in a fable is a post-Aesop invention added to the original. Some are not even moral but merely counsel on prudence or dish out worldly wisdom based on observation of people's behavior. Others are not expressed in epigrammatic form and are only implicit in the narrative. Still others, as S.A. Handford notes, are more immoral than moral—for example, "how to get the better of an enemy (or even of a friend), how to keep a whole skin by subservience to the possessors of power, how to profit by other men's misfortunes and mistakes, and in general how to turn everything to good account for oneself."

5. Crying Game

Myth! The Greeks originated the fable about the boy who cried "wolf."

It seems fairly well established that, while most of the fables did not come from the same person, the same people—the Greeks of Asia Minor—crafted them. Still, there is evidence that the Greeks lifted many of their ideas from the Indians, the Egyptians, and the Assyrians. It is even likely that one of the most classic of these fables—about the boy who cried wolf—was based on either Chinese folklore or Chinese history.

Everyone familiar with Aesop knows about the young shepherd who, bored with watching his sheep, decided to play a prank on the villagers by shouting, "Wolf!" In some versions, he had his comeuppance when a real wolf ate him in the end, while in others, the wolf merely ate his flock. It is no longer certain which of the two versions is the original, but researchers have succeeded in tracing the basic plot to the rich literature of the East, specifically China. The history of the place suggests that literature may have influenced—or been influenced by—a real-life event involving the Chinese emperor Yuang Wan of the Mongol Dynasty, who "cried wolf" as a way of spreading alarm to confuse his enemies.

6. Creature Feature

Myth! The fable "A Case for Patience" proves foxes would do anything to get corn.

The fable entitled "A Case for Patience" tells about a half-starved fox who crept into the hollow of an oak-tree to get at some bread and meat left there by shepherds. After eating, his stomach became so distended that he could not get out again. Another fox who was passing by and heard his complaint told him, "Well, stay there till you are as thin as you were when you went in; then you'll get out quite easily."

Horace in his *Epistles* has a version in which the fox enters a corn bin, but as noted by A. S. Handford, "Richard Bentley was so outraged by this—since foxes do not eat corn—that he proposed to read *nitedula* (shrew-mouse) instead of *vulpecula*." There are other fables that contradict facts of natural history, and which no doubt Bentley found equally disturbing. What makes his kind of reaction amusing is that it shows little tolerance for the slightest inconsistency, yet takes for granted the biggest incongruity for which fables are famous, which is that animals talk and act like human beings.

II

A Gander At The Goose

On Nursery Rhymes

"Good, better, best. Never rest until good be better.
And better best."

•

Charles Perrault

1. Goose Story

Myth! **Mother Goose, neé Elizabeth Foster Goose, had her first book published by Thomas Fleet in 1719.**

Although what is popularly known of Mother Goose is limited to the figure that is often depicted in children's books—a colonial housewife riding a huge high-flying goose—there are claims that this mysterious rhymer and storyteller is a mythic rendering of a real person. One appeared in a magazine article in the mid-nineteenth century, alleging that Elizabeth Foster Goose invented some nursery rhymes and her son-in-law, printer Thomas Fleet, published them in Boston in 1719 in a book titled *Songs for the Nursery, or Mother Goose's Melodies for Children.* Elizabeth Foster was born in Boston in 1665, married one Isaac Goose (or Vergoose) at age 27, and reared sixteen children, six of whom were her own and ten her husband's. But no one is really certain that Fleet published a book in 1719, or that if he did, it was the collection of rhymes and jingles that the widowed Elizabeth composed for the benefit of his oldest child. A copy of the work or any indication of what it contains has yet to be found.

Queen Bertha, wife of Pepin the Short and mother of Charlemagne, has also been mentioned—in fact, long before Elizabeth—as the inspiration for the fantasy figure. She was said to have had a peculiarity—webbed feet—and for this reason was called Queen Goosefoot. She often posed in pictures sitting at her spinning wheel and telling stories to children seated around her, leading some to believe she was at least the model for the Mother Goose illustrations.

These two contenders notwithstanding, there has been a consensus that Mother Goose is none other than Charles Perrault, who popularized the concept of fairy tales and the name of their mythical teller. He could have been Father Goose, of course, but the title has already been appropriated for Walt Disney as the leading animator of Perrault's fairy world.

2. Not Suitable for 5 and Under

Myth! Mother Goose rhymes were designed as verses for little children.

There is evidence that Mother Goose rhymes and songs, while decidedly English in origin, existed long before Thomas Fleet had any book published in 1719. Panati notes that, in the eighteenth century and before, they were not children's verses at all but stanzas from bawdy folk ballads, tavern limericks, popular proverbs, romantic lyrics and social satire. The only true rhymes composed for the nursery were rhyming alphabets, infant games and lullabies. The adult material was later sanitized at the onset of the Victorian era and their application extended by making them suitable for children. Many of the lyrics were based on actual people and contained hidden symbolisms or significance—a further indication that they were originally intended to be appreciated by adults. Little Jack Horner, for instance, was the Bishop of Glastonbury, England; Jack Spratt was a fat churchman named Archdeacon Pratt; Little Boy Blue was the influential sixteenth-century statesman and cardinal Thomas Wolsey; and Humpty Dumpty may have been either King Richard III or a nobleman close to him, both of whom, like their fictional counterpart, met an untimely end.

The belief that nursery rhymes are basically children's fare stems from the idea that the silly-sounding verses have a juvenile meaning and demand only a literal translation. Those who take a more than cursory look are surprised to learn that, on the contrary, nursery rhymes have a lot to say about the real world, and that even the most familiar ones offer mature stuff completely different from what they came to know as children. Consider the 350-year-old lines: "Pat-a-cake, pat-a-cake, baker's man! / So I will, master, as fast as I can: / Pat it, and prick it, and mark it with T, / Put it in the oven for Tommy and me." The letter 'T' is usually taken as the initial for Tommy based on the context, but since the name Tommy does not occur in all versions, it seems more likely that the 'T' was intended to be the sign of the cross and not the initial of a person. The custom in the Medieval Ages, when the rhyme came about, was to mark various baked goods with the sign of the cross, often depicted as a T, a relic of this practice being the hot cross bun. Another verse, "See-Saw, Margaret Daw," was originally sung in the seventeenth century by builders, purportedly in accompaniment to the to-and-fro motion of a two-handed saw. But some folklorists say that in those days, the term "Margaret Daw" was slang for a prostitute. They are inclined for this reason to support the bawdy suggestion that "see-saw" is a description of how a prostitute moves while she is engaged in her trade.

The beginnings of some rhymes are well established, but others have murky or alternative sources. For instance, the rhyme "Mary, Mary, quite contrary" originated in the eighteenth century with both a religious and a secular meaning. The Catholic view is that "silver bells" are "sanctus bells" of the mass, "cockle shells" are badges worn by pilgrims, and "pretty maids all in a row" are ranks of nuns marching to church services. Mary is none other than the Blessed Virgin. The secular and more popular thinking is that "Mary" is Mary, Queen of Scots, who was "quite contrary" in her tastes and preference for things French. Her "pretty maids" were her four ladies-in-waiting all named Mary: Mary Seaton, Mary Fleming, Mary Livingston and Mary Beaton. The cockleshells were the decorations on an elaborate gown given to her by the French dauphin.

"Ride a Cock-Horse (to Banbury Cross)," a product of pre-18th century England, is about "a fine lady upon a white horse." It is believed that the reference is to Lady Godiva, the eleventh-century noblewoman of Coventry who, according to her legend, rode naked on a white horse to protest her husband's tax impositions. But Panati offers another alternative. The "fine lady," he says, may have been Celia Fiennes, daughter of a Member of Parliament in the 1690s, and the phrase "To see a fine lady" may have been a corruption of "To see a Fiennes lady." Lady Fienne is a logical candidate because her family owned a castle in Banbury, and she had a reputation for riding magnificent horses on long stretches of the English countryside.

3. A Short Lamb's Tale

Myth! Sarah Josepha Hale wrote the nursery rhyme "Mary Had a Little Lamb".

Sarah Josepha Hale became famous for composing the nursery rhyme "Mary Had a Little Lamb," which was first published in her name in the September 1830 issue of *Juvenile Miscellany*. It later became known that the 24-line verse was based on a real incident involving ten-year old Mary Sawyer, who had a pet lamb that followed her to the schoolhouse at Redstone Hill in Boston one day in 1817. Mary's brother talked her into hiding the lamb under her shawl and sneaking it inside. The teacher discovered the indiscretion when she called upon Mary to recite the day's lesson and the sheep followed her to the front of the class.

Mary Sawyer confirmed this story a half-century later (at which time she was already Mrs. Mary Tyler), but denied it was Hale who did the verse. She said it was John Roulstone who, as a young man, had seen her and her lamb walk to school, and had been so amused by the sight that he recorded it in rhyme. Hale merely added a couple of moralistic stanzas of her own before printing the whole poem in her magazine. Despite Hale's insistence that she was the sole author, the restored Redstone schoolhouse now bears a memorial plaque crediting Roulstone for the first three quatrains of the poem and Hale for the rest. Notwithstanding the cloud on its authorship, the work became so popular that when Thomas Edison invented the phonograph, the first sound he recorded on it was the poem "Mary Had a Little Lamb."

4. Humongous Human Goose

Myth! Charles Perrault coined the name 'Mother Goose'.

Charles Perrault, a French lawyer-turned-writer of fairy tales, wrote Tales *of Times Passed* in 1697. On the frontispiece of his edition was pictured an old woman engaged in spinning and telling stories to a man, a girl, a boy and a cat. A placard near the picture says *Contes de ma Mere l'Oye*, which, translated, means "Tales of My Mother Goose." The book contained fairy tales rather than nursery rhymes, but it was ahead of Thomas Fleet's reputed 1719 publication in the use of the name Mother Goose.

It is nevertheless unlikely that Perrault himself invented the name or character of Mother Goose. According to Andrew Lang, the term was employed as early as 1650, half a decade before Perrault, in Lorret's *La Muse Historique.* Perrault may have lifted it from an even earlier source—either the "Frau Gosen" of German folklore or an imaginary French housewife known for her incredible tales.

5. Goose Dressing

Myth! Old Mother Hubbard and Jill are two of the more popular females in nursery rhymes.

There are two famous female nursery rhyme characters that were actually males in their real-life incarnations. The first is Old Mother Hubbard, whose rhyme was written by Sarah Catherine Martin in 1804. Martin apparently based her piece on a poem published in 1803 by T. Evans under the title of "Old Dame Trot, and Her Comical Cat," but which had been known for almost a hundred years, having been published originally in 1706. As the principal character in a satire, *Mother Hubbard's Tale*, Mother Hubbard herself was a popular cartoon figure in 1590 whose real-life model was the eighth-century French martyr St. Hubert, patron saint of hunters and dogs. The saint was a matronly-looking cleric, the bishop of Tongres-Maestricht, who died at Tervueren on May 30, 727, following injuries suffered while hunting.

The second female-cum-male is Jill of the famous Jack-and-Jill tandem who "went up the hill to fetch a pail of water." Jack was the influential sixteenth-century Cardinal Wolsey, and "Jack fell down and broke his crown" means Wolsey failed in his efforts to negotiate a peace between France and the Holy Roman Empire of the Hapsburgs in 1518, causing the full-scale war that involved Britain. Jill is portrayed in a 1765 British woodcut of the rhyme as a boy named Gill. According to some folklorists, Gill is Cardinal Wolsey's close colleague, Bishop Tarbes, who accompanied him on his frustrated peace missions. The bishop is depicted as a female in the rhyme for no other reason that that he wore long robes as his official attire.

6. Dum-dee-dum-dum-dum

Myth! Lewis Carroll invented the names "Tweedledum and Tweedledee" for the two little fat men in his book *Through the Looking Glass.*

Lewis Carroll used the names Tweedledum and Tweedledee for two little fat men that Alice encounters in the book *Through the Looking-Glass.* These funny but bizarre characters are so alike in appearance and mannerism that Alice is unable to tell them apart except through the names embroidered on their jackets. This is probably why the nicknames Tweedledum and Tweedledee are often given to any two people or groups resembling each other so closely that they are practically indistinguishable.

Actually, it was John Byrom (1692-1763), not Carroll, who invented the names for the purpose of satirizing two quarreling schools of musicians between whom there was very little difference. One school had for its champion Giovanni Battista Bononcini (1670-1747), with whom the Duke of Marlborough and most of the nobility sided, while the other was led by George Frederick Handel (1685-1759), who was supported by the Prince of Wales, Alexander Pope and John Arbuthnot. It was from this feud that Lewis Carroll obtained the idea of two almost identical twins preparing to go to battle over a damaged rattle without really meaning to. Carroll helped popularize the phrase and its fantasy setting, but it is Byrom who must be credited for coining the names in mockery of persons who think and act the same way yet still find the occasion to engage in needless squabbles.

7. Reborn in the Nursery

Myth! The nursery rhyme characters Jack Horner, Old King Cole and Humpty Dumpty are all fictional.

'Old King Cole', 'Jack Horner' and 'Humpty Dumpty' are titles of nursery rhymes about certain people, long regarded as mythical, and their strange doings. But there was actually a King

Cole in Britain during the third century, although nothing much is known about him. All we know from the song is that he "was a merry old soul" whose idea of fun was to smoke a pipe, drink from a bowl (probably a jug or glass of wine), and listen to his "fiddlers three." Robert of Gloucester said he was the father of St. Helena and consequently grandfather of the Emperor Constantine.

Little Jack Horner wasn't a king but an emissary named Thomas Horner, who was sent by the bishop of Glastonbury to deliver some deeds of title to King Henry VIII. Placed in a Christmas pie, the deeds were to be a bribe to his majesty to dissuade him from confiscating the richest Roman Catholic abbey in the kingdom. During the trip, Thomas (his name was later changed to Jack to suggest a 'knave') dipped his hand in the pie and pulled out a "plum," i.e., stole a deed to a private estate called Mells Manor, into which he later moved his family and where his descendants continue to live today.

Finally, Humpty Dumpty was King Richard III, who is said to have been a hunchback and, therefore, "egg-shaped," and the fall from the wall is an allusion to the beating he took from Henry VII at the Battle of Bosworth. His defeat was so convincing and his reputation so shattered that the York line could not be put "together again," i.e., restored to the crown, which was usurped by the Tudors.

III

Evergreen Tales From The Neverland

On Fairy Tales

"Every man's life is a fairy tale
written by God's fingers."

•

Hans Christian Andersen

1. Unbending Ending

Myth! **Most fairy tales end with the line, 'And they lived happily ever after'.**

Misled by our childhood memories, we are surprised to learn that no real fairy tale ends with the phrase, "and they lived happily ever after." Of the earliest known English forms of such tales, only a few—perhaps not more than five—wind up with words to that effect. A large number of fairy tales, in fact, do not end happily at all. Students of the genre point out that in some, not even the hero or heroine escapes with their life.

We think of fairy tales in terms of Cinderella, about a poor, hard-working drudge who is transformed by magic into the belle of the ball. After reading through a wide collection of these tales, we realize that what puts Cinderella on par with the others is not a happy ending but one that restores the character to a previous reality. Indeed, for the Cinderella story, the closing phrase, "And she lived happily again," would have been more appropriate. In both the Walt Disney and Charles Perrault versions, Cinderella is not a menial or an ordinary girl. Rather, she is a beautiful and contented heir until her stepmother and stepsisters take over the family home and abuse her. Contrary to the popular understanding that she is a miserable creature made happy in the end by magical intervention, she is actually a cheerful girl who, while having to suffer temporarily, ends up being happy again. In other fairy tales, the restoration may be to a previously unhappy or tragic state, but the pattern is the same.

How fairy tales begin is a different matter. Most, particularly those for younger children, open with the line, "Once upon a time." But the phrase, though commonly used in the English translations of Hans Christian Andersen and the Brothers Grimm, has never been unique to this kind of stories. According to the Oxford English Dictionary, 'once upon a time' is a stock phrase used in oral and written storytelling in the English language since at least 1732. The phrase occurs most frequently in narratives produced by and for children, as well as in the retellings of myths, fables, and folklore.

261

2. A Life quite Ordinary

Myth! **Most fairy tales are based on the concepts of royal romance and magical transformation.**

It's disappointing to learn that the traditional story opener and ender we liked to hear as kids are not necessary fixtures of the fairy tale. It's doubly disappointing to know that the 'Cinderella' concepts of royal romance and magical transformation are not usually found in fairy tales either. The two elements are present in such classics as 'Snow White and the Seven Dwarfs', 'Sleeping Beauty', 'Beauty and the Beast' and 'The Frog Prince', but these stories are in the minority. In most of the tales, royalty is absent and transformation to a state of bliss is effected not by magic but by the perfect love of one person for another. Any magical change that occurs is really a disenchantment, or the breaking of a spell. The only transformation is of a character degraded by some curse at the beginning of the story and later restored to his or her original form.

3. Loathsome Spirits and Lithesome Sprites

Myth! **The most common character in fairy tales is the fairy godmother.**

We sometimes argue ourselves hoarse on who is the most common character in fairy tales. If children were given the vote, the clear winner would be the fairy godmother.

The fact is there are no characters common to fairy tales. Princes and princesses, giants and witches, and fairies and fairy godmothers are all familiar types, but they are not common as common is. A fairy tale generally contains some supernatural element that is clearly imaginary, yet it is seldom about fairy-folk and may not necessarily even feature an enchanted person. Andersen and the Brothers Grimm did not often use wish-givers or enchanters as characters in their stories, and much less did Charles Perrault. The Grimms featured elves, giants and animals transformed into people and vice-versa, but hardly any fairies. Probably because of the rich history of witchcraft in Scandinavia in the middle ages, Andersen deployed more witches in his stories than any other type of magical creatures.

Unlike the tales themselves, the term 'fairy tale' is modern, having entered the language only in the eighteenth century. The origin is France—not Perrault, as some would expect, but his contemporary, Madame d'Aulnoy, whose *Contes des fees* was published in 1698 and translated into English the following year as *Tales of the Fairys*. Why Madame d'Aulnoy used the term 'fairy tale' when there are practically no fairies in her work is unclear. Nevertheless, the phrase caught on and by 1752 was well established.

Most people learn about fairy godmothers from fairy tales and Walt Disney films, not realizing that the concept is much older than the stories themselves. According to the lore, fairies originally had only one function, and this was to appear in a household soon after a birth and bestow various gifts upon the newborn child. If the baby's family treated them with tact and sensitivity, they rewarded the infant with gifts of beauty, tranquility and loving kindness. Otherwise, if any of them were improperly treated at their reception, they would add some curse or taboo that would affect the child for the rest of its life.

The fairy myth has been corrupted over time by numerous fallacies, one of which is that fairies possess the power of invisibility. The original belief is that birds, horses, dogs, cattle and all other animals see fairies clearly, whereas humans see them between two blinks of an eye and thus catch only fleeting glimpses. Human inability to focus properly on fairy beings is very likely the basis for saying they are invisible. The notion that there is a separate habitat known as Fairyland is also revisionist. What tradition dictates is that fairies co-exist with us in our own world, although some species live in societies inside hollow hills or in the great mounds of earth, known as barrows or tumuli, that prehistoric tribes erected either as forts or as monuments to dead chieftains. And the entire fairy race is not limited to the court of Queen Titania and Prince Oberon, who are indeed the overall rulers of the little people but whose subjects are spread all over the globe.

4. Grimm Reality

Myth! The Brothers Grimm invented the fairy tales that they wrote.

The best-known writers of fairy tales, aside from Hans Christian Andersen, are the brothers Jacob and Wilhelm Grimm. It is often believed that, like Andersen, the Grimms invented the stories themselves. This is not so. The siblings did not produce originals but only reworked folk tales gathered from earlier collections and by word-of-mouth from other storytellers. They were compilers, not authors, and even in this regard, they were not dedicated folklorists. Their 1812 masterpiece, *Grimms' Fairy Tales*, was only a by-product of their professional interest in language, grammar and history.

According to most references, the claim that the two obtained their materials "wandering about the country, gleaning from peasants and the simpler townspeople a rich harvest of legends, which they wrote down as nearly as possible in the words in which they were told," is a hoax. The Grimms were German ultranationalists who only pretended to write down tales told by peasants and common folk as if they were tapping into an authentic German oral tradition. In fact, their major sources were educated, middle-class and French. Most were well-to-do friends and relatives who provided the brothers with stories that they radically rewrote to their own taste, later passing them off as genuine German folktales.

5. A Mythifying Dane

Myth! Hans Christian Andersen was a gentle aristocrat who specialized in writing fairy tales for children.

In 1952, Danny Kaye portrayed Hans Christian Andersen as a kindly aristocrat who devoted himself entirely to writing fairy tales. The movie role, according to the critics, is "completely fabricated." The real Andersen was born in 1805 to a sickly

264

shoemaker and an illiterate washerwoman. He got over his desperate circumstances to become the author of the famous *Tales, Told for Children* at the age of thirty and eventually the master of the art fairy tale. However, he also authored plays, novels, poems, travel books and several autobiographies. The first six years of his productive life (1829-1835) were in fact devoted almost exclusively to writing plays, although none was successful.

Andersen's children's stories are not strictly children's fare and do not conform to the popular mold of fairy tales. According to the Britannica, they are "informed by moral realism rather than wish fulfillment," and the villains are "not fantasy characters but rather human weaknesses—vanity, snobbery, or selfish indifference." Many of the tales are deeply pessimistic and end unhappily, deviating entirely from the 'ugly ducking to graceful swan' norm for which Andersen is popularly known.

Finally, his literary works, diaries and letters reveal Andersen not as a kindly gentleman but as an ambitious, high-strung, vain and sensitive man. Contrary to his myth, nobility was not manifest in his appearance, attitude or behavior. It is not true he was the illegitimate son of the future King Christian VIII of Denmark, or an aristocrat who was well cared for and allowed to grow up in respectable middle-class stability.

6. Malice in Wonderland

Myth! Love and friendship prevail even as unwarranted sex and excessive violence are taboo in fairy tales.

Since fairy tales were designed for children, they can't have too much sex and violence. Right? Wrong. In fact, even though the fantasy field is no stranger to sex and violence, these elements are more common in fairy tales than in ordinary folklore. The animated versions are relatively sanitized for family consumption, but in the original tales, violence is portrayed with tasteless abandon and sex is only a whit subtler.

For example, in the Grimms story of the Little Mermaid, the witch cuts out the heroine's tongue, she doesn't get to marry the Prince, she fails to kill him with a magic dagger, and she jumps into the ocean and dissolves into sea foam. Versions earlier than Perrault's feature a scene of Cinderella's stepmother cutting off the toes (ach!) and heel (ouch!) of her eldest daughter so her foot could fit into the slipper. In a Hungarian version of the Frog Prince, it wasn't a kiss but sex that transformed the enchanted frog into a prince. After the frog had spent the night with the girl and turned into a handsome youth, "they hastened to celebrate the wedding, so that the christening might not follow it too soon." Snow White's stepmother arranges her murder, doves peck out the eyes of Cinderella's stepsisters, Briar Rose's suitors bleed to death on the hedge surrounding her castle, and a mad rage drives Rumpelstiltskin to tear himself in two. These are just a few of the graphic descriptions of murder, mutilation, cannibalism, infanticide and incest that run through the gamut of fairy tales and are so uncharacteristic of what we remember of them.

In fact, the spinners of fairy tales originally intended their works for adults, even though in many cases, they regarded as their source the tales that servants or other women of lower class would tell to children. It was only in the modern era that the tales were recast in other versions in response to parental demands to make them suitable for children. The Brothers Grimm concentrated mostly on eliminating sexual references by way of compensating for the increased violence that was inflicted particularly on the villains. With the onset of the Victorian era, the tales were stripped even of the violence and redesigned to teach lessons, as when Cinderella was made to contain temperance themes. There were protesters, of course, including Charles Dickens ("In an utilitarian age, of all other times, it is a matter of grave importance that fairy tales should be respected") and psychoanalyst Bruno Bettelheim, who believed the expurgation "weakened (the tales') usefulness to both children and adults as ways of symbolically resolving issues."

7. Starting on the Wrong Foot

Myth! Cinderella's slippers are made of glass.

The story of Cinderella has hundreds of versions, most of which describe the heroine's slippers (not shoes) as being made of gold, silver, or rare metal, sometimes bedecked with gleaming gems. Other versions use conventional materials like leather, cloth or fur. The later stories based on Perrault make mention of glass slippers, presumably so the prince can see through them and detect any attempt at fraud. Glass has since become the standard, although how it got into the picture was purely unintentional. In the earliest French renditions, Cinderella wore *pantouffles en vair*, or 'slippers of white squirrel fur', but Charles Perrault confused the word *vair* with *verre*, or 'glass', and inserted the latter in the title 'Cinderella: or, the Little Glass Slipper'.

Perrault would seem to have committed another error by failing to specify if the slipper was for the left or the right foot, but historians tell us he didn't. Perrault could not possibly have distinguished between the right slipper and the left because there was no way of making a distinction in those days. Until well into the 19th century, shoes and slippers in Europe and even in the US were made by hand and could be worn on either foot.

The Grimms version throws two more slippers into the story, and in that respect differs from Perrault's (and Disney's). The Grimms' heroine attends a three-day festival, and each day she loses a slipper. Beginning with the first day, the Prince makes an unsuccessful search throughout the kingdom, until on the third, he has the palace stairway coated with pitch to catch her slipper one last time.

---

8. While She was Sleeping

Myth! In many fairy tales, the heroine's love interest is named Prince Charming.

The name Prince Charming is often associated with fairy tales in which a handsome royal scion saves the heroine from a spellbound or unhappy condition. The word has crept into everyday language to mean any girl's hero, the man of her dreams, the one she hopes will save her one day from a dreary existence. This is a misconception because there is no prince by that name in any known fairy tale, whether written or animated. In the stories, the heroine is usually named but the hero is anonymous, and the sole exception—Sleeping Beauty's Prince Philip—is given his appellation only in the Disney film.

Both Disney and Perrault show Sleeping Beauty as a sixteen year-old who falls into a one-hundred-year sleep, during which she does not age a bit. Based on real time, however, she is 116 years old and at least two generations older than the Prince when he wakes her up. In 1636 Giambattista Basile wrote the classic story on which the fairy tale is patterned as part of his Pentamerone, and in it we are not told how long Sleeping Beauty slept, although it is made clear that she grew older during her stupor. She was a teen-ager when placed under the spell, and was a mature woman when she woke up. A married nobleman hunting in the woods, who had discovered our heroine, kissed and then raped her, and while still asleep, she gave birth to twins who suckled at her breasts.

9. Bears on her Back

Myth! 'Goldilocks and the Three Bears' is one of the most beloved of fairy tales.

For one reason or another, many stories that are traditionally regarded as fairy tales have been given a second look and adjudged as not true to the mold. For example, 'The Yellow Dwarf', 'Thumbelina', and 'The Tinder Box' are now seen as purely literary tales. 'Little Red Riding Hood' and 'The Three Bears' have nothing magical about them other than that the animals can speak. Some that are truly magical, like 'The Three Wishes' and 'The Princess on the Pea', are fables rather than tales of romance. The stories about Tom Thumb, Jack the Giant Killer, Puss in Boots, Hansel and Gretel, and Rumpelstiltskin, while providing their share of marvelous events, are essentially adventure yarns and only incidentally romances.

By way of example, 'Goldilocks and the Three Bears', despite its unknown origins, continues to be regarded by most people, including teachers and critics, as a fairy tale. Actually, it is not a fairy tale but a children's story believed to have begun with the British poet laureate Robert Southey in 1837. Southey's principal character was originally an ugly old crone, but during the next seventy-five years of retelling, she metamorphosed into a young

268

girl called Silver-Hair in 1849, Golden Hair in 1868, and finally Goldilocks in 1904. The story was once described as the only instance in which 'a tale that can be definitely traced to a specific author has become a folk tale'.

This distinction lost ground in 1951, when Southey's authorship was placed in doubt with the discovery of a manuscript of 'The Story of the Three Bears' in the Osborne Collection of Early Children's Books at the Toronto Public Library. The new find was an 1831 'nursery tale' rendered in verse and embellished with drawings. Apparently, it had been offered as a birthday gift to a little boy named Horace Broke by his 32-year-old maiden aunt Eleanor Mure. The story, though six years older, differed from Southey's version in only a few respects. The central character was the same old woman but the bowls in the parlor contained milk rather than porridge. While Southey's intruder jumped out of the window when discovered and was seen no more, Eleanor Mure's verses ended with the bears musing among themselves as to what to do.

Southey may not have been the original author of Goldilocks and the Three Bears, but it is concededly the Briton who immortalized the tale and his text that has become the standard for most versions.

---

10. Fantasie Francais

Myth! The fairy tale genre originated in France.

The lesser-known Charles Perrault (1628-1703) has a body of work that's even more famous than those of Andersen and Grimm; having preceded the other two by almost two hundred years, this French author offers a better claim to the title of inventor of the modern fairy tale. Perrault laid the foundation for the new literary genre, with classic tales like 'Little Red Riding Hood', 'Sleeping Beauty', 'Puss in Boots'', 'Cinderella', 'Bluebeard' and 'Donkeyskin'. His most famous stories are still in print today and have been made into operas, ballets (e.g., Tchaikovsky's Sleeping Beauty), plays, musicals and films, including many of the highly-successful animated features of Walt Disney, Pixar and DreamWorks.

This is not to say, however, that the fairy tale originated in France. According to most historians, the likeliest venue for the invention of the genre is—you guessed it—ancient Egypt, with Confucius' China running a close second.

---

11. Wolf Bait

Myth! The concept of the wolf as a woman chaser evolved from the story of Little Red Riding Hood.

People believe justice was served when a wolf-hunting human in 'Little Red Riding Hood' did in a woman-hungry wolf. Little did they know the hunter never figured in the original story. In all of the early versions, including Charles Perrault's, Little Red Riding Hood and her grandmother were both killed and devoured by the wolf. It was only because illustrators refused to provide any artwork for the gruesome ending that later revisionists spared Red through the intervention of a saving mechanism, in most of the versions a hunter.

The Brothers Grimm's adaptation, written one hundred twenty years after Perrault's, is the only one that spares the grandmother as well. However, she survives only after she and Red go through the ordeal of being swallowed whole by the wolf. A huntsman rips open the wolf's stomach with a pair of scissors and frees both.

It was once believed that the concept of a 'wolf' as a man who spends much of his time chasing women came from the misadventures of Red Riding Hood and her grandmother, if not from the earlier nursery rhymes that featured the wolf as a villain. These sources were eventually disproved, however, when it was revealed that the term acquired its current colloquial signification in the US only about 1930, and it had no link whatever to any fairy tale or nursery rhyme.

12. Up a Tree

Myth! The expression 'fi, fie, fo, fum' is first heard from the mouth of the giant in 'Jack and the Beanstalk'.

The expression 'fe, fi, fo, fum', which is common to most British tales of blood-lusting giants, was made popular by the ogres in 'Jack the Giant Killer' and in some versions of 'Jack and the Beanstalk' (the two Jacks are not one and the same, as is often believed). But it did not originate in these stories or in any other fairy or folk tale.

The first known instance of its use is in an English adventure story of the fifteenth century, as a war cry made by a warrior when he sighted an enemy approaching. The expression was next mentioned by Thomas Nashe, who, in his 1596 work 'Haue with You to Saffron-Walden', wrote "Fy, fa, fum, I smell the bloud of an Englishman." Later, Shakespeare mentions the phrase in a line in King Lear, written c. 1605, through the character Edgar mouthing snatches of old verse during his assumed madness: "Childe Rowland to the darke Tower came, / His word was still, fie, foh and fum, / I smell the blood of a Brittish man." The Nashe quote presumably also referred to Childe Rowland, not to a giant, and provided the basis for the Shakespeare line.

According to scholars, none of the stories of a giant uttering the expression can be traced to a date earlier than the 18th century, and no tradition of magical giant-killing tales is evident in early English oral folklore.

13. Seven Footmen

Myth! Disney's Snow White and the Seven Dwarfs is faithful to the Grimms' original.

The first published version of Snow White and the Seven Dwarfs (or Dwarves, to the grammatically inclined), by the Italian Giambattista Basile in his Pentamerone, calls the heroine Lisa. Two hundred years later, the Brothers Grimm heard the story from their two sisters-in-law and renamed the heroine Snow-drop. Snow White is Disney's own invention, and so are the names of the seven dwarfs.

Disney brought the Grimms' version to the screen in 1937, but was not completely faithful to it. He left out that part in the German original in which the queen, believing the heart that was brought to her to be Snow White's (in fact it was a young boar's), had it salted and ate it. Disney also eliminated the Grimms' account of the queen's fate, particularly her donning red-hot slippers of iron and dancing until she dropped dead.

Disney is the only one who has Snow White revived by a kiss, an obvious plagiarism of Sleeping Beauty. In all other versions, she wakes up when an accident dislodges the apple from her lips. In the Disney and Grimm versions, Snow White was seven years old when abandoned in the woods and apparently not much older when murdered. How she could have matured into a young woman while confined in a small glass coffin is something to think about. Basile provides a magical but rational element: the coffin is a wooden casket that is made to grow long with Lisa over the years.

14. Foot-bound for the Ball

Myth! Cinderella is a French fairy tale.

The notion that Cinderella was born in France was first suggested when the French folklorist Charles Perrault included the story in his *Tales of Times Passed* published in Paris in 1697. It was later brought up that Perrault merely retold a Scottish tale about Rashin Coatie, a lovely impoverished girl with three abusive stepsisters and a wicked stepmother.

Panati now tells us that the earliest known version was not from Scotland but from China, where the original name of Cinderella was Yeh-hsien. Written between AD 850 and 860, the Chinese tale contains the essential Cinderella elements: a stepmother and her ugly daughter, a fairy (a magic fish), a ball (a Chinese festival), a prince (a wealthy merchant), and a golden slipper. The recorder was Taun Ch'eng-shih, one of history's

272

earliest folktale collectors, who wrote that he first learned the story from a servant who had been with his family for years.

The story of Yeh-hsien has obvious similarities with, and appears to be the pattern for, over 700 extant versions of the tale in scores of languages. Still, there is doubt that Taun Ch'eng-shih's rendering is the original. According to People's Almanac No. 2, in a nature myth that goes back even further than the ninth century, "Cinderella, representing the dawn, is persecuted by her foul-tempered sisters, representing the dark clouds of night, and is ultimately rescued by the sun—the handsome prince."

---

15. Little Green Baddies

Myth! Some apples contain toxic elements that may prove fatal to the eater.

The story of Snow White has done much to compound the already negative image of the apple as a purveyor of injury and even death. It all started with Eve, of course, when she bit into the forbidden fruit and tempted Adam to do the same, bringing about evil in the world. An apple allegedly caused the legendary 10-year conflict called the Trojan War, while in real life, the fruit, with razor blades imbedded in it, has become a Halloween icon.

Then comes the child's myth of the Barefoot Boy promoting the old wives' tale that an apple's greenness by itself will cause a stomachache. There is no medical proof that this is so. According to the United States Department of Agriculture, the stomach has no way of differentiating between ripe and unripe apples. Green or otherwise, apples will not cause sickness provided they are "eaten slowly and sufficiently chewed."

Experts do point out that there is some difference between ripe and unripe fruit that may cause some disturbance in the stomach. The unripe apple contains more acid and long-chain pectin, which produce gas in the stomach, and people differ in their ability to handle acids and gas in the digestive system. For this reason, some people will have problems eating green apples, but not to the point of making them sick.

All of the above seek to put the apple in some disrepute, but what proposes to hack down the apple tree completely à la George

273

Washington's myth is the belief that the pit of the fruit contains cyanide. This is only partly true, however. Apple seeds are mildly poisonous because they contain a small amount of amygdaline, a cyanogenic glycoside, but a large amount would need to be chewed to have any toxic effect.

16. Fruit Fatale

Myth! In the original fairy tale, the queen gives Snow White a poisoned apple.

The possibility of the forbidden fruit not being an apple looms large in both the Genesis story and the one about Snow White. In the classic fairy tale, the evil queen can't live with the idea that Snow White is fairer than her, and plans to do away with the maiden. She makes several attempts to kill Snow White, first by pulling her lace tight in order to stifle her breath, and second by gifting her with a poisoned comb, but Snow White survives both. In her third and final attempt, the queen offers our heroine a poisoned apple, which puts her into a deep sleep "for a long time." She is awakened only when a piece of the apple stuck in her mouth is dislodged while the prince is carrying her coffin away.

In early appearances of the fairy tale, the poisoned apple wasn't around; instead, the witch-queen applies a poisoned stab (Celtic) to, or places a poisoned ring (Armenian and Greek) on, the girl's finger and delivers her into a death-like trance. The Brothers Grimm are believed to have concocted the idea of the apple for their own version after adopting the main plot from older sources.

IV

Life Is A Riddle And Man Is The Answer

On the Greek Classics

"The difficulty is not so great to die for a friend,
as to find a friend worth dying for."

•

Homer

1. Oedipus Wrecked

Myth! Oedipus was the first known sufferer of Oedipus complex.

An Oedipus complex is when a son feels an excessive erotic love for his mother and a corresponding hatred or hostility for his father. Sigmund Freud, the first to analyze this psychological condition, chose the name because he saw some similarities with the myth of Oedipus. However, Freud's implication that Oedipus was the first known victim of the aberration is not correct. In Oedipus complex, it is essential that the fantasizing child know exactly who his parents are. Unlike a true sufferer, our mythical hero did not, and hence could not have harbored any filial feelings when he killed his father and married his mother. Being totally unaware of his relationship to either parent at the time, he had no understanding of the true nature of his acts albeit they were voluntary.

As a baby, Oedipus had been left alone to die because of an oracle's prediction that he would one day kill his father. He was saved and brought to King Polybus of Corinth and his wife Merope, who nurtured him as their own son. Grown up to manhood in the belief that the two were his real parents, he decided to leave home to prevent the prediction from happening. He was journeying near Delphi when he met his real father, King Laius of Thebes, and killed him in a quarrel. The Thebans, not suspecting that Oedipus was their ruler's slayer, elevated him to the vacant throne as a reward for solving the riddle of the Sphinx. Pressed by his new position, Oedipus married Jocasta without any inkling that the widowed queen was his true mother.

To lift a plague that had struck Thebes, the oracle ordered that the murderer of Laius be discovered and expelled from the city. Oedipus was found out, whereupon he took out his eyes and Jocasta committed suicide. Critics say that, by meting on himself a gruesome and undeserved punishment, Oedipus showed an abnormality far more serious than the one named after him.

2. Belling the Cat

Myth! The Greek Sphinx originated from Homer's story of Oedipus.

The Sphinx is commonly perceived as a one-of-a-kind monster, with the body of a lion and the head of a woman, which is how it was depicted in Greek mythology. The creature made its most awesome appearance in the story of Oedipus, the tragic hero who, like all travelers before him, had to answer a riddle posed by this mythic mutant before he could enter the gates of Thebes. "What is it," asked the Sphinx, "that goes on four legs in the morning, on two legs at noon, and on three legs in the evening?" Oedipus' hapless co-adventurers, failing to give the right answer, had been eaten alive, but Oedipus, who was not expected to fare differently, so unnerved the monster with his correct reply of "man" that it was driven to suicide.

These two legendary characters had their separate stories to tell in Greek mythology, and only in Greek drama would they have their fateful encounter with each other. It is believed neither the Sphinx nor its riddle was an original part of the Oedipus myth, as Homer, Oedipus' creator, never mentioned the creature, while Hesiod sponsored the Sphinx' debut without referring to Oedipus. It was the great tragedian Sophocles who brought the two together, obviously to prove that Oedipus was clever and intelligent and not as dense as he had acted throughout his ordeal.

Sophocles' Sphinx has been qualified on occasions as (a) a plot device invented by the ancient Greek scriptwriters; (b) "a purely psychological symbol, representing the complexity and duality of the human mind;" or (c) a mother image, which Oedipus was made to demolish to avenge the early years of parental abuse. According to critics, whatever the Sphinx's reason for being was, it couldn't justify that monster's intrusion into a story that's "focused on human feelings, and human reactions to terrible human events. It seems as out of place as Godzilla in New York and Sicily of Coppola's Godfather trilogy."

3. Electra Connection

Myth! Electra was the first known female in fact or fiction to suffer from Oedipus complex.

Freud, who had used the term 'Oedipus complex' for both sexes, disdained the way his rivals coined the term 'Electra complex' for the process in girls. According to some analysts, this was more from hubris than from the belief that Electra's story had totally no bearing on the subject of his study.

Where a girl becomes attracted to her father and antagonistic toward her mother, the term used is 'Electra complex', after the daughter of Mycenae's King Agamemnon and Queen Clytemnestra of Greek mythology. Electra loved Agamemnon so much that when she learned it was her mother who had caused her father's death, she had her killed. Unlike Oedipus, Electra was always fully aware of her parents' identities, but like Oedipus no parallel can be drawn between the mythology and the eponymic psychiatric condition. Electra's love for her dead father was not sexual but familial, albeit it was so strong and pitying that it created in her an overwhelming urge to destroy her mother. Modern psychoanalysts agree that Electra's consuming passion against Clytemnestra was righteous anger and should not be confused with the jealousy or the sexual envy that is normally associated with an erotic relationship.

4. Neutered by the Gods

Myth! The Sphinx is a gender-specific figure, most likely a female.

The first indication that our perception of the Sphinx is flawed is from the ancient Greeks themselves, who referred to the monster as a 'she' even while others considered it a 'he'. Apparently for no other reason than to amuse, the creators—Hesiod in particular—developed a female image for the character while giving it a mixed masculine-feminine physical appearance.

278

The Sphinx has the full muscular body of a lion (not a lioness), but its face is that of a woman. In some art, its hair is cut short, like a male, or spread on its shoulders like a lion's mane, yet we see a pair of very feminine breasts on its manly chest. According to speculation, the Sphinx might have been a hermaphrodite, as some mythological creatures turned out to be, although there is really no reason that it should be.

The next indication is from the relics of other ancient cultures in which the Sphinx in some variation or other figured prominently. The Oedipus myth is uniquely Greek, but the character of the Sphinx was obviously lifted from Middle-Eastern lore, which features a whole species of this creature that was predominantly male. The Egyptian sphinx (which Hesiod called Andro-Sphinx) was definitely a man-lion combination when the builders of the great pyramids of Egypt appropriated the form for their monuments. The head of the pharaoh Khafre (c2550 BC) adorns the famous Great Sphinx at Giza, proving beyond doubt that the creature had a male personality. Unfortunately, like the other sphinx monuments, Khafre's headdress has been so eroded by time that it now looks like the hair of a woman. An Egyptian sub-specie, the crio-sphinx, has the head of a ram or a falcon and is undoubtedly male. The sphinxes of Persia, Assyria, and Phoenicia have male heads that sport beards and long curly hair.

Two features that could have helped define the Andro-sphinx's gender are its nose and its beard, but both are missing from its face. Regarding the first, it is said that while France was taking over Egypt, some of Napoleon's soldiers got drunk and accidentally fired a cannonball at the figure, hitting it in the face and damaging its nose. The beard may have gone the same way, though no one really knows.

5. That Darn Cat Again

Myth! The Greeks copied their version of the sphinx from the Egyptians.

The Greeks chose the Andro-Sphinx for their model but also deviated from it in many respects. They used the Sphinx typically as a symbol of wisdom and malignance, whereas the Egyptian sphinx, especially in its earliest forms, was often associated with divinities and was used as a symbol of protection. The latter had no mysterious or deceitful nature, projecting instead a benign presence as it sat in the Valley of the Kings outside the pyramid of Khafre. In physical appearance, the Egyptian sphinx did not have wings and was recumbent, compared to the Greek Sphinx, which was in a sitting posture on her tall perch at Thebes. And unlike the Giza structure, the early Greek sculptures were never monumental, only decorative.

The Greek Sphinx is a low-end figure, a stupid and uncouth monster despite her matronly appearance, unlike its Egyptian counterpart, which is heroic. Most mythologists have judged it as having no iconic or other significance, being merely a literary embellishment or a thing of the imagination. Apparently, the Greeks have succeeded in maintaining some dimension for the creature only by endowing it with a monstrous appetite for riddles and human flesh and killing it off in the most preposterous manner.

After her moral defeat by Oedipus, the Sphinx is said to have thrown herself from her high rock on Mount Phikion and died, but the more popular version is that she devoured herself to end it all. Critics ask why anyone, even a fictional monster, would commit a spectacularly impossible suicide over a riddle that, although supposedly taught by the Muses, could be answered by any 10-year-old human with the proper intuition. Most importantly, of course, is why present the Sphinx as a mother figure filled with affection and compassion, yet, without any qualm, portray it in the same breath as the very embodiment of wrath.

6. Looking a Gift Horse in the Belly

Myth! The Greek gift of a wooden structure to the unwary Trojans is known in classic literature as the Trojan Horse.

The first breakthrough in that almost endless conflict called the Trojan War occurred when the Trojans accepted a gift of a huge wooden horse from the Greeks during a lull in the fighting. Unknown to the Trojans, the horse contained Greek warriors who would later sneak out during the night to pillage Troy.

The term 'Trojan Horse' poses the first incongruity about this wooden animal: in all classic literature, the name used is "the Wooden Horse of Troy," and even this gives no hint that the device was of Greek origin. The curious Trojans dragged in the great structure, with room inside for thirty men and their weapons, after it was found "abandoned" outside the city (that there was no "gift" in the real sense knocks down Virgil's rationale for the proverb, "Beware of Greeks bearing gifts"). In the dead of night, the hidden invaders sneaked out and, according to the popular version, started sacking and burning the city. The official story, however, is that they first opened the gates of the city to their waiting cohorts outside, who then joined them in pillaging Troy. The military hoax, a brainchild of the wily Ulysses, ended the ten-year siege and entered the language as a synonym for deception. The tale itself—part of the Homeric saga—has remained almost unequalled as a theme of narrative poetry and a tragic centerpiece of mythology.

Most people believe the Trojans were caught totally unaware by the ruse, but they were not. The priest Laocoon declared the Horse a fraud, hurled a spear into its flank, and heard the telltale hollow sound. Unfortunately, his protestations and demand that the creature be burned did not move the unbelievably gullible Trojan generals. To silence Laocoon, the gods on the side of the Greeks sent two great sea serpents to kill him and his twin sons. The famed prophetess Cassandra, a daughter of Troy's King Priam, also saw through the deception but could not raise the proper alarm. Having previously spurned the advances of the god Apollo, she had been cursed to tell the truth every time but never to be believed.

---

7. When a Twin Peaks, the other Twin Falls

Myth! The twins Remus and Romulus were the legendary founders of Rome.

According to tradition, the twin sons of Mars with Rhea Silvia, daughter of King Numitor of Alba Longa, founded Rome in 8 BC. Ordered drowned by their uncle Amulius, Remus and Romulus survived to become leaders of a band of adventurous youths, later settling in the place where they had been saved. Romulus built a wall around the site, then killed Remus when the latter jumped contemptuously over it. The victim of the fratricide was soon forgotten, and it is solely in honor of Romulus that the settlement was named Rome.

The myth of Remus and Romulus was invented in 4 BC, many years after Virgil created his Trojan hero Aeneas, who mythologists claim was the real founder of Rome. Virgil's *Aeneid*, written c. 29-19 BC, covers Aeneas' exploits in the Trojan War and his founding of Lavinium, the parent city of Alba Longa and Rome. When Virgil produced his literary masterpiece, Augustus had just taken over the bankrupt Roman world, which was reeling from the chaos following Caesar's assassination. Virgil, fired with enthusiasm for the new order, believed it was time to produce a great national hero and a founder for "the race destined to hold the world beneath its rule."

The ancient Romans showed their preference for Aeneas by dating the founding of Rome to 754 BC, as shown on their markers and monuments.

8. Breathless but Breastless?

Myth! Amazon women were so-called because they cut off their left breasts at an early age.

The Amazon legend is the fountainhead of every female-dominated society, real or fictional. It is about a race of militant superwomen who lived on the coast of the Black Sea near the southern borders of Turkey, with their capital at Themiscyra. Lacking men but spurning them, they propagated by trysting with males in nearby settlements, then returning to their own colony to await the results. A male infant was returned to his father (or, according to some historians, strangled), while girls were raised according to a strict regimen and a set of female-oriented standards.

At adolescence or thereafter, each girl's right breast was burnt off or excised so that it would not get in the way when she pulled a bowstring or hurled a javelin. We are told this accounts for the name 'Amazon', from the Greek *a-mazos*, meaning, "lacking a breast." Most etymologists demur, pointing out that the prefix *a* before the Greek word *mazos*, for breast, denotes amplitude and not a lack of. Historians themselves don't cater to the myth of the Amazons as being single-breasted by choice. From their perspective, Amazon women were "tall, lithe, and full-breasted, their limbs powerful from constant exercise, their features stern and noble and their gaze sharp and challenging."

'Amazon' quite possibly evolved from a foreign name, although not of the famed river of South America. Known as the River Sea at the time of its discovery, the Amazon was renamed for the Amazon women of legend rather than vice-versa. This occurred when a Dominican friar who chronicled the Amazon expedition of Spanish explorer Francisco de Orellana in 1541 saw female warriors leading the Indian attacks on the Spanish boats.

---

9. Sour Graping over an Apple

Myth! A controversy over an apple caused the ten-year Trojan War involving gods and heroes.

The story begins at the wedding of the hero Peleus and the water nymph Thetis, parents of the redoubtable Achilles. All the gods and goddesses are in attendance, except Eris, the goddess of discord, who was not invited. Out of spite, Eris steals one of Hera's golden 'apples', inscribes it "Property of the Fairest," and then tosses it onto a banquet table. When the ensuing scramble does not produce a winner, Zeus decides to have the dispute settled among the three major contenders—Hera, Aphrodite and Athena—with Paris as judge.

Aphrodite, after offering Paris the hand of the world's most beautiful woman as bribe, gets his nod. But the promised lady happens to be Helen of Troy, who is already espoused to King Menelaus. When Paris returns home to Troy with his all-too-willing bride, it is just a matter of time before mythology's bloodiest conflict, the Trojan War, erupts. The claim that Paris may have abducted Helen does not mitigate the silliness of the carnage that kills some of the world's greatest legendary heroes.

Because of what it started, the golden 'apple' is called the

Apple of Discord, but only half the description is apt. Until the 17th century, 'apple' was used in religion, mythology and folktales as a generic term for any fruit other than berries but including nuts. This raises the odds that the apple of the Mediterranean may be any fruit at all, including the indigenous apricot. In fact, the ancient Greeks had the same word for both 'apple' and 'sheep', which means that the prize Paris awarded to the fairest woman in Olympus may not even be a fruit.

Incidentally, like the Trojan Horse, Helen of Troy was Greek, not Trojan. It was only when Paris took Helen to his homeland as his secondhand bride that she became Helen of Troy. In Euripides' *Trojan Women*, Helen admits going with Paris on her own volition, discrediting the popular belief that she was abducted. Shenkman refutes this, saying "it's unlikely she ever would have eloped. FitzRoy Raglan, an expert in world history, reported that he could find no instance in history 'in which a queen has eloped with a foreign prince, or anybody else'." Most other critics dismiss the issue with the comment that ancient fantasy figures like Helen are better off being interpreted by mythographers than by modern historians.

Helen's beauty and fate are encapsulated in the eternal line, "Is this the face that launched a thousand ships/ And burnt the topless towers of Ilium?" The words are sometimes attributed to Homer, but it was actually composed by Christopher Marlowe (1564-93) for the title character of his play 'Dr. Faustus'. The tenor doesn't seem to be original with Marlowe either, for in 'The Dialogues of the Dead' written by the great satirist Lucian (125?-210?) and translated by M. O. Macleod, the character Menippus says: "Was it then for this that the thousand ships were manned from all Greece, for this that so many Greeks and barbarians fell, and so many cities were devastated?"

V

Altered States

On Death and Metamorphosis in Mythology

"But why must the Argives fight the Trojans?...
Are Atreus' sons the only men who love their wives?"

•

Achilles

1. Flower Children with Blooming Egos

Myth! The Greek youth Narcissus gave his name to a flower.

According to Edith Hamilton, the "charming tales of lovely young people who, dying in the springtime of life, were fittingly changed into spring flowers, have probably a dark background" and "can be associated with the idea of human sacrifice." She was no doubt referring to the common fate of Narcissus, Adonis and Hyacinth, three promising youths who were either fancied or pitied by the gods and turned literally into flowers.

Pining for his image in a pool every single minute, Narcissus wastes away and dies, leaving only a small white and gold flower to mark his place. And so, the famous blossom of the genus *Narcissus* was born. Ovid told the tale, and Samuel Taylor Coleridge followed in 1822 by coining the term 'narcissism' to describe Narcissus' obsessive self-admiration. Most are surprised to learn that, unlike 'narcissism', the name of the flower did not come from but was rather given to Narcissus. According to Plutarch, the real source of 'narcissus' is the Greek word *narko*, or 'numbness', which is reputedly the effect one gets from eating the flower's petals. *Narko* fathered other English terms, such as 'narcolepsy', 'narcotic', and the slang expression 'narc'. When the myth got started, the flower was already called *narcosis*, meaning the plant that produces numbness or palsy.

The narcissus is sometimes confused with the anemone, a flower that another beautiful youth of mythology, Adonis, left behind when he died. Fortunately, the anemone is not saddled by the irony of Adonis' name, which suggests handsome masculinity even though he was only a boy and an effeminate one at that. According to Ovid, the goddess Venus was looking at him when she accidentally sat on one of Cupid's arrows and was immediately captivated.

This leaves the hyacinth as the only flower to adopt the name of a beautiful youth of Greek mythology. The hyacinth supposedly grew from the spilled blood of its namesake, Hyacinth, who was beloved of both Apollo and Zephyrus the West Wind. Virgil says that Zephyrus became so jealous of Apollo, whom Hyacinth favored, that one day, while the three were playing games,

Zephyrus caused the god to misdirect a discus throw and kill Hyacinth.

2. Ledan Egg

Myth! Zeus changed himself into a swan to seduce the goddess Leda.

The magical transformation of humans and gods into birds is a class by itself. Cycnus, son of Apollo, leaped off a cliff and was changed into a swan because his friend Philius refused to give him the bull that Hercules helped capture. What's odd about this account is that there are two other incidents in Greek mythology involving a Cycnus who is changed into a swan. Cycnus, the son of Sthenelus, dove repeatedly into the river Eridanos attempting to retrieve Phaeton's body. The gods turned him into a swan to relieve him of his pity. Cycnus, king of Colonae and the son of Poseidon, was also changed into a swan after his death at the hands of Achilles in the Trojan War.

Perdix, the mythical inventor of the drawing compass and the saw, was turned into a partridge by Minerva when his envious uncle Daedalus, under whom he was apprenticed, threw him to a premeditated death from the Acropolis. Thus, the Greek word for partridge is *perdix*, which actually shouldn't be because, as mythographer Apollodorus pointed out, the boy's real name was Talos and it was his mother who was called Perdix.

One of the favorite scenes in Renaissance art—that of a beautiful maiden consorting with a swan—was drawn from the myth of Zeus and Leda. The story begins when Zeus discovers Leda bathing one day, and this stirs up his carnal desires. Disguised as a huge swan, he approaches and takes advantage of the Spartan queen. Their union begets Helen of Troy, the most beautiful woman in the world, and Pollux, one of the Gemini twins.

Leda is actually a rehash of the older and more authentic myth of Nemesis. According to Hesiod, Nemesis is a pretty daughter of the goddess Nyx who takes on a series of disguises to evade the pursuit of a lustful Zeus. The god, appearing as a swan, finally catches up and surprises Nemesis posing as a goose.

287

Leda was apparently an attempt to fit the story of Nemesis into the Trojan War mold to make it more alluring particularly for new readers. Beauty embraced by a bird is harder to imagine than two birds mating, but the odd pairing is decidedly more erotic. Moreover, Leda has a softer image than the somewhat masculine Nemesis. As the Greco-Roman personification of just retribution, the latter comes on too strongly as a persistently threatening foe.

Revisionists offer to reconcile the characters of Leda and Nemesis by explaining that, while Helen was indeed the result of the union of Zeus with Nemesis, someone chanced upon the egg and—for reasons not known—threw it between the thighs of Leda as she sat on a stool with her legs apart. When Helen was hatched, Leda nursed the young chick (pun intended) and brought her up as her own.

3. Hard to Swallow

Myth! The gods changed Philomela into a nightingale.

King Tereus of Thrace rapes his sister-in-law Philomela, then cuts out her tongue and imprisons her to prevent the story from leaking back to his wife Procne. The latter finds out anyway from clues provided by a tapestry that the mute Philomela weaves in prison. In retaliation Procne kills her son Itys and serves cooked bits of him to her husband, later telling him what she has done. The sickened Tereus is about to kill both sisters when the gods intervene and change Procne into a swallow and Philomela into a nightingale.

This is the Greek legend that Roman writers, notably Ovid, made popular without knowing they had confused the traditional fates of the two sisters. According to Hamilton, it is really Philomela who is turned into a swallow, "which, because her tongue was cut out, only twitters and can never sing." Procne becomes the nightingale, the bird whose "song is sweetest because it is saddest. She never forgets the son she killed." The error has become the basis of a misconception that runs through the whole of English and American poetry, deceiving even T. S. Eliot— reputedly the most scholarly poet after John Milton—who mentions the transformation of Philomela into a nightingale in his most famous poem, 'The Waste Land'. Another myth-loving poet, Samuel Taylor Coleridge, commits the same fallacy much earlier in his piece 'The Nightingale'.

4. Which Twin is the Phony?

Myth! **Castor and Pollux were twins.**

Somewhere in the zodiac is the constellation Gemini (Latin for 'the Twins'), which the brothers Castor and Pollux symbolically represent. According to the myth, Castor was slain by a suitor of one of the daughters of Leudippus. Pollux (who was immortal unlike Castor) grieved so deeply that Zeus placed them both in the heavens.

Few people realize that the Gemini, though born at the same time and of the same mother, were not really twins. In fact, they were not even full brothers. What is more, Castor was legitimate whereas Pollux was a bastard. This anomalous relationship can only be explained by the strange manner in which the two were conceived. The boys' mother, Queen Leda of Sparta, was already pregnant by her mortal husband Tyndareus when impregnated by Zeus in the guise of a swan. She bore two eggs—one, sired by her husband, hatching Castor and Clytaemnestra, and the other, by Zeus, producing Pollux and Helen.

An occurrence involving fraternal twins by different fathers, though remote, is biologically possible. The phenomenon is called superfecundation. Semantically speaking, however, Castor and Pollux are not fraternal twins but two in a set of quadruplets. Whatever may be the proper word for this strange sibling formation, Clytaemnestra, not Pollux, is the rightful half of the Gemini.

5. Days of Heaven

Myth! **The Greek 'alkyon' bred on the sea during 'halcyon days'.**

289

According to etymologists, the main influence for the phrase 'halcyon days' (pronounced *halkion*, not *hal-sigh-on*), a synonym for 'the good old days', was a Greek belief concerning a species of birds called the *alkyon*. It was claimed that, as cousins of the kingfisher, the *alkyon* made their nest and laid their eggs on the ocean during the winter solstice, making sure that the weather remained gentle and cloudless for two weeks. The Greeks called this fortnight of calm *alkyonides hemerai* and the Romans *alcyoni dies*. The terms, later rendered into English as 'halcyon days', were not based on the name *alkyon* but on the Greek word *hals-kyoi*, meaning 'sea-conceiving' in reference to the bird's main feature.

However, the real source of 'halcyon days' is the myth that gave rise to the belief and not the belief itself. 'Halcyon' is from Alcyone, daughter of Aeolus, king of winds, who with her husband Ceyx, son of the Morning Star, blasphemed the gods. Transformed into a kingfisher, Alcyone was left at the seashore, and when the roiling waters threatened to destroy her nest eggs, Zeus took pity and commanded that the seas be still for fourteen days. In Ovid's version, Ceyx drowned in an accident, and Alcyone, discovering her husband's body on the shore, threw herself into the sea. After this act of self-immolation, both were miraculously transformed into 'halcyons' and given the power to calm the waters.

Originally, 'halcyon' didn't mean 'prosperous' but 'peaceful', and 'halcyon days' referred to a period not only in the past but also in the present and future. Compounding these fallacies is the known fact that kingfishers like other birds breed on land and never on the sea.

6. How Now, Brown Cow?

Myth! Hera transformed Io into a cow after catching her dallying with Zeus.

Among the myths of chase and transformation, there is the tale of the Nereid Arethusa, a huntress whom Alpheus fell in love with and pursued. Unwilling to marry, she fled to the island Ortygia in

Sicily and there turned into a fountain. Daphne is changed into a laurel tree while fleeing from Apollo (who chases her out of love), but is later changed back into a woman. Sometimes it is the pursuer who is metamorphosed, as in the myth of Orion who, while pursuing the Pleiades, was changed into a constellation complete with a girdle, sword, club and lion's skin.

According to the popular retelling of a Greco-Roman legend, Hera, wife of Zeus, catches him dallying with Io, and as punishment she transforms the maiden into a cow. As originally told by the poets Aeschylus and Ovid, however, it is Zeus who causes Io's transformation in order to hide her from Hera's condemnation and the punishment she is sure to inflict. Hera, who fails to catch the couple *in flagrante* and is the one outwitted, discovers the deception anyway, and taking the beast from Zeus, leads her to a place where she can be guarded by Argus, a monster with hundreds of eyes all over his body. In the end, Io finds peace when Hermes liberates her, and after being comforted by Prometheus, she reaches the Nile and is restored to her pristine self by Zeus.

Most everyone is aware that Io's name was given to the Ionian Sea, along which she ran on her way to the Nile. What is less evident is that the Bosporus, meaning Ford of the Cow, was also named after her, as this was the other sea she traversed during her flight.

Certain inconsistencies and irregularities found in metamorphic myths make it almost impossible to set rules and clear categories for them. For instance, some transformations, like Philomela's, are effected by the gods as a reward, and others, such as Io's, as a punishment. Hamilton narrates the story of Philemon and Baucis, who were changed into an oak tree and a lime tree, respectively, in their old age in gratitude for offering hospitality to Zeus and Hermes when they had come disguised as mortals. On the other hand, the Apulian Shepherd was changed into an oleaster tree as punishment for mocking some dancing nymphs. Then, there is Hierax, who was changed into a hawk as punishment for informing Argus that the god Hermes was stealing Io; however, as a favor from Apollo, Daedalion was also transformed into a hawk while leaping from a cliff, crazed by the death of his daughter, Chione.

7. United Front

Myth! **The first hermaphrodite resulted from the fusion of Hermes and Aphrodite.**

Combining the names of the Olympian immortals Hermes and Aphrodite forms the word 'hermaphrodite', which means any being possessed of the physical traits of both sexes. While this may suggest that the first hermaphrodite resulted from the fusion of Hermes and Aphrodite, the legend states that the two did not fuse but united sexually to produce a son, Hermaphroditus, who grew up to be the world's first gay.

According to the more reliable version, Hermaphroditus wasn't gay, and was in fact a strapping fifteen-year-old boy when espied by a water nymph named Salmacis. One day, while the boy was taking a dip, the smitten Salmacis slipped in and grabbed him. Holding him tight, she prayed that their two bodies would never again be separated. The gods heard the prayer, and slowly, the nymph's body merged with the boy's until they were one.

The myth was invented not so much to explain the origin of homosexuality as to justify tolerance for the practices associated with it. Unfortunately, the tale falls short even of this task by failing to grasp the difference between a hermaphrodite and a homosexual. Hermaphroditus and Salmacis, whose fused bodies retained the physical endowments of both sexes, were transfigured into a hermaphrodite, not a homosexual. The latter has the biological trappings of only one sex, although manifesting the behavioral characteristics of the other sex. Some historians claim that in ancient Greece, where it was common for men to be bisexual if not homosexual, there was no awareness of homosexuality as an overall psychological condition. In fact, no term existed for the behavior, only various expressions referring to specific homosexual roles and attitudes.

8. Morphing Addict

Myth! **Morpheus was the Roman god of sleep.**

Morpheus, the god of dreams who can change shapes and mimic voices, is the logical name source of the word 'metamorphosis'. Due to a fallacy, however, Morpheus is better known as the origin of 'morphine', a word that has a lot to do with sleep but nothing to do with form or shape. The reason: medieval and Renaissance poets like Chaucer and Spenser tag Morpheus as the god of sleep and not of dreams, confusing him with his father Somnus (Greek: Hypnos). This accounts for why the Laurence Fishburne character in the 1999 movie *The Matrix*, though named Morpheus and residing in a dream world, never undergoes physical transformation.

Similarly, while it seems logical to relate the word 'argosy' to Jason's *Argo*, one has nothing to do with the other, etymologically or otherwise. *Argo* is actually based on Argus, the craftsman who built the great ship on Jason's request for use in his pursuit of the Golden Fleece. The *Argo* could accommodate fifty oarsmen and a crew, which eventually consisted of nearly every hero of the day, from Heracles to Theseus. "Argosy," on the other hand, dates back to the sixteenth century, during a period when merchant vessels plied a brisk trade with England from the Italian port of Ragusa, now in Yugoslavia and called Dubrovnik. A ship hailing from this port was "a Ragusa," which was rapidly corrupted on the dockside to "a Ragusy," and finally to "argosy."

Finally, it is worth mentioning that Mars, the Roman god of war, is the name source for the word "martial" but is totally unrelated to the verb "to march." The latter comes from the French *marcher*, "to walk," originally "to trample," which is in turn derived from the Latin *marcus*, "hammer."

9. Beaus and Eros

Myth! **The Greek god Eros was a blind baby who never grew old.**

Eros, being the cutest thereabouts, turned everybody on in Olympus, except that he was blind. Young people who are just beginning to wake up to love's stirrings know him better as Cupid, the name given him by the Roman successors to the Greeks.

293

However, the blindness of Eros is a post-classical invention, and so is his being a baby. Hesiod saw him originally as a very old god, but for some reason, he aged in reverse, growing younger in the art of each passing century. By the fourth century BC, he was a spoiled and mischievous child-god, son of Aphrodite, who was inclined to tantrums and practical jokes that drove his elders in Mount Olympus crazy.

The Greek dramatist Euripides was the first to mention that he was an archer, armed with arrows of gold and lead. The golden arrows would inflame their target's passions, while the leaden arrows had just the opposite effect, inspiring only disgust and hatred. Because these missiles were fired indiscriminately, it often happened that one was hit by the golden arrow and became lovesick, and the object of his or her fancy was hit by the leaden arrow and was repelled.

Eros' performance over the ages was haphazard and inaccurate, which is probably why, in later times, people thought him blind, the mythic personification of the saying "love is blind." But because of the difficulty of portraying natural blindness on canvas, artists merely place a blindfold on the god as their convention for showing love's inability to distinguish between old and young, good and bad, and god and mortal.

Eros is often rendered as a cherub (pl: cherubim) with a nimbus round his head. The tyke apparently got his nimbus well ahead of his human counterpart, St. Valentine. The nimbus, it must be recalled, began in history as a symbol for pagan gods, who were bestowed this attribute by Hindu, Greek, and Roman art. Eventually, despite the absence of a proper reference in Scripture, the Church allowed it as an artistic way of glorifying the image of Christ and the saints.

10. No Need to Exorcise

Myth! **Demons in Greek mythology and legend were bad spirits that opposed the will of the gods.**

As incompatible as it may sound, there was a time in Greek mythology when demons were not evil. Although they eventually became minions of Hades and his underworld, they used to be the agents of all the gods in their dealings with men. The *daimon* was Homer's concept of the active aspect of a god, and other writers would later give it a quasi-divine personality invisible to mortals. This guardian spirit was entrusted with the fate of each man, and effected the gods' will with respect to that individual. Hesiod speculated "there were precisely 30,000 *daimones*, the spirits of those lucky people who had lived during the so-called Golden Age."

Since they administered Zeus's judgments, the *daimones* were also gods, albeit nameless and low-ranked. Unfortunately for them, they were the first immortals to go when Christianity decided to clean up the pagan temples. To ease the changes and make their teachings more palatable, the Christians refrained from condemning the old gods outright while persuading the converts to have the Greek pantheons exorcised of the minor ones. In the process, the *daimones* were made to assume an evil nature and an undeserved association with the devil, culminating in the transmutation of the term into the English "demons."

---

11. Brute Force

Myth! Hera's favorite, the heroic Hercules, performed twelve mighty labors as penance for the murder of his family.

Heracles, or Hercules as he is popularly called, was born to Queen Alcmene of Tlryns in Argolis after Zeus had visited her bed in the guise of her husband Amphitryon. It is said that the hero came out prodigiously strong because his conception took three hectic nights of continuous lovemaking.

What is not readily apparent is why he was named Heracles, meaning "Hera's glory," when that goddess, as the real wife of Zeus, had no reason to be happy with this proof of her husband's indiscretion. In fact, Hera despised Heracles so much for becoming the apple of Zeus' eye that in his eighth month, she sent a pair of deadly snakes to kill him in his crib. But as expected, the extraordinarily gifted infant, giving a preview of things to come, strangled the creatures with his bare hands. Many believe Heracles' name is not original but was borrowed from a hero more to Hera's liking—the real-life prince Heracles of Tlryns, on whom the myths were based.

The obstinate Hera, intent on her design to destroy or disgrace Heracles, caused him to become temporarily mad and to kill his own family. As penance for this homicidal outburst, Heracles placed himself at the service of King Eurystheus of Tlryns, who dispatched the hero on a series of near-impossible missions requiring largely the killing or capturing of a fabulous animal or monster. Homer and Hesiod, who were the earliest to describe these exploits, refer to them as the "Labors of Heracles," without specifying their number. It was only in later writings that this was set at twelve, presumably to match the signs of the zodiac.

VI

Monster Menagerie

On Monsters in Mythology

"Sssssssss."

•

Medusa

1. Killing 'em Softly with her Song

Myth! The Lorelei was a beautiful siren that sat on a rock on the bank of the river Rhine.

Ordinarily, the word 'siren' summons up the romantic image of a beautiful sensual woman who seduces men with her charms. Mythology transforms the image into a mysterious creature that lurks on lonely shores and invites misfortune through its exquisite singing.

The eight known sirens in legend were originally water nymphs that banished themselves to a remote island when they lost a singing contest to the Muses. In revenge, they would pose on the rocks and sing songs of such sweetness that mesmerized sailors abandoned ship and swam ashore to certain death. Of the slew of heroes and mighty men who encountered the sirens, only Ulysses (in Homer's version) and Jason survived the ordeal.

In real life, a siren is a mud eel, a great disappointment to the many whose vision of the creature is that of a beautiful mermaid. Both the siren of mythology and the mermaid had sweet voices, which accounts for why a siren, according to some stories, could easily change into a mermaid to make itself more physically seductive to seamen. But the similarity ends where a shocking difference begins. A mythical siren was a monster even more ugly than a mud eel, with the body of a bird as big as an adult human, the head of a crone, and a taste for human flesh. It pounced on sailors who, enticed by its singing, swam to shore, then ate their flesh that it shredded with its talons.

There is a German folk tradition about a siren looking like a mermaid and sitting on a rock that juts steeply on the right bank of the Rhine near Bingen, opposite St. Goar. The remarkable echo one hears in the vicinity is said to come from the creature while she combs her hair and sings songs in an effort to lure ships and sailors to their ugly fate. The poem 'Die Lorelei' by Heinrich Heine and two operas of the same title, one produced by Max Bruch in 1864 and the other not quite completed by Mendelssohn, have made the story famous. The word 'Lorelei' (also 'Loreley', 'Lorelie' and 'Lurlei') has entered popular usage and most lexicons as the name of the siren—somewhat of a misnomer, since

298

to most people who are unaware of the myth 'Lorelei' is just the name of a rock and not of a being.

2. Bullheaded Cretan

Myth! The Minotaur was a bull with a man's head.

A careful peek at a monster menagerie from Greek mythology will reveal that most if not all of the specimens are a combination of body parts belonging to various species of real or fictional animals and humans. The human part is usually the head, as though it were to endow the monster with human personality or reason. Thus, the Sphinx has the head of a woman and the body of a lion; sirens have female heads attached to the bodies of fish or birds; and harpies have the heads of maidens perched on the bodies of vultures. The infamous Medusa has a woman's head and the scaly body of a dragon, while Theseus' quarry, the Minotaur, is sometimes depicted as a man's head on the body of a bull. A monster usually has a female head, as opposed to a demigod, such as the half-horse centaur or the half-goat satyr, which has a male head.

In the real myth, however, the Minotaur is described as having the body of a human and the head of a bull. This is how Picasso portrays it in various renditions. The monster, son of a magnificent white animal that mated with Pasiphae, wife of King Minos of Crete, was imprisoned in a   labyrinth because it liked to kill and eat people. However, non-impressionists prefer to show the man-animal combination in reverse perhaps because they cannot envision the ridiculous idea of a bull's head feeding on human flesh.

3. Doom Box

Myth! Pandora unwittingly released every known misfortune into the world from a box.

The phrase 'Pandora's box' is a metaphor for anything that appears harmless on the outside but which, when indulged, causes limitless harm. The literal reference is to a vessel that Zeus entrusted to Pandora's husband with instructions that it should never be opened.

Pandora, the mythological equivalent of Eve, was fashioned by the gods out of clay and sent to earth, where Prometheus's brother Epimetheus accepted her as his wife. Zeus had earlier given Epimetheus a box, with instructions that it should never be opened. But Pandora, epitomizing both the curious and the naive, took the lid off, and out sprang disease, plague, envy, hatred, and every other evil previously unknown to man. Pandora slapped the lid back on, but it was too late, for the only thing remaining in the box was hope.

Contrary to what is generally accepted, Pandora was sent to earth not to please man but to punish him. Her mission was to serve as Zeus' revenge for the bounties, including fire, that Prometheus had given humankind without the god's consent. She herself was a veritable Pandora's box, a wonder to behold but capable of causing incalculable harm. The gifts she received at her wedding (Pandora means 'gifted by all') made her what the ancient Greeks imagined women to be—"an evil to men, with a nature to do evil."

As its name indicates, Pandora's famous container is popularly perceived to be a box. In support of this, Edith Hamilton uses the words 'box' and 'casket' interchangeably, deviating from Hesiod's original *pithos*, meaning a jar for storing grain. The earliest period to use the phrase 'Pandora's box' is the sixteenth century, when humanist Erasmus of Rotterdam apparently confused *pithos* with *pyxis*, 'box'. In a version as old as Hesiod's, the receptacle contained virtues instead of vices, and all flew out to the people when she opened it, except hope, which stayed to console her.

---

4. Stalking Heads

Myth! Of all the famous monsters of mythology, Hydra had the most number of heads.

Cerberus, one of the members of a monster family bred by Typhon, was a three-headed canine with a serpent's tail and a mane of snakes. Hades chained this literal hound of hell on the underworld side of the river Styx to see that no living person trespassed and no spirit departed. Anyone that did so without throwing 'a sop to Cerberus'—i.e., a bribe or appeasement to distract the dog—would be eaten.

As described by Hesiod, the dog originally had no serpent or snakes to augment its powers. However, it sported not three but fifty heads, or more than five times those of its sibling, the terrible Hydra, another of Typhon's monstrous offspring. The Hydra was a serpent with nine heads, the ninth being immortal, and was specially trained in wickedness by Hera. One of Heracles' labors was to rid Lerna of this monster, but each time he chopped off a head, two more grew in its place. It was only with the help of his nephew Iolaus, who seared each stump with a brand, and by burying the immortal head under a great rock, that Heracles was able to put the Hydra to rest.

In other versions of the myth, the number of heads on the Hydra varied from seven to one hundred. In their most benign incarnations, the serpent topped the dog seven heads to three, and at their worst, the ratio was two of the serpent to one of the dog. Still and all, the monster with the most 'heads' was neither Cerberus nor the Hydra but Medusa, whose hair was a swarm of snakes numbering in the hundreds.

5. Choice of Harms: Hell or High Water?

Myth! Scylla was as much a deadly threat to sailors as Charibdys was.

According to popular understanding, the two mythological horrors Scylla and Charibdys posed equally dire alternatives, and to avoid one was to be exposed to the other. Hence, the expression 'between Scylla and Charibdys', meaning between a rock and a hard place, or, in plainer language, a mid-course between perils.

As described by Homer in his *Odyssey*, Scylla was a six-headed man-eating monster that dwelt in a cavern in the Strait of Messina

301

on the face of a high cliff overlooking a narrow channel of the sea. Each head was on a long neck, and from every ship that passed each mouth seized a sailor. Charibdys, a deadly whirlpool that sucked down water and regurgitated it three times a day, was on the Sicilian side of the strait beneath a wild fig tree on the opposite rock from Scylla.

It became Ulysses' dilemma to sail between these two perils, on the one hand trying to avoid the loss of his crew to the monster, and on the other the loss of his ship to the whirlpool. Ulysses had the bad luck of losing to both, with himself barely surviving by clinging to the fig tree near Charibdys.

Ulysses' ordeal bears out the popular belief that one extreme was as bad as the other, but Homer strikes down the colorful metaphor by revealing that Charibdys, though less ugly, was the more dangerous.

6. Goodbye Tai Fung, Hello Harry Cane

Myth! The word 'typhoon' evolved from Typhon, a terrible dragon that stirred up sea storms.

The word 'typhoon' is said to have evolved from the character in Greek mythology called Typhon, a terrible dragon with one hundred serpents' heads and many mighty hands and feet. Typhon was so evil and deadly that of all the gods, only Zeus could put up a fight by hurling lightning bolts at the monster. Zeus cast him into the bosom of Tartarus, devoid of his fire but still potent enough to stir up sea storms.

Because of geography, however, the etymological connection between the mythical creature and the eponymous typhoon appears flimsy. Since tropical disturbances are totally alien to Greece, it is doubtful that the ancient Greeks who devised the myth ever saw a typhoon in their lifetimes.

However, there is a similarity in sound between 'typhoon' and Typhon, on the one hand, and the Chinese *tai fung*, or 'big wind', on the other, enough to indicate that 'typhoon' and Typhon may have proceeded, albeit by independent routes, from *tai fung*. Presumably, the Chinese phrase, which was adopted by the Urdus to become the word *tufan* ('a tempest, a hurricane'), provided the concept used by other Asian and Near-Eastern societies as the basis of their myths about sea gods and sea monsters. It was probably one of these myths that found its way to ancient Greece and was recast into the tale of Typhon. At the same time, the word 'typhoon' developed from the Urdu noun *tufan*, entering the English language via the late sixteenth century *touffon* and the early nineteenth century *tay-fun* and *ty-foong*.

It may be that Typhon was an earlier concept than *tai fung*, or that the homonymy is entirely coincidental. The point, however, is that, between one and the other, *tai fung* is more likely the etymological source for 'typhoon'.

7. One-eyed in Gaza

Myth! The mythological Cyclopes were demigods that hounded Ulysses.

Most people think Polyphemus the Cyclops (plural: Cyclopes) is a creature of classical mythology. In truth, this giant and his ilk were creatures of Greek classical literature, having been invented by the great poet Homer to bedevil Ulysses in the Odyssey.

According to Hesiod, there were only three mythological Cyclopes, each of whom had one eye and was handy with a forge. They were named Arges, Steropes and Brontes, sons of Gaia and Uranus and brothers of the Titans. Chained at an early age by their father, they were later freed by the Titan Cronus, who used them to depose Uranus. But Cronus, worried about their skills, cast them down into Tartarus once he was safely in power. Zeus liberated them again so they could fashion the thunderbolts that would help him overthrow the Titans. Ironically, they ended up being destroyed by Apollo after an errant thunderbolt struck down the sun god's son Asclepius.

The Cyclopes of Homer, though they were also gigantic and one-eyed, were not demigods but monsters that inhabited Sicily. They were far more numerous—there were at least a hundred of them—and much less civilized. Homer tried to pass them off as descendants of the mythological Cyclopes, despite their lack of the skills or the inventiveness that distinguished their namesakes. In the end, he could only show them as huge, simple-minded shepherds who preferred to feed off the raw meat of their flocks notwithstanding their ability to build a fire. Worse, they had a connoisseur's taste for human flesh, which they tried to indulge every time a passing ship provided the opportunity.

8. Getting Kraken Ready

Myth! Perseus rode Pegasus to slay Medusa and afterwards display her head to the Kraken.

The combination of Sir Laurence Olivier and Ray Harryhausen's special effects did little to save the movie *The Clash of the Titans* from critical damnation when it debuted in theaters in 1981. Like "Greek mythology in some alternate universe," the plot is a mishmash that confuses Perseus' defeat of the Gorgon with Bellerophon's slaying of the Chimaera. In the film, Perseus rides Pegasus to reach the Gorgon's lair and kill her. Later, he displays Medusa's head to a monster called the Kraken, who is turned to stone by its deadly gaze.

In the myth, Perseus' magical means of transportation is the winged sandals that he extorts from the three Gray Women, with Pegasus nowhere in sight. Only when Perseus kills the Gorgon does the fabled winged horse make its entrance, by springing from the blood of Medusa after her head is cut off. Pegasus flees, at which point Bellerophon takes over and catches the animal. Our new hero rides the horse and from his perch kills the three-part monster Chimera with his arrows.

The legend approaches a climax when King Polydectes of Seriphus commands Perseus to secure Medusa's head and forever rid the kingdom of this notorious pest. After the task, Perseus returns to Seriphus to find his mother fighting the amorous advances of the tyrant. Perseus corners Polydectes and pulls Medusa's head out of the sack, petrifying the king both figuratively and literally.

The Kraken never did figure in the ancient tale. This anomaly of Roman mythology would not emerge from its sea roost until well into the Middle Ages.

304

VII

Ain't No Ordinary Folks

On American Folk Heroes

"I can lay on my back, look up at the stars
and it seems almost as though I can see the angels praising God,
for he has made all things for good."

•

Johnny Appleseed

1. Babe in the Woods

Myth! The figure of Paul Bunyan emerged from the campfire stories of North American lumberjacks.

People are wrong in assuming that Paul Bunyan, reputed king of the lumberjacks, is a creation of folklore, particularly the legends that came out of the timber drives in French Canada and Michigan. Paul, though a mythical person, did not emerge from the imagination of common folk but is a spontaneous product of modern commercialism. Writers and advertisers invented him in the 20th century—in the 1920s, to be exact.

His originator was not one James Stevens, as some believe, but a young advertising writer for the Red River Lumber Company in Minnesota named W. B. Laughead, who based the legendary strongman on a French-Canadian logger in the 1830s named Paul Bunyon. Laughead printed facts and anecdotes about Paul—all made up, of course—in a little booklet that he gave to customers. As sales grew, the legend of Paul grew even bigger. His feats—such as cutting the Grand Canyon of the Colorado by dragging his pick behind him—were embellished with each retelling. Soon, Paul had Babe, his blue ox, who was so strong she could be hitched to forty miles of winding road and pull it straight and true. Later, there was Ole, the blacksmith who had a special iron mine on Lake Superior that he kept going twenty-four hours a day just to keep Babe shod.

Paul is no more authentic a folk hero than any of the fantasy figures that help promote products on TV today. But his inclusion in almost every collection of American folk tales proves he has a uniquely endearing quality that no amount of debunking has been able to blemish.

2. Untrained Engineer

Myth! Jones was a legendary rounder and womanizer whose name was lifted from the initials of the city of his birth.

Contrary to popular belief, the character of Casey Jones is not legendary but real. John Luther Jones was nicknamed Casey because he was born near Cayce, Kentucky, not in K. C. (Kansas City) as many presume. Casey was not a 'rounder' in spite of the words of the ballad (''Casey Jones was the rounder's name''); a 'rounder' in railroad parlance is a worker who moves from job to job, whereas Casey was a steadfast employee who stayed with his line, the Illinois Central, until his death. His train was a speedy number called the Cannonball Express.

He was a large, handsome man who stood six feet 4 inches, with a reputation for speed on the rails and for being rewarded with the best runs and the newest and fastest trains. His reputation for womanizing, attributed to him by lines sometimes added to the ballad (''Go to bed, children, and hush your cryin', / 'Cause you got another papa on the Salt Lake Line''), is apparently untrue. Mrs. Jones, who died in 1958 in Jackson, Tennessee, at the age of ninety-two, waged a crusade after her husband's death to dispute the implications of the words, and was apparently successful in doing so.

---

3. Derailed Objective

Myth! Casey saved many lives from the two-train crash in which he died.

Before perishing in the collision that occurred on April 29, 1900, at 4:00 A.M. near Vaughan, Mississippi, Casey was able to shout, "Jump, Sim," to his fireman Simeon Webb, but Sim was the only other person on board either train. Contrary to popular reports, Casey was not driving the train on his own run when it happened. On that same night, just after Jones pulled into Memphis, the engineer of the return run turned up sick, so Jones agreed to work a double shift. Jones eagerly determined to make up for the one hour and 15 minutes that the train was already delayed.

A stone marker in Jones's Kentucky hometown, in commemorating the crash, states that it occurred "by no fault of his." Actually, the evidence points to negligence as the cause of the accident, and that negligence was apparently Casey's alone. It was his love for speed and a reckless desire to keep to schedule no matter the conditions that pushed Jones to do an average 60—at times over 100—against a normal rate of 50 miles per hour. Speeding full-throttle through darkness and fog, the tired Jones missed a flagman's signal that a freight train lay dead ahead on the tracks.

According to Casey's widow, his black engine wiper, Wallace Saunders, composed the ballad and began singing it a few days after the wreck. However, the song most people know today as 'Casey Jones' is a slightly different tune with entirely different words. It was published about 1902 and copyrighted in 1906 by Shapiro and Bernstein of New York.

4. Tall Tales from the Saddle

Myth! Pecos Bill is wholly a product of cowboy folklore.

Of the same mythic proportions as Paul Bunyan is Pecos Bill, a legendary American cowboy born in the 1830s and immortalized in numerous tall tales of the Old West during the American westward expansion. Among his 'achievements' are the invention of calf roping, the practice of cattle branding, and the creation of the six-shooter (and Western movies to boot!). On a level involving superhuman courage and prowess, he learned to ride a cyclone like a bronco and use a rattlesnake for a whip; he also had something to do with why coyotes howl at the moon, how the Rio Grande got dug, and how the Painted Desert became so colorful.

Pecos Bill's fantasy story was first published by Edward O'Reilly in the Century Magazine as 'The Saga of Pecos Bill' in 1923, after which it continued to grow as other writers, such as S. E. Schlosser, Charles E. Brown and Harold W. Felton, added to his tales in other publications. It was given the Disney treatment with two movies: *Melody Time* in 1948 and *Tall Tale: The Unbelievable Adventures of Pecos Bill* in 1995. More feats were invented for the cowboy hero through other media, such as in 'Pecos Bill,' a song written by Eliot Daniel and Johnny Lange and sung in Euro Disney's Frontierland. As several post-O'Reilly

308

writers have noted, Pecos Bill has adapted well even in the Argentines and is now part of their culture.

Despite O'Reilly's insistence that he only learned about Pecos Bill second hand from cowboy storytellers, students of folklore have been unable to authenticate any oral accounts of the character from those sources. Critics believe the claim that O'Reilly's book was a mere compilation of tall tales told by real cowboys is itself a tall tale and Pecos Bill is nothing but a media creation. One expert concludes that the cowboy wonder was a formula concocted by a few men who rehashed Greek and Mesopotamian myths and applied them to a Wild West setting. He was, in someone's words, "a product of popular culture more than of American folklore."

O'Reilly may not have created the basic figure of Pecos Bill, but it was most certainly he and his successors that killed the hero and his girl friend off. On their wedding day, Pecos Bill's lover Slue-Foot Sue attempted to ride his horse Widowmaker, but the animal pitched Sue so high that she almost hit the moon. When her steel-spring bustle continued to bounce her, Bill was forced to shoot her to keep her from starving. Pecos Bill's own death is somewhat controversial. Some say that he died from drinking fishhooks with his whiskey and nitroglycerin; others insist that he died laughing at a Boston dude pretending to be a cowboy as he swaggered into a bar.

5. Johnny, we Hardly Knew Ye

Myth! Johnny Appleseed accidentally mixed weeds with the apple trees he sowed all over the Midwest.

Most Americans know Johnny Appleseed as a poor hermit who wore a coffee sack for a dress and a tin kettle for a cap and sowed apple seeds all over the Midwest. According to his myth, Johnny stuck pins and needles through his flesh without getting hurt, walked barefoot in below-zero weather without freezing his toes, befriended wild animals, and ran through unfamiliar forests at twelve miles per hour without the aid of a compass. The bad news about Johnny is that he mistakenly mixed destructive dog fennel weed with the apple seeds he sowed. What makes it even worse is that, for the most part, Johnny is not myth. Most of his feats are obviously manufactured, but the man himself was real and his most celebrated achievement—sowing apple seeds on more than 100,000 square miles of America—actually happened.

The man behind the legend was one John Chapman, born in Leominster, Massachusetts, on September 26, 1774. The two basic versions of his life story clash on many points but converge on a central detail—he produced most of the apple orchards we see in Ohio and Indiana today. The looser rendering of the tale states that after being jilted by his girl, Johnny wandered for forty years, sowing apple seeds he collected from the cider mills of Pennsylvania over miles of Midwest terrain. He walked barefoot, dressed only in a coffee sack with holes cut in it for arms and legs, his long hair falling on his shoulders and his head covered by a tin kettle working part time as a cap. The historical view diminishes the legend considerably when it describes Johnny as neither a poor bumpkin nor a hermit but a well-liked nurseryman whose contribution "lay in moving his nurseries west to keep abreast of the receding frontier." He was successful and by the end of his life had accumulated more than 1,200 acres of land. By at least one account, he dressed just like everybody else in the region down to Indian moccasins on his feet.

Some say Johnny was completely unaware that the apple seeds he was sowing had been mistakenly mixed with the destructive weed called the dog fennel. Thus, all along the route that he took in the great Midwest, particularly Ohio, one will find the weed growing wherever there is an apple tree. What seems more likely, according to researchers, is that Appleseed knew what he was doing and did not err when he sowed the weed. He had great faith in the power of medicinal plants, administering them to any Indians and settlers he found sick along the way. He propagated these plants whenever convenient and encouraged others to do so. Since he believed, like everybody else, that dog fennel relieved fever, he scattered the seeds throughout Ohio and Indiana. The foul-smelling weed spread from barnyard to pasture, sometimes growing as high as fifteen feet. "Today," says a writer, "exasperated Midwestern farmers still cannot rid their fields of the plant they half humorously call 'Johnnyweed'."

6. Drillmaster

Myth! **The story of John Henry is an outstanding example of Afro-American myth.**

Like Casey Jones, John Henry is erroneously regarded as a mythical person. He is not only real, but the incident that made him a legend actually happened. John was a black person working to help build the Big Bend Tunnel for the C. & O. Railroad. He was the best man in a group whose job was to drive long rods of steel deep into the rock. Under their foreman, Captain Tommy, they made holes in the rock, and when these were deep enough, another group put nitroglycerin, mica powder or dualin into the holes to blow away the rock huge chunks at a time. A third group cleared the debris to prepare the site for further work.

One day a man came along and tried to peddle a steam drill to Captain Tommy. Afraid that the machine might unduly displace his people, he challenged the salesman to allow John to compete with the steam drill over a period of nine hours. "If the steam drill wins, I'll buy it. But if John Henry wins, you give me the steam drill and five hundred dollars," Captain Tommy said. John Henry beat the machine by three holes, but he died from exhaustion, fulfilling his own prophecy that he would "die with my hammer in my hand." It is said that he was buried with a hammer in each hand, since it was his practice to use two twenty-pound hammers in his work.

VIII

Animated Lives

On Disney Characters in Fact And Fiction

"What I love most about rivers is you can't step
in the same river twice, the water's always changing, always flowing."

•

Pocahontas

1. The Thief of Beijing

Myth! **Aladdin was an Arab.**

Most people think the fabulous collection called *The Arabian Nights' Entertainment* is Arab folklore written originally in Arabic. Thus, in Disney's 1993 interpretation of Aladdin, every detail is Arabian in texture and characterization—except for one song that a nationalist organization says contains lyrics insulting to the Arab people.

Actually, the tales have been told in a wide variety of places—India, Iran, Greece, Turkey, Iraq and Egypt—with their common point of origin as the Orient, from where the Mongols brought them to the Middle East. The collection familiar to the West is more properly called *The Thousand and One Nights*, originally from Syrian and Egyptian texts and variously translated, notably in French by Antoine Galland and in unexpurgated English by Sir Richard Burton.

The frame story, which is set in Central Asia ('the islands or peninsulae of India and China'), is probably Indian, although the names of its chief characters are Iranian and those of the rest are mostly Arabic. Aladdin himself is not clearly identified by nationality, but the principal location of the story makes it likely that he is Chinese. The genie that he summons from the magic lamp builds him a palace in China, and he wins the love of the daughter of the Sultan of China. His palace is transported to Africa, but when he recovers the lamp, he returns with both wife and palace to China to live happily for many years.

2. Indian Corn

Myth! **Pocahontas saved Captain John Smith from execution by the Indians.**

Captain John Smith was on the verge of being executed by the Indians when Chief Powhatan's favorite daughter, Pocahontas, intervened. She covered Smith's head with her own and held tight

313

to his body with her hands. Powhatan, stirred by his daughter's devotion, relented—and Smith was saved.

Many historians are not entirely sold on the story, convinced that at least the part involving Pocahontas is bunk. For one, Smith, who was then the appointed leader of the Jamestown colony, did not mention the Pocahontas episode in a book he wrote in 1608, which was shortly after its supposed happening. For another, none of the other Virginia colonists in their letters home ever mentioned the incident, and neither did any contemporary writers.

Not until 1624, in *The General History of Virginia*, did Smith tell the story of his 'rescue'. But on this date, Pocahontas could no longer provide corroborative support because she was already dead, and had been so for seven years. It is also odd that Smith's 1608 account presents Powhatan as uniformly friendly, yet the 1624 *History* portrays him as a potentially dangerous savage. The latter book recounts that twelve Indians brought Smith back to the camp, whereas his earlier work mentions only four. Finally, Smith's known reputation for exaggeration makes historians suspect that his planned 'execution' by the Indians was really his initiation into the tribe, with Pocahontas' participation as part of the ritual.

Whatever a novelist or scriptwriter might make of the strange relationship between Captain John Smith and Pocahontas, he would only have his imagination to stand on. According to tradition, the two were lovers, but Smith himself didn't make this claim when he wrote about his rescue by the Indian maiden. Though Smith was not married nor betrothed to anyone, he could not have wooed Pocahontas because she was only 11 years old at the time. Even her subsequent marriage to John Rolfe was far from being the culmination of a romance, as she was then a captive of the settlers and was still the wife of a tribesman named Kuocum.

With the 1995 *Pocahontas*, Disney created a myth within a myth, deviating as he did from the original folklore. It's probably just as well that the film is animated and its theme of New World adventure and racial romance is attuned to the younger generation. Critics say a live action version appropriate for a more mature audience would have to begin only at the time Pocahontas went with John Rolfe to England, where she was treated as a princess and became an overnight celebrity. The story would continue after her death of smallpox and her burial in the English town of

Gravesend, with Rolfe returning to the New World and getting killed in 1622 in an Indian attack led by his own uncle-in-law. The finale would show their son, Thomas Rolfe, deciding to settle in Virginia to found a line that would include the Marshalls, the Jeffersons and the Lees, not to mention the second Mrs. Woodrow Wilson.

3. Maid in China

Myth! The story of Mulan was adapted from an English language children's book.

Mulan (1998), about a Chinese girl who disguises herself as a boy to join the Imperial Army in place of her handicapped father, is based on a children's book by Robert San Souci. Despite—or because of—the juvenile antics of an inept but boisterous mini-dragon and a slaphappy cricket, the animated fantasy adventure does well to deliver its message of honor, heroism and sacrifice to fans of all ages. However, Disney could have made a much larger impression, even with the film's unpolished graphics, by declaring that the story was lifted from a famous Chinese ballad written and sung about 1,500 years ago during the Northern Dynasties (AD 420-589). A footnote in the credits might also have pointed out that certain significant details of the plot have a basic authenticity that most Asian writers and historians have accepted over the centuries.

Presaging Disney's *Mulan* are several live action movies produced in China, Taiwan and Hong Kong, from 1937 to the 1990s. Devoid of Hollywood flair but heavy on Chinese martial scenes, their scripts have all been inspired by the ancient ballad about a female dressed up as a male warrior who attains the rank of general and quits the army in her early thirties to go back to her peaceful life of weaving. Yet opinions differ on how much of the ballad is fiction and how much is historical fact. "It's sort of like Robin Hood in Chinese," observes one critic. "There are any number or versions and contradictory telling of the basic story that have been done in China over the past 1,500 years."

For one, there is no agreement on Mulan's surname—Zhu, Wei and Mulan were used by various writers, although the Ming writer

Xu Wei called her Hua and it was his version of the tale that became the most popularly known. Mulan's time frame is also vague: one version said she served the Sui dynasty (589-618), another put her exploits at the beginning of the Tang dynasty (618), and yet a third placed her during the reign of Emperor Xiaowen (467-499) of the Northern Wei dynasty. The last date appears to be the most relevant, considering that in the ballad, Mulan's emperor is referred to as 'khan', a fifth century title. 'Khan' is not an indigenous Chinese word but comes from the vocabulary of the nomads on China's northern frontier, raising the possibility that Mulan did not belong to Chinese mainstream culture but to a minority immigrant race. Finally, Mulan was said by some to have emerged from the Wan County in Hebei, and by others the Shangqiu province in Henan. A third opinion was that she was a native of the Liang prefecture in Gansu. One thing seems certain, though: Hua Mulan hailed from a region known as the North China (or Central) Plain.

The most fundamental criticism against Mulan has to do with whether a story like hers could have happened in traditional Chinese society where women were a submissive and non-aggressive lot. Those who believe it cite as support the fact that lady combatants disguised as males were not unheard of in other places and climes, including even the US during the Civil War. In China, the sheer number of real-life heroic stories that verge on the fictional raises the probabilities dramatically. Interestingly, part of Mulan's popular tradition holds that, consistent with the common practice for ancient and medieval Chinese military families to train their daughters in the arts of war at an early age, Mulan was already an accomplished martial artist before she joined the army.

4. Opening Davy's Locker

Myth! Davy Crockett's life was completely true to his heroic image.

The little that we knew about Davy Crockett before Walt Disney discovered him can be summed up in one line: he was a Western folk figure who stood somewhere between Daniel Boone and Kit Carson. Disney's take on Davy as the 'King of the Wild

316

Frontier' and a subsequent John Wayne film about the Alamo (1960) bolstered the belief that Davy was bigger than any of the other frontiersmen of his time, being one of the Alamo defenders who fought to the death and sacrificed themselves for a patriotic cause.

Of French Huguenot descent, Crockett's family name was originally Crocketagne, while his first name wouldn't be Davy until after his death. He sired several children, having been married twice, not counting the one evidenced by a contract preserved in the Dandridge, Tennessee courthouse even though it was never celebrated. He was elected Tennessee representative to the US Congress in 1826 and 1828, lost his re-election bid in 1830, then regained his seat in 1832. In 1834 he published his autobiography, *A Narrative of the Life of David Crockett*, and in the same year ran for re-election, which he lost. In 1835 he lost yet again, compelling him to quit his home state in disgust and move to the then Mexican territory of Texas.

Long before Walt Disney built his myth, Davy's autobiography was already being held out as a fraud that contained mostly tall tales of adventure and heroism. One improbable item in the *Narrative*, which was immediately discredited (but retained in the song 'The Ballad of Davy Crockett'), is his claim that he killed a bear at the age of three. True to the suspicion that Davy did not write the *Narrative* himself, being poorly educated, it would soon be revealed that the work was ghostwritten by his political supporters, the Whigs, to improve his standing as a frontier hero and a possible successor to Democrat Andrew Jackson. Today critics insist the true Davy Crockett was neither like the figure in the autobiography nor like the clean-shaven hero portrayed by TV's Fess Parker. In spite of Disney's build-up and the craze for all things Crockett that it created in the 1950s, Davy continues to be seen as a laggard and a drunk who deserted his wife and children, a 'scout' who hired a substitute to fight his battles against the Indians, and a congressman who failed to get reelected because of one of the worst absentee records in Congress. Harvard University awarded the American folk hero an honorary degree, apparently unaware that he was technically an illiterate and had once been a juvenile delinquent.

It is popularly believed Davy died defending the Alamo, but a controversial diary written by a Mexican participant in the attack disclosed that he was one of the few who survived and were later

317

executed by General Sta. Ana. Eyewitness reports that he was on a downslide, spending most of his time drinking and carousing in the Alamo and proving to be a liability to the garrison, have raised doubts that he fought gallantly and competently in the end. A statement publicly issued by Crockett himself has provided a clue to the real reason he was at the Alamo on that fateful occasion. In 1835, having suffered his second consecutive defeat for re-election to the US House of Representatives, he said, "I told the people of my district that I would serve them as faithfully as I had done; but if not ... you may all go to hell, and I will go to Texas." And so he did, offering his services to the Provisional Government of Texas for six months on the promise of a land grant of 4,600 acres as payment.

IX

Shadows In The Myth

On King Arthur and Robin Hood

"For every man, there is a purpose which he sets up in his life.
Let yours be the doing of all good deeds."

•

Robin Hood

1. 13Th Century Fox

Myth! Robin Hood was a real figure in 13th-century England.

As early as the 16th century, Robin Hood was being treated as though he were an established historical figure. Henry VIII knew of him, and so did William Shakespeare. Later, some historians would dignify him as the disinherited earl of Huntington, and his bow and arrows would be proudly displayed as museum pieces in Kirklees Hall, Yorkshire, where his grave is pointed out in the park. Others, like the 19th-century Shakespearean scholar Joseph Hunter, wrote about finding concrete evidence that Robin was real. Many today give his legend the same factual accreditation, believing that its consistency with the general history and social conditions of the English medieval period is sufficient to qualify it as true.

Contrary to his flesh-and-blood reputation, little can be said to support the authenticity of Robin Hood. There were undoubtedly daring outlaws that inhabited Sherwood Forest during his period, and some even had names strikingly similar to Robin's. Various histories introduce us to Robert Hood of Wakefield or Barnsdale in Yorkshire; Robyn Hode, a humble servant to King Edward II; Roberd Hude, an almost illegible name on a gravestone at Kirklees; and Gilbert Robynhod of Sussex. Others, like Hereward the Wake, the last Anglo-Saxon chieftain to resist the Norman Conquest of 1066, became famous for their own Robin Hood-like exploits. But these parallels are obviously not enough to link a true-to-life character to the legend and to make a real Robin out of a mere Robin Hood look-alike. The misery of the period would have just as likely spawned a legendary as a historical outlaw who stole from the rich to give to the poor, and in Robin Hood's case, it happened to be the former.

Historians have used the name 'Robin Hood' at various times without any serious intent of determining who its rightful owner is or whether it has one at all. Some believe 'Robin Hood' was only a pseudonym commonly used by English rebels, revolutionaries, bandits and poachers of the period. Others say it could have been applied as a temporary tag on unknown persons involved in medieval court proceedings, in much the same way the name 'John

Doe' is encountered today in open police files and cold cases. A writer notes that during the turbulent days of the English aristocracy, 'Robin Hood' was an iconic signature affixed by many to statements of protest, defiance and solidarity against real or imagined oppression.

2. Once a Shining Spot

Myth! **The British folk hero Arthur was a flesh and blood king.**

Despite the mythification of King Arthur's reign, many believed he was real, among them Henry II of England, who was thoroughly convinced that Arthur founded the royal line leading down to him. The earliest of Arthur's publicists, Geoffrey of Monmouth, lived in the twelfth century, which is probably why people tend to associate the legendary monarch with that era. Arthur is called 'the once and future king' because, according to Monmouth and another publicist, Sir Thomas Malory, Arthur is fated to return someday.

Many modern historians assume Arthur lived, but not as a king. His character has been traced to two minor figures that belonged to a far earlier period than what legend has assigned to Arthur's Camelot. One is a general named Artorius and the other is the warlord Riothamus, who fought under other chieftains or princes as a mercenary to stop the Anglo-Saxon invasions of fifth-century England. As one writer puts it, the man behind the myth was "not a medieval Briton on a white charger but a Roman who rode armorless on a Roman horse the size of a modern pony."

Disbelievers say there could not have been any knights around Arthur because these cavaliers appeared in Europe only in the eighth century and in England several centuries after that. Also, while romanticists equate Camelot with South Cadbury Castle in southwest England, there is no proof people got to live in castles before the Norman Conquest in the eleventh century. Equally doubtful is the claim that Arthur's body was discovered by monks in the twelfth century in a hollow log buried somewhere in the vicinity of Glastonbury Abbey near Somerset. Most historians concur that the cause of the confusion between Avalon, Arthur's mythical burial place, and Glastonbury was an etymological error.

3. Gay Blade

Myth! Robin Hood was a dashing ladies' man.

The Robin Hood persona has always been that of a dashing ladies' man, thanks to Errol Flynn's definitive performance in the 1938 classic. This was briefly interrupted in 1976, when Sean Connery brought the character out of Hollywood hibernation and presented him as a tired old bachelor trying to rekindle an insipid romance with Maid Marian.

A twenty-year research has revealed that the historical model for Robin Hood was a gay who had Edward II for a lover. Edward was the real-life king whose only claim to fame is the unique way he was assassinated: he was sodomized with a red-hot poker. The same source confirms that there never was a Maid Marian, adding that in the absence of any other woman in Robin's mythical or real life, he was possibly a misogynist.

Robin, it is said, met Edward in a forest, and after he was pardoned for his brigandage, went to work for His Highness in London. The ensuing friendship became the subject of one of the first stories to be published about the outlaw, 'A Gest of Robyn Hode'; this was produced in the form of a lengthy poem by a London printer in the late 1400s but probably written about eighty years earlier. Recently, proof was unearthed in the form of official royal records that Edward actually did go on a hunting trip to Yorkshire and Nottingham between April and November 1323, and he did employ a Robyn Hode at his London Court at about that time.

Nottingham authorities admit the veracity of the meeting but claim it was another Robyn Hood—the one from Yorkshire—who was involved. The revelation appeared in a brochure that the Nottingham Tourism Committee prepared and released to the public in 1988. Its basis is a book, *Robin Hood*, by Professor James Clarke Holt, Master of Fitzwilliam College in Cambridge. The Nottingham people are understandably quick to acknowledge the existence of Robin look-alikes, to ward off claims derogatory of the personal and geographical circumstances long established by legend and tradition for their hero.

---

4. Jacks to the King

Myth! **Merlin built the round table for King Arthur to seat his appointed knights.**

King Arthur's legendary court was centered on the Round Table, around which he gathered his most trusted knights. According to the Table's own fabled past, Merlin the Magician built it at Carduel to seat 28 persons.

The original story assigns ownership of the table to Uther Pendragon, who gave it to King Leodegraunce of Cameliard, who in turn gave it to King Arthur when the latter married his daughter Guinevere. The round shape, it is said, was to prevent arguments about precedence from breaking out, but later revisions of the myth skirted the idea by setting up a favored seat, the Siege Perilous, for the knight whose destiny was to reach the Holy Grail. Contrary to the common belief that Arthur commissioned all the 150 Knights of the Round Table, Gawain and Tor were the only ones the king personally appointed. One hundred knights came with the furniture piece when Arthur accepted it from his father-in-law, and Merlin put another 28 in their seats (this is apparently why some insist the table could accommodate only 28). The remaining 20 were for those who would later prove themselves worthy of the standards set by Arthur for his gallants.

The concept of the Round Table is not entirely legendary, however. One such table, good for 12 knights, is shown in Winchester, inherited from Henry III's time by Henry VIII. In the eighth year of Edward I, Roger de Mortimer established a Round Table at Kenilworth for "the encouragement of military pastimes," and about 70 years later, Edward III erected a splendid table 200 feet in diameter at Windsor.

5. Errant Lineage

Myth! Merlin was King Arthur's father, Mordred his son or nephew, and Excalibur the sword he pulled out of a magic stone.

Mordred was the evil knight who usurped King Arthur's kingdom while he was away and plotted to take Queen Guinevere from Lancelot so he could marry her himself. His acts caused King Arthur's demise as well as his own and the consequent dissolution of the Round Table.

Mordred is sometimes described as Arthur's son and at other times his nephew, but the conflict is quickly resolved by the revelation that, as Arthur's son by his half-sister, he was both. The king's incestuous relationship with his sibling so offended the Victorians that this aspect of the legend was excised from the original during their era.

If Arthur's parenthood was controversial, his pedigree was even more so. Geoffrey of Monmouth wrote that he was the son of Uther Pendragon, a king of Britain who sired him by raping Ygerna, the beautiful wife of the Duke of Cornwall, through trickery. The Victorians also omitted this part for its prurience, but it has since been restored in print and can even be seen visually in the 1981 film *Excalibur*. In an effort to make Arthur's origin consistent with the story of the sword in the stone, Bullfinch tags Merlin as Arthur's father—a revision of the line that Ygerna only surrendered Arthur to Merlin so he could be protected against the prediction that pretenders to Uther's throne would kill him.

Incidentally, the movie *Excalibur* may have corrected a fallacy but creates another by confusing the origin of Arthur's magic sword. It shows Arthur laying claim to the throne by pulling Excalibur out of a stone, contravening the basic myth that the Lady of the Lake gave him the sword sometime during his reign.

6. Wiz of a Star

Myth! Merlin was dressed in a flowing robe, with a tall conical hat on his head and a magic wand in his hand.

The 1963 Disney animation The *Sword in the Stone* portrays Merlin in his most cartoonish—a sorcerer wearing a tall conical hat and a flowing robe, and waving a magic wand over a crystal bowl. The film did not invent the stereotype, as it was totally in accord with the wizard's popular image. However, if the studio had taken more time to research the figure, they would have discovered that there was a real Merlin and that he was less flamboyant than imagined.

One of those suspected to be Merlin is a Welsh bard and part-time prophet named Myrddin. The trouble with this character is that he was alive long after Arthur's time, in fact nearly a century later. Others agree with Geoffrey of Monmouth that the real-life Merlin was about 30 years Arthur's senior, although some critics say Geoffrey made Merlin much older than Arthur only for the sake of a good story. According to this view, Merlin was not a name but a title, and its owner was a bishop named Dubricius, who crowned Arthur.

In either case, Merlin was Welsh and a sorcerer, which easily qualify him to be a Druid, one of the last from this strange priesthood. He was supposed to have been murdered, in the realistic version by shepherds and in the fantasy version by the Lady of the Lake, of whom he became enamored and to whom he offered to teach magic. She refused to become his mistress and finally used one of his own spells to bind him and entomb him in a cave.

---

7. Tighted Englishman in green Hood

Myth! Robin Hood's standard attire included green tights.

There are homoerotic undertones in the phrase 'Men in Tights', which is the subtitle of Mel Brooks' 1993 take on the Robin Hood story. The suggestion is that, accurately or not, those Lincoln green tights Robin wears in his movies and elsewhere project a gay image for this gallant. It may be that men's tights in Robin's days were actually close-fitting breeches and an acceptable fashion of the times. Still, Robin, if he were real, would not have been caught wearing them, as they would have proved flimsy and impractical for forest living. Actually, Hollywood's depiction of Robin in tights was based largely on Victorian stage plays in which most of those who played his character were women who loved to wear tights to show off their legs.

One thing more: the outlaw's costume was not always Lincoln green. In one story, Robin is described as wearing red while leading his merry men into Nottingham in June. The name 'Robin' happens to be related to the Latin *robus*, meaning red, a hint that red was really his favorite color. Robin's persona may yet be involved in a third color; in many of his tales, Robin Hood is also nicknamed 'Brown Robin'. Whatever was the true color of Robin's attire, Lincoln green was one of the eye-pleasing elements that gave Errol Flynn that dashing look and his movie an IMDB five-star rating. Lincoln is a reference to the English town where the material for Robin's costume was supposedly woven, while the color is one of the deeper hues of green believed to have been preferred by Robin because it camouflaged well in a Sherwood Forest setting.

8. Lanced a Lot

Myth! Sir Lancelot and Queen Guinevere were lovers.

It is ironic that the knight of the Round Table everyone seems to know is the most enigmatic of all. Lancelot is popularly believed to be a British original of the Round Table whose special friendship with the King ended abruptly when he was discovered carrying on a clandestine affair with Queen Guinevere.

In fact, Lancelot was a johnny-come-lately and French. It was his Gallic charms more than his secret love for Guinevere (which, contrary to what most literary sources claim, never culminated in an adulterous affair) that incurred the blind jealousy of Arthur and, through Modred's machinations, indirectly caused the destruction of Camelot.

Fans who fell in love with the Lancelot character in the Broadway play *Camelot* may be disappointed to know that he was never in the original British-Celtic legends of Arthur and the knights of the Round Table. His origins actually lie in the twelfth-century work of the French writer Chretien de Troyes, who made him out as the hero of a series of amorous adventures, none of which involved Guinevere. Thomas Mallory, who wrote his version of Arthur while languishing in prison for crimes ranging from robbery to rape, lifted Lancelot wholesale from French literature to perk up the British legend.

9. Time Bandit

Myth! Maid Marian and Richard the Lion-Heart were the closest persons to Robin Hood.

Several Hollywood interpretations of Robin Hood's legend portray Maid Marian as a relative of King Richard the Lion-Heart. In The *Adventures of Robin Hood* (1938), she is a protégé of Prince John, brother of Richard, and in *Robin Hood: Prince of Thieves* (1991), she is Richard's cousin. Marian's kinship to a historical figure is obviously one of the elements designed to lend credence to the Robin Hood story.

The legend is a muddled timetable of events spanning several centuries. The outlaw's thirteenth-century origins separate him by almost three hundred years from his love interest, Maid Marian, who is a sixteenth-century damsel in most writings. There is an attempt to rationalize the historicity of Robin through Richard the Lion-Heart, but the two were never contemporaries. The outlaw of Sherwood Forest (or Barnesdale Forest, as in the early ballads) was erroneously brought back to the monarch's time in the twelfth century by a pedigree that an eighteenth-century antiquary fabricated.

The confusion in Robin's annals is worsened by the anachronisms that abound in his movies. The 1991 Kevin Costner vehicle stands out for its boggled scenes in which various things make 'untimely' appearances. For instance, gunpowder was not used in Europe until the late thirteenth century, while the telescope was invented only in the sixteenth century. Other examples are a Saracen sword, which came later than the broadsword of the period; 'wanted' posters of Robin Hood, which couldn't have been printed until the fourteenth century; and a codpiece (apparent on the sheriff of Nottingham), which debuted in the fifteenth century.

The early books and ballads about the prince of thieves are also full of anomalies. In *A Lytell Geste of Robyn Hode*, printed in 1420 by Wynkyn de Worde, Littel John is not a giant outlaw but a normal-sized fellow named Lytell John or John Lytell. Historian Thomas Slemen notes that, in those days, the 'merry' in 'merry men' merely meant that their story had a happy ending, but "down the centuries the word has become confused with the carefree living-off-the-land philosophy of Robin's men." The ballads locate most of the action in south Yorkshire, bringing them outside the jurisdiction of the sheriff of Nottingham. These same sources reveal why music, literature and the movies are generally quiet about the fate of Robin and his principal adversary. As described in the ballads in poetic but grisly detail, the sheriff was shot to death with arrows and then beheaded. Robin fared even worse: he was bled to death by a prioress whose own lover was slain and thrown to the dogs.

X

Stone Cold Dead

On Monuments to Myths

"And should I be willing to do this, wilt thou give me leave?"

•

Lady Godiva

1. Fantasy in Concrete

Myth! The Little Dutch Boy was a real live hero from Haarlem.

One of our greatest childhood heroes was a child himself. He was the Little Dutch Boy who, after thrusting his finger into the hole of a leaking dike to save his town from being destroyed, died. His story suggests that he succumbed to the pressure brought upon his finger by the water on the other side of the dike. Unfortunately, this will never be confirmed in the absence of a medical report or coroner's investigation.

Nobody knows when the Dutch boy, also called the Hero of Haarlem, lived, or indeed if he lived at all. All we are sure of is that the story is American, not Dutch, and is about the son of a dike worker who, on his way home just before dark, heard the sound of water and saw it trickling down from a hole in the dike. He immediately thrust his forefinger into the hole and started shouting for help. All night long he hollered but no one heard, until the next morning, still plugged in, he was spotted by a priest who alerted the maintenance crews.

The integrity of the story has been challenged so many times there should no longer be any question that the whole thing is a pure literary invention. Not the least of its blatant fallacies is the idea that one chubby finger of a boy can stop a whole dike from leaking and finally disrupting. Equally ludicrous is that a boy can die from mere water pressure on that finger. It is said that the Dutch people are deeply ashamed of the story, although this did not stop the Dutch Tourist Office from pretending the boy was real and having a statue of him erected in 1950 in the town of Spaarndem, which is nowhere near Haarlem. This monument to fictional heroism has been a favorite of sightseers, who continue to be fascinated by the deed it glorifies without realizing it is an all-American concoction. The basis of the whole fantasy is the 1865 juvenile classic *Hans Brinker, or the Silver Skates* by the American writer Mary Mapes Dodge, in which the Hero of Haarlem appears as the title character in a story being narrated by a teacher to a group of school children. Dodge's novel is so dominated by the legend it has produced that even people today

330

believe that Hans Brinker and the nameless boy who plugged a hole in the dike are one and the same.

2. Where have All the Symbols Gone?

Myth! **The Dutch invented the windmill.**

Some of our Dutch friends hazard the point that it's not really the boy they are honoring, but the dike as an inanimate object that the boy was hoping to protect by his act of valor. The dike happens to be a national symbol of the Netherlands, and the monument is apparently a demonstration of the extent to which people will go to preserve that symbol.

And yet, Time reports, the dike is fading fast both as a symbol and as a landmark of the Netherlands. The Dutch have concluded that wresting their land from water through the use of dikes has in many instances become too costly and damaging. The manipulation has played havoc with water tables, sunk the lowlands further, and polluted fields and aquifers. Consequently, they have adopted a plan, approved in 1990, to return almost one-tenth of the present farmland to forest, wetlands and lakes. Bulldozers have been punching holes in dikes to let a river spill into flood plains and recreate alluvial forest.

The dike is only one of the three most ubiquitous features of the Dutch countryside, the second being the stork, also long a national symbol of the Netherlands. According to the same report from Time, the Dutch have realized that constant manicuring of the land and use of chemicals to increase their yields of flowers, vegetables, meat and produce have driven out numerous native plant and animal species. Even the daisy is dwindling, and larger creatures like the stork have disappeared. Eighty per cent of the world's storks are now located in Spain.

With the dike and the stork on their way out, what remains of the venerable symbols of the Dutch is the windmill. But the windmill is more a symbol of Iran than of the Netherlands. Though the device is a common sight in Europe, it did not originate there. Rather, it was a product of Arab and Persian ingenuity and was widely used in the Middle East long before it reached the continent. The earliest known structures, in the fashion of sails attached to vertical-axis center posts to pick up the wind from either direction, date to about 644 BC in Seistan, on the borders of Iran and Afghanistan. Back in the 12th century, crusaders saw the strange objects dotting the Iranian landscape, and only then was knowledge of windmills brought to Europe to make an impression in Holland

---

3. Apple of Bill's Eye

Myth! The William Tell legend is beloved to the Swiss but the majority of them don't believe it's true.

It happened in the late thirteenth century, when the Swiss began to stir against the tyrannical influence of the Hapsburg rulers of Austria, especially Albert I. William Tell, the famous Swiss patriot, was compelled to shoot an apple off his son's head, but had the prudence to reserve a second arrow for the Austrian bailiff Gessler in the event the child was killed. This is probably the most popular tale to come out of Switzerland, and Tell himself has been almost beatified as a Swiss national hero by its constant retelling worldwide.

For reasons not easy to understand, the usually pragmatic Swiss are most serious in dignifying Tell's tale as history, with 60 percent believing (according to a recent survey) that their hero existed. They built a chapel to the archer in 1338 on Lake Lucerne, which they say was the spot where the whole apple-shooting incident took place. A block of stone from that chapel was Switzerland's official contribution to the building of the Washington Monument. Yet their own Historical Society is unequivocal in announcing that both Tell and Gessler are wholly fictional characters. At least one canton, that of Schwyz, couldn't live with the lie and in 1890 ordered the Tell legend to be erased from its history textbooks.

Like most other legendary heroes, William Tell is replicated outside his own country, for example in England, which has its Sir William of Cloudesley. But Tell could have been a copy himself. The Norwegians produced their folk hero Egil hundreds of years before the 16th century chronicler Aegidius Tschudi came up with the original Tell version, and a similar tale was told as early as the twelfth century in Persia.

---

4. Barebacked Rider

Myth! Lady Godiva is a mythical figure celebrated in an annual English pageant.

It is not entirely clear if this popular lady of merry old England was a real human being. Historical-sounding names and places give the story a patina of truth, but the overall flavor is still folkloric. There was a Lady Godiva who lived in the 11th century and who pleaded with her ruthless husband Leofric, the Earl of Mercia, to ease up on his subjects and reduce the tax they had to pay. But there is no record that, like the Lady Godiva of legend, she rode shamelessly naked on a white horse through the English town of Coventry in order to convince her husband.

Undoubtedly, while the legendary lady's story has some basis in the life of the real Godiva, the famous ride is only a fictional embellishment. The idea was very likely borrowed from an annual English pageantry, which, as portrayed by the misericord carving in Coventry Cathedral, featured a woman riding a goat. Oddly, the first known celebration involving a naked lady on a white horse was launched long after Godiva's name had become a synonym for exhibitionist, and was precisely to honor the legend. Still, the ride was not mentioned until 1236, in the chronicle of Roger of Wendover, or nearly 200 years after the real Godiva's death at about the time of the Norman Conquest in 1066. Several centuries later, a 1670 article by the Earl of Oxford added the character of Peeping Tom, the town tailor who peeped through a knothole in the shutter of his shop despite Leofric's order not to look at the lady.

Whole communities of people fantasizing about a person who should have been but never was can be found not only in Europe but in other places as well. Paul Bunyan is a pure product of Yankee imagination, yet his awesome frame stands heroically on some serious-looking monuments from Minnesota to California, as if to say that it's the spirit and not the flesh that counts.

5. A Muse Meant for the Gods

Myth! Polyhymnia was the Greek patron of music.

The mythical sources of artistic inspiration for the Greeks were the Muses, of whom there were nine. Hesiod named them Clio, Thalia, Melpomene, Calliope, Euterpe, Erato, Terpsichore, Urania and Polyhymnia. Should we ask which one was the patron of music and singers, the answer, surprisingly, would be no one. Only Polyhymnia had a special interest in music or singing, and this was limited to hymns. The others dabbled in history, comedy, tragedy, epic poetry, lyric poetry, erotic poetry, the dance and astronomy, respectively.

In another sense, it was everyone. The Muses when invented by the Greeks weren't specialized and didn't have the individual attributes that would later be assigned to each by the Romans. They were regarded as a group, with Calliope as their leader, and collectively they inspired kings and poets. The totality of the Muses' arts was called *mousikos*, and the artist, whether a bard, a dancer, a historian or a dramatist, was a *mousike*. The Greeks considered song the highest art and believed the Muses' principal talent was singing. In due time, the term *mousikos* came to be more particularized to mean what we know it today—the art of combining pleasant sounds, or 'music'.

The Romans distorted the Greek concept when they assigned specific areas of interest to the Muses, and worse, when they failed to provide a rational basis for the assignment. Thus, there was a Muse for astronomy although it was a science and not an art, two Muses too many for poets, and none for true artists like painters and sculptors.

6. Gold Diggers of 1595

Myth! The fabulous quest of New World explorers was a long-lost city of gold called El Dorado.

Gaily bedight, a gallant young knight, in search of El Dorado—this is the opening line of a famous poem by Edgar Allan Poe about a fabled quest many adventurers and explorers undertook during the early years of the New World. The poem is an affirmation of the popular belief in 16th century Europe that El Dorado was a long-lost city of gold located deep in the American jungle. Later reports would assert that there was no city of gold, only a man and a lake of gold. El Dorado was El hombre Dorado, meaning 'The Golden Man', chief of a tribe who lived on an island named Manoa in the middle of a lake somewhere in South America. Each morning, the priests coated his naked body with resin and then blew gold dust all over the sticky surface, and each evening he washed the gold dust off in the lake. This practice continued for so many centuries that a great deposit of gold dust is said to have accumulated on the lake floor. Augmenting the dust were golden trinkets that the natives threw into the lake one day each year according to tribal tradition.

Many a Spanish conquistador tortured and killed, often only to be killed themselves, in their quest for El Dorado. The real objective was not so much the 'Golden Man' as the place from which his subjects were mining the precious metal. Thanks to this focus on a lost city of gold, the impression has remained that El Dorado is the name of a place rather than of a person. The most famous searcher is Sir Walter Raleigh, who convinced King James I to release him from the Tower of London so that he might seek the fabulous source. When he returned empty-handed, James was so disappointed he had Raleigh beheaded.

7. Playing the Piper's Song

Myth! The Pied Piper was a figure in medieval legend that abducted 130 children of a German town.

Contrary to popular belief, the story of the Pied Piper of Hamelin originated not as legend but as fact. Two 16th-century houses in the Westphalian town of Hamelin (or Hameln, the correct German name) bear inscriptions commemorating the abduction of 130 of its children by a stranger on June 26, 1284. The underlying story is that on this date a piper appeared and offered to rid the community of its rats in exchange for a fee of 1,000 guilders. The bargain was sealed, but after the piper had played his pipe through the streets and lured the rodents to a mass drowning in the Weser River, the townspeople refused to pay. The piper returned to Hamelin on St. John's Day and with his playing enticed the children into a cave in the Koppenberg Mountain. As soon as they had entered, the entrance of the cave closed behind them and all 130 were trapped forever. Until the 19th century, two crosses had stood on the mountain to mark the spot where the children were last seen.

This strange account, which has become the stuff of the Brothers Grimm's 'The Pied Piper of Hamelin', is remarkably similar to other tales of pipers, magicians and father figures who spirited away children in European and Middle Eastern folklore. Its earliest known record dating back to the 15th century makes no mention of a piper, leading some mythologists to believe the reported disappearance might have been an allegorical allusion to either the Children's Crusade of 1212, the battle of Sedemunde in 1260, or the Black Death that raged through Europe from the mid 1340s to the late 1360s. All these events are well-known disasters that wiped out large numbers of Europe's children, especially Germany's. On the other hand, the oldest monument to the story is a stained glass window placed in the Church of Hamelin c. 1300, or more than a century earlier than the report. This was supposedly destroyed in 1660, but based on the surviving descriptions, the famous German cryptographer Hans Dobbertin (1952-2006) created a modern reconstruction of the window. The work showing the colorful figure of the Pied Piper and those of children dressed in white is touted generally as a memorial to a tragic event that marred the city's otherwise tranquil history. However, while research has been conducted for centuries, there are a few odd facts (e.g., rats were only added to the story in c. 1559) that have prevented historians from reaching a consensus on what really happened.

❊○❊

LIST OF TOPICS IN THIS VOLUME

SCIENCE & PHILOSOPHY

Global Movement
Three from Galileo's Proofs
Henry and Lizzie: A Love Story
Oil Alone
Down-to-Earth Principle
Looking Over one's Shoulder
Rub-a-dub-dub
Pressure in the Right Places
Mr. Smithson Goes to Washington

Nature Studies
Ole Blue Cheese
The Moon has Two Faces
Look, Sky Walkers!
24 Carrot Sticks and a One Pound Cake
To the Ends of the Earth
Round as an Egg
How Levelly the Sea
The Long and Short of 24 Hours
Somewhere under the Rainbow
The Straight Story
Snap Judgment
Hair to Dye for
Horrorscope Signs
Father of the Pride
The Sssssound of Music
Suicide Kings
When Giants Swam the Seas
In the Company of Man
Bye bye Birdie
Whither the Winter Weather?
Up and Down the Poles
Horns Aplenty
They Live?

ART & LITERATURE

The Folly In Leonardo's Folio
The Smile becomes Her
The Lady was no Dame
She was no Lady, she was his Wife

The Lady shows her Hand
Cherchez l'Homme
Italian Cosmetic Job
Making Eyes all the Time
Her Life on the Rocks
The Lady shows her Worth
The Lady has a Medium
The Lying Apostles
Maker's Dozen
Thirteen at Dinner
A Brooder in the Brood
Holy Graffiti!
When Last is First
Rejuvenating an Old Master

Creation And Recreation
Horned Dilemma
Exemplars of Piety
An Unfinished Statement
Signature Art
Horizontal Perspective
Multiple Dimensions
End in View

Masters Of Art
Lending an Ear
Day into Night
Op Art
Portrait of the Artist as a Whistler
After Death Experience
Dollar Portrait
Painting by the Book
Sign of the Greek

Black And White In Color
Color it Black
Pigments of the Imagination
Primal Senses
Shades of Hades
Color it Dead
Dreamscape
Southern Blackface

Flower Perfect
Green Passions
Dark Waters
Managing the White Pieces
Bullish Tendency
Meet Roy G. Biv
Proof of Life
Legally Blonde
Panic Button
Hot Styles are Cool (and Vice Versa)

According To Doyle

First on the Crime Scene?
Needling Questions
Gumshoe in Steele Trappings
The Hounds of Baker Street
Rules of Deception
Eliminate to Illuminate
Welcome to the Doyle House
Art of the Double Doyle
Say it Again, Basil
In his Own Image
Whose Name is it, Anyway?

Murder On Her Mind

A Mysterious Affair with Style
Rx for Murder
As Plain as Miss Jane
Dead Man's Mirror
Warning Miranda
Murderers Row

Culture Vultures

Gertie was no Dinosaur
Generation X'd
The Sweaty Smell of Success
An Intense Interest in Tents
A Hawthorne in his Side
Twain Spotting
Mad about Alice
Wooly Retorts from a Dotty Lady
Just a Jokey Jane

Zola Power
A Case for Hard-boiled Yeggs
Poster Fodder
Does it have 'Encyclopedigree'?
His own Worst Enemy
Homo is the Hero
Never these Twins shall Meet
John woos Priscilla as Miles' Stand-in?

Malappropriate Language
Their Slips showed
Goldwyn's Follies
The Boner Collection
The Owl behind the Howler
A Queer old Dean

Slices Of Shakey's
A Poet by any Other Name
A Life in Three Acts
Of Shylocks and Shysters
Fingers are All you Need at Shakey's
Not to the Manner Born
Ham Maybe, but Bacon Never
Shakespeare for Dummies
Rivals in Arms Deal
Romeo Bleeds
Regarding Henry
Last Seen with Rosencrantz & Guildenstern
English Spoken Here

English Waffles And Danish Sophistries
Two Danish Tarts
Protestant Queen
The Ploy's the Thing
In a Spectral Manor
Polonaic Wisdom
Fine Dining at the Front
More than Meets the Eye

FILM & MUSIC

A Failure To Communicate

Don't Snarl when you Say That
Minors' Extravaganza
When you See this Bogie, just Whistle
Celluloid Passport
Breaking the Sound Barrier
Eye-lashing in a Small Town
Three and three from Two
Is that Mae West or is it Just Silicone?
A Butler did it
Swedish Message
Choosing Bubbles
Those Itchy-bitchy Years

The Hitch In Hitchcock
Spy up his Nose
The Twist at the End of the Stairs
Lowdown on a High Crime
Long Distance Slaying
"I was Rebecca's Altar Ego"

Celebrity Rolls
Pie in your Eye
A Naked Half-Wit
The Rat Packer's Way
The Sorcerer's Apprentice
Wonder Boy
All Ears
The Best Year of his Life
Head Turner

Music In A Falsetto Voice
British Air Apparent
Better Sung than Red
A-kickin' we will Go
Long, Long Ago
Sing a Song of Six Pence
Rest Stop
A Handle on Handel
Out of Time and Place
Whose Side were they on Anyway?

FANTASY & MYTHOLOGY

Animal Farm
Ease up on Aesop
Fabulous Fabulator
Wildcat Strike
Nature of the Beast
Crying Game
Creature Feature

A Gander At The Goose
Goose Story
Not Suitable for 5 and Under
A Short Lamb's Tale
Humongous Human Goose
Goose Dressing
Dum-dee-dum-dum-dum
Reborn in the Nursery

Evergreen Tales From The Neverland
Unbending Ending
A Life quite Ordinary
Loathsome Spirits and Lithesome Sprites
Grimm Reality
A Mythifying Dane
Malice in Wonderland
Starting on the Wrong Foot
While She was Sleeping
Bears on her Back
Fantasie Francais
Wolf Bait
Up a Tree
Seven Footmen
Foot-bound for the Ball
Little Green Baddies
Fruit Fatale

Life Is A Riddle And Man Is The Answer
Oedipus Wrecked
Belling the Cat
Electra Connection

Neutered by the Gods
That Darn Cat Again
Looking a Gift Horse in the Belly
When a Twin Peaks, the other Twin Falls
Breathless but Breastless
Sour Graping over an Apple

Altered States
Flower Children with Blooming Egos
Ledan Egg
Hard to Swallow
Which Twin is the Phony
Days of Heaven
How Now, Brown Cow?
United Front
Morphing Addict
Beaus and Eros
No Need to Exorcise
Brute Force

Monster Menagerie
Killing 'em Softly with her Song
Bullheaded Cretan
Doom Box
Stalking Heads
Choice of Harms: Hell or High Water?
Goodbye Tai Fung, Hello Harry Cane
One-eyed in Gaza
Getting Kraken Ready

Ain't No Ordinary Folks
Babe in the Woods
Untrained Engineer
Derailed Objective
Tall Tales from the Saddle
Johnny, we Hardly Knew Ye
Drillmaster

Animated Lives
The Thief of Beijing
Indian Corn
Maid in China

344

Opening Davy's Locker

Shadows In The Myths
13th Century Fox
Once a Shining Spot
Gay Blade
Jacks to the King
Errant Lineage
Wiz of a Star
Tighted Englishman in green Hood
Lanced a Lot
Time Bandit

Stone Cold Dead
Fantasy in Concrete
Where have All the Symbols Gone?
Apple of Bill's Eye
Barebacked Rider
A Muse Meant for the Gods
Gold Diggers of 1595
Playing the Piper's Song

SELECTED READINGS

Adams, Cecil, *The Straight Dope*, New York: Ballantine Books, 1986

Adams, Cecil, *More on the Straight Dope*, New York: Ballantine Books, 1988

Agel, Jerome and Glanze, Walter D., *Cleopatra's Nose, The Twinkie Defense, & 1500 Other Verbal Shortcuts in Popular Parlance*, New York: Prentice Hall Press, 1990

Alterman, Eric, *When Presidents Lie,* London: Penguin Books, 2004

Aron, Paul, *Unsolved Mysteries of History,* New York: Barnes & Noble Books, 2000

Aron, Paul, *More Unsolved Mysteries of History,* New York: Barnes & Noble, 2004

Aron, Paul, *Did Babe Ruth Call His Shot?,* New Jersey: John Wiley & Sons, 2005

Barham, Andrea, *The Pedant's Return,* New York: Bantam Books, 2006

Barthel, Manfred (translated by Howson, Mark), *What the Bible Really Says*, New York: Wings Books, 1992

Battle, Kemp P., *Great American Folklore*, New York: Barnes and Noble, 1992

Boardman, Barrington, *Flappers, Bootleggers, "Typhoid Mary" & the Bomb*, New York: Harper & Row, 1968

Boller, Jr., Paul F., *Presidential Anecdotes*, New York: Penguin Books, 1981

Boller, Jr., Paul F. and Davis, Ronald L., *Hollywood Anecdotes*, New York: William Morrow, 1987

Boller, Jr., Paul F. and George, John, *They Never Said It*, New York: Oxford University Press, 1990

Boller, Jr., Paul F., *Not So!,* New York: Oxford University Press, 1995

Boorstin, Daniel J., *The Discoverers*, New York: Random House, 1983

Boorstin, Daniel J., *The Creators*, New York: Random House, 1992

Breuer, William B., *Daring Missions of World War II,* New Jersey: Castle Books, 2001

Breuer, William B., *Deceptions of World War II,* New Jersey: Castle Books, 2001

Brokaw, Tom, *The Greatest Generation,* New York: Random House, 1998

Brown, Anthony Cave, *Bodyguard of Lies*, London: W. H. Allen & Co. Ltd., 1977

Brown, Peter H. and Pinkston, Jim, *Oscar Dearest*, New York: Harper & Row, 1987

Botting, Douglas & the Editors of Time-Life Books, *The Pirates*,

Virginia: Time-Life Books, 1978

Bullis, Don, *The Old West Trivia Book*, California: Gem Guides Book Company, 1993

Carnes, Mark C. (ed.), *Past Imperfect,* New York: Henry Holt and Company, 1996

Cole, Sylvia & Lass, Abraham H., *The Dictionary of 20th-Century Allusions*, New York: Ballantine Books, 1991

Cowley, Robert (ed.), *What Ifs? Of American History,* New York: G.P. Putnam's Sons, 2003

Craughwell, Thomas J., *Urban Legends,* New York: Barnes & Noble, 2000

Crofton, Ian, *Brewer's Cabinet Of Curiosities,* London: Weidenfeld & Nicolson, 2006

Davis, Kenneth C., *Don't Know Much About History*, New York: Avon Books, 1992

Davis, Kenneth C., *Don't Know Much About Geography*, New York: Avon Books, 1993

Davis, Kenneth C., *Don't Know Much About Mythology*, New York: Harper, 2005

Davis, Kenneth C., *Don't Know Much About World Myths,* New York: HarperCollins, 2005

Davis, Kenneth C., *Don't Know Much About Anything,* New York: Harper, 2007

Del Re, Gerard & Patricia, *History's Last Stand*, New York: Avon Books, 1993

Dickson, Paul & Goulden, Joseph C., *Myth-Informed*, New York: Putnam Publishing, 1993

Diefendorf, David, *Amazing...But False!,* New York: Sterling, 2007

Donald, David Herbert, *Lincoln*, London: Jonathan Cape, 1995

Durant, Will, *Caesar and Christ*, New York: Simon and Schuster, 1944

Durant, Will, *The Age of Faith*, New York: Simon and Schuster, 1950

Durschmied, Erik, *How Chance And Stupidity Have Changed History,* New York: MJF Books, 1999

Eastman, John, *Retakes*, New York: Ballantine Books, 1989

Editors of Time-Life Books, The, *Visions and Prophecies*, Virginia: Time-Life Books, 1988

Editors of Time-Life Books, The, *Feats and Wisdom of the Ancients*, Virginia: Time-Life Books, 1990

Evans, Harold, *They Made America,* New York: Back Bay Books, 2004

Evans, Ivor H., *Brewer's Dictionary of Phrase and Fable*, New York: HarperCollins, 1991

Farquhar, Michael, *A Treasury of Deception,* New York: Penguin, 2005

Farquhar, Michael, *A Treasury Of Foolishly Forgotten Americans,* New York: Penguin, 2008

Feldman, David, *Why Do Pirates Love Parrots*, New York: Collins, 2007

Filler, Louis*, The Muckrakers*, Chicago: Henry Regnery Company, 1968

Flexner, Stuart Berg*, Listening to America*, New York: Simon & Schuster, 1982

Flexner, Stuart and Doris, *The Pessimist's Guide to History*, New York: HarperCollins, 2000

Fox, Robin Lane*, The Unauthorized Version*, New York: Vintage Books, 1993

Funk, Charles Earle, *Thereby Hangs A Tale*, New York: Harper & Row, 1985

Gardner, Martin, *The Magic Numbers of Dr. Matrix*, New York: Dorset Press, 1990

Gardner, Martin, *Science Good, Bad and Bogus*, Buffalo: Prometheus Books, 1989

Garrison, Webb, *Behind the Headlines*, Harrisburg: Stackpole Books, 1983

Garrison, Webb, *A Treasury of White House Tales*, Nashville: Rutledge Hill Press, 1996

Gentry, Curt*, J. Edgar Hoover*, New York: W.W. Norton & Co., 1991

Goldberg, M. Hirsch, *The Book of Lies*, New York: Quill / William Morrow, 1990

Gore, Chris, *The 50 Greatest Movies Never Made*, New York: St. Martin's Griffin, 1999

Gottlieb, Agnes Hooper et al., *1000 Years, 1000 People,* New York: Barnes & Noble, 199

Graham, Lloyd M., *Deceptions and Myths of the Bible*, New York: Citadel Press, 1975

Greenberg, Gary, *101 Myths of the Bible,* New York: Barnes & Noble, 2000

Greig, Charlotte, *Conspiracy,* New York: Barnes & Noble, 2003

Gribbin, John, *The Scientists,* New York: Random House, 2002

Griffin, Lynne & McCann, Kelly, *The Book of Women*, Maine: Bob Adams, 1992

Haining, Peter, ed., *A Sherlock Holmes Companion*, New York: Barnes & Noble, 1994

Hamilton, Edith , *Mythology*, Boston: Little, Brown and Co., 1942

Handford, S.A. (transl.), *The Fables of Aesop*, London: Penguin Books, 1964

Hardwick, Michael, *The Complete Guide to Sherlock Holmes*, New York: St. Martin's Press, 1986

Hay, Peter, *Movie Anecdotes*, New York: Oxford University Press, 1990

Haycraft, Howard (ed.), *The Art of the Mystery Story*, New York: Grosset & Dunlap, 1946

Haycraft, Howard*, Murder for Pleasure*, New York: Carroll & Graf

Publishers: 1984

Hayward, James, *Myths & Legends of the Second World War*, Stroud, Sutton Publishing, 2003

Hendrickson, Robert, *World Literary Anecdotes*, New York: Facts on File, 1990

Hendrickson, Robert, *American Literary Anecdotes*, New York: Facts on File, 1990

Hendrickson, Robert, *British Literary Anecdotes*, New York: Facts on File, 1990

Herbert, A. P., *Uncommon Law*, London: Methuen & Co., 1964

Hersch, Hank and Bechtel, Mark, *Classic Rivalries,* New York: Sports Illustrated Books, 2003

Holden, Anthony, *Behind the Oscar*, New York: Plume, 1993

Holland, Barbara, *Hail to the Chiefs*, New York: Ballantine Books, 1990

Holt, Patricia Lee, *George Washington Had No Middle Name*, New Jersey: Citadel Press, 1988

Innes, Brian, *Fakes & Forgeries,* New York: Reader's Digest, 2005

Isaacson, Walter, *Pro & Con*, New York: G. P. Putnam's Sons: 1983

Jackson, Robert, *Unexplained Mysteries of World War II*, New York: Gallery Books, 1991

Jeffers, H. Paul, *History's Greatest Conspiracies,* New York: Barnes & Noble, 2004

Jennings, Peter & Brewster, Todd, *In Search of America,* New York: Hyperion, 2002

Johnsen, Ferris, *The Encyclopedia of Popular Misconceptions,* New York: Carol Publishing, 1994

Johnson, Paul, *Modern Times*, New York: Harper Collins, 1991

Jones, Judy and Wilson, William, *An Incomplete Education*, New York: Ballantine Books, 1987

Kahn, David, *The Code-Breakers*, London: Weidenfeld and Nicolson, 1967

Kerr, Philip, ed., *The Penguin Book of Lies*, London: Viking Press, 1990

Keyes, Ralph, *"Nice Guys Finish Seventh,"* New York: Harper Perennial, 1993

Kick, Russ, *You Are Being Lied To,* New York: MJF Books, 2001

Kick, Russ, *Everything You Know Is Wrong,* New York: Barnes & Noble Books, 2002

Lane, Sheldon, ed., *For Bond Lovers Only*, New York: Dell Publishing, 1965

Lass, Abraham H., Kiremidjian, David & Goldstein, Ruth M., *Dictionary of Classical, Biblical, & Literary Allusions*, New York: Ballantine Books, 1988

Leighton, Isabel, ed., *The Aspirin Age*, 1919-1941, New York: Simon and Schuster, 1965

Lindskoog, Kathryn, *Fakes, Frauds & Other Malarkey*, Grand Rapids:

349

Zondervan Publishing House, 1993

Llewellyn, Sam, *Small Parts In History*, New York: Barnes & Noble, 1992

Lloyd, John & Mitchinson, John, *The Book Of General Ignorance,* New York: Harmony Books, 2006

Loewen, James, *Lies My Teacher Told Me*, New York: Simon & Schuster, 1995

Loewen, James, *Lies Across America*, New York: Touchstone, 1999

Lorie, Peter, *Superstitions,* New York: Simon & Schuster, 1992

Macrone, Michael, *By Jove!,* New York: HarperCollins, 1992

Macrone, Michael, *Brush Up Your Shakespeare!,* New York: Harper Collins, 1990

Magee, Bryan, *The Story Of Philosophy,* New York: Barnes & Noble, 2006

Manser, Martin, *Melba Toast, Bowie's Knife & Caesar's Wife*, New York: Avon Books, 1990

Matthews, John, *Pirates*, London: Carlton Books, 2006

McCullough, David, *Truman*, New York: Simon & Schuster, 1992

Montagu, Ashley and Darling, Edward, *The Prevalence of Nonsense*, New York: Dell, 1969

Moore, Laurence, *Lightning Never Strikes Twice*, New York: Avon Books, 1994

Morrow, Ed, *The Grim Reaper's Book of Days*, New York: Carol Publishing Group, 1992

Most, Glenn W. and Stowe, William W. (eds.), *The Poetics of Murder*, New York: Harcourt Brace, 1983

Nash, J. Robert, *Darkest Hours*, New York: Simon & Schuster, 1977

National Insecurity Council, The, *It's A Conspiracy*!, Berkeley: Earth Works Press, 1992

Opie, Iona & Peter, *Classic Fairy Tales*, New York: Oxford University Press, 1980

Page, Michael & Ingpen, Robert, *The Time-Life Encyclopedia of Things That Never Were*, Virginia: Time-Life Books, 1988

Panati, Charles, *Panati's Extraordinary Origins of Everyday Things*, New
York: Harper & Row, 1989

Panati, Charles, *Sacred Origins Of Profound Things,* New York: Penguin, 1996

Pappas, Theoni, *The Joy of Mathematics*, California: Wide World Publishing / Tetra, 1989

Pappas, Theoni, *Mathematical Scandals*, California: Wide World Publishing/Tetra, 1997

Pearson, John, *James Bond*, London: Colins Publishing, 1986

Perkes, Dan, *Eyewitness to Disaster*, New York: Gallery Books, 1985

Platnick, Kenneth B., *Great Mysteries of History*, New York: Dorset

Press, 1987

Poirier, René (transl. by Crosland, Margaret), *Engineering Wonders of the World*, New York: Barnes & Noble, 1993

Poundstone, William, *Big Secrets*, New York: Quill, 1983

Poundstone, William, *Bigger Secrets*, Boston: Houghton Mifflin Company, 1986

Poundstone, William, *Biggest Secrets*, New York: William Morrow & Co,. 1993

Powell, Michael, *Forbidden Knowledge,* Massachusetts: Adams Media, 2007

Randi, James, *Flim-Flam!,* New York: Prometheus, 1982

Rawson, Hugh, *Devious Derivations*, New York: Crown Publishers, 1994

Reader's Digest, The, *Great Cases of Interpol*, Hong Kong: Reader's Digest, 1982

Reader's Digest, The, *Facts & Fallacies*, New York: The Reader's Digest Association, 1988

Rees, Nigel, *The Nigel Rees Book of Slogans & Catchphrases*, London, Unwin Paperbacks, 1984

Rees, Nigel, *A Word in your Shell-like, London: Trafalgar Square, 2007*

Roberts, Andrew (ed.), *What Might Have Been,* London: Phoenix, 2005

Robertson, Patrick, *The Guinness Book of Movie Facts & Feats,* New York: Abbeville Press, 1991

Rogers, Tom, *Insultingly Stupid Movie Physics,* Naperville: Sourcebooks Hysteria, 2007

Rosenbaum, Ron, *Travels with Dr. Death*, New York: Penguin Books, 1991

Rosenberg, Bernard & White, David Manning, eds., *Mass Culture: The Popular Arts in America*, London: Collier-Macmillan, 1964

Rowan, Richard Wilmer, *33 Centuries of Espionage*, New York: Hawthorn Books, 1967

Rowse, A. L., *William Shakespeare*, New York: Harper & Row, 1963

Sanders, Dennis & Lovallo, Len, *The Agatha Christie Companion*, New York: Berkley Books, 1989

Sanello, Frank, *Reel v. Real,* New York: Taylor Trade Publishing, 2003

Shenkman, Richard & Reiger, Kurt, *One-Night Stands with American History*, New York: Quill, 1982

Shenkman, Richard, *Legends, Lies & Cherished Myths of American History*, New York: Harper & Row, 1988

Shenkman, Richard, *Legends, Lies & Cherished Myths of World History*, New York: Harper Collins, 1993

Shirer, William L., *The Rise and Fall of the Third Reich*, New York: Exeter Books, 1987

Stewart, Desmond and the Time-Life Editors, *Early Islam*, New York: Time-Life Books, 1972

Tamarkin, Bob, *Rumor Has It,* New York: Prentice Hall, 1993

Thornton, Willis, *History: Fact & Fable*, New York: Dorset Press, 1992

Tiballs, Geof, *The Olympics' Strangest Moments,* London: Robson Books, 2004

Tuleja, Tad, *Fabulous Fallacies*, New York: Harmony Books, 1982

Vankin, Jonathan and Whalen, John, *Based On A True Story,* Chicago: Chicago Review Press, 2005

Walker, Barbara G., *Woman's Encyclopedia of Myths and Secrets*, San Francisco: Harper & Row, 1983

Wallace, Robert and the Editors of Time-Life Books, *World of Leonardo*, New York: Time, 1966

Wallace, Robert and the Editors of Time-Life Books, *World of Rembrandt*, New York: Time, 1968

Ward, Philip, *Panama Hats, Crocodile Tears and Other Common Fallacies*, New York: Barnes & Noble, 1993

Wecter, Dixon, *The Hero in America*, Michigan: The University of Michigan Press, 1963

Weir, Stephen, *History's Worst Decisions,* New York: Metro Books, 2009

West, Nigel, *A Thread of Deceit*, New York: Random House, 1985

Whitehouse, Arch, *Espionage and Counterespionage*, New York: Doubleday, 1964

Wiley, Mason and Bona, Damien, *Inside Oscar*, New York: Ballantine Books, 1988

Williams, Hywel, *Days That Changed The World,* London: Quercus, 2006

Wills, Gary, *What Jesus Meant,* New York: Penguin Books, 2007

Winter, Gordon and Kochman, Wendy, *Secrets of the Royals*, New York: St. Martin's Press: 1990

Wise, David and Ross, Thomas B., *The Invisible Government*, New York: Bantam Book, 1964

Wright, Mike, *What They Didn't Teach You About The 60s,* California: Presidio, 2001

Zich, Arthur, and the Time-Life eds., *The Rising Sun* (World War II), Alexandria: Time-Life Books, 1978

————*Mysteries of Mind, Space & Time*, Westport, Conn: H. S. Stuttman Inc., 1992

————*The New Encyclopedia Britannica*, 15th Ed., Chicago: Encyclopedia Britannica, 1994

————*The Truth About History,* New York: Barnes & Noble, 2